ALWAYS YOUNG FOR LIBERTY

a biography of
WILLIAM ELLERY CHANNING

ALWAYS
YOUNG FOR LIBERTY

by
ARTHUR W. BROWN

SYRACUSE UNIVERSITY PRESS

to my mother,

HELEN EVELYN BROWN

PREFACE

The purpose of this study is to re-define William Ellery Channing's life and work for a generation which knows him almost solely by association with other, more familiar names. Ever since his death in 1842, Channing's memory has been treated with respect—usually, indeed, with deference—in accounts of the development of American thought. Modern students of the intellectual and moral growth of the early American Republic bow courteously in Channing's direction and then move quickly on toward other men and other stages of that growth. As a result, although Channing's name is familiar today, it is so chiefly because of its connection in one way or another with the names of many of his young contemporaries who made more dramatic, if not always more permanent, contributions to the American cultural heritage. Channing has become a kind of nodding acquaintance: almost everybody knows him slightly; few know him well.

The time is right for a re-appraisal of Channing on his own merits. A new study in the light of modern scholarship is particularly desirable at a time which is very similar to Channing's own. Like us, Channing lived in an age when liberty had to be defended and bolstered on every front, and when powerful forces were seeking security at the expense of individual liberties. His chief aim was the preservation of national honor without the destruction of individual rights, which he sought to achieve through his carefully developed doctrine of social regeneration, self-reliance, and self-culture. With this doctrine he helped to lead his own minority group to its eventual place in the sun without once changing his basic ideas of freedom of speech or worship or compromising his belief in liberty as a guiding principle of human existence. The story of this leadership should be an inspiration to the thoughtful reader of mid-twentieth-century America.

Although space does not permit individual mention of all those who have assisted in completing this book, I wish to extend my thanks to each and every one who has made my task easier. In particular, I should like to acknowledge my gratitude to my colleagues Thomas F. O'Donnell and Charles E. Samuels for their valuable criticism and advice. Mere words are small tribute to pay to Professor Edwin H. Cady, whose inspiration and encouragement have never failed me. I owe much also to Ralph F. Strebel for his friendly support as well as the time and opportunity to complete my research. In countless ways this book is a monument to the patience and forebearance of my wife, Dorothy.

My thanks are also due for the efficient and prompt library service granted wherever I inquired. To the personnel of the Boston Public Library, the Houghton Library and the Divinity School Library at Harvard University, the Massachusetts Historical Society, the Meadville Seminary Library, the Newport Historical Society, the New York Public Library, and the Rhode Island Historical Society, I am under the deepest obligation.

ARTHUR W. BROWN
May 1956
Utica, New York

CONTENTS

I cannot praise a fugitive and cloistered virtue,
unexercised and unbreathed, that never sallies out
and sees her adversary, but slinks out of the race,
where that immortal garland is to be run for,
not without dust and heat.

Areopagitica

CHAPTER ONE

FREEDOM'S LEGACY

WILLIAM ELLERY CHANNING was born on April 8, 1780, in Newport, Rhode Island, in the midst of the Revolutionary War. Although he hated war with a passion few men have exceeded, he was fated to live out his lifetime of devoted service to mankind and God during an era of conflict on a bewildering series of civil, military, intellectual, and spiritual fronts. Yet his own most significant battle was inward and resulted in as complete a victory as any man of the spirit might hope to win over self, flesh, and worldly temptation.

On both sides of his family, William Channing was fortunately born. John Channing, his grandfather, was a prosperous Newport merchant whose influence was widespread in commercial circles during the lush pre-revolutionary days. His father, the founder of the New England branch of the Channings, had emigrated from Dorsetshire in England. Beyond this Dorsetshire line, the family history becomes obscure. There were Channings in Newton Abbot, Devonshire; and their coat of arms (three moors' heads) indicates an alliance with the distinguished Canning family, which could trace its descent from the Canynges of Bristol, merchant princes of the fifteenth century. But somewhere in the march of time, the Channings had lost the Midas touch: when John Channing, Jr. died, he left his widow in near penury.

With a courage that the world has come to take for granted of our pioneers, Mary Antram Channing managed to support herself and family in respectable if very slender circumstances. Her second son, William—the father of William Ellery—was born in Newport in June, 1751. Like his son after him he came into a world filled with war, for the French and English were contending bitterly at that time for possession of the golden Empire in the uncharted West.

When William was old enough to attend college, Grandfather Channing still had enough money to send him to Nassau Hall, a small school in Princeton, New Jersey; and he was enrolled in 1765, one class ahead of Philip Freneau and James Madison. His liberality of mind and winning personality quickly brought him into the circle of which Philip Freneau, James Madison, Henry Brackenridge, Aaron

1

Burr, and Henry Lee were members. The currents of political liberalism, which were beginning to blow through Nassau's Halls, eddied
about William as well as about firebrands like Freneau and Brackenridge and drew him into the same college enterprises.

Having graduated in '69 from the "hotbed of Whiggism," as Princeton was sometimes called, William missed the dramatic bonfire of 1770,
when Princetonians, robed in black gowns, burned the letters of merchants who had failed to keep their non-importation agreements. But
he read the commencement poem of that year, and praised the exultant
note of nationalism that throbbed and pulsated in every line of "The
Rising Glory of America," the poetic product of the fertile minds of his
classmates Philip and Henry.

William left Princeton with as thorough an education as America
then offered, even if it was perhaps less liberal than that of his contemporaries at Harvard and Yale. In his Junior year Princeton had
welcomed a new President, a man of action rather than words, and Old
Nassau had undergone severe change. The new Head was Dr. John
Witherspoon, a Scots divine, who had earned many enemies by his attack on the moderates in the Church of Scotland. Witherspoon, a
charter member of the school of *saeva indignatio,* a man who felt no
attraction toward the doctrine of benevolence, sank his barbs deep into
the tender hides of the young Scottish divines until they retaliated by
harassing him politically and religiously. When Princeton invited him
to become its President, he hesitated only momentarily. The growing
clamor against him brought a speedy decision to emigrate to America.
Soon after he was installed in 1768, Nassau's halls were buzzing with
news of his one-man revolution.

Unlike the college president of the twentieth century, Witherspoon
was short on administration and long on instruction. His teaching program, for example, was heavy enough to make even the over-worked
college instructor of a mass education system flinch. In addition to his
course in moral philosophy, he lectured to the Juniors and Seniors
upon chronology and history, composition and criticism, Hebrew and
French.

But the doughty Scot spent most of his energy confuting the Berkele-
ian system of metaphysics which had infiltrated among the tutors and
students of Nassau. Whatever rosy dreams the student body and faculty
might have had for gaining a proselyte in Witherspoon were soon dissipated. He first reasoned them down, then ridiculed their new "fad,"
and finally drove it from the College. To him Berkeley's philosophy of
immaterialism was utter nonsense. Reasoning depended upon the dic-

tates of common-sense, which were either simple perceptions or intuitions. They could no more be proved than you could prove the axioms of mathematical science. With this gospel he won over the most recalcitrant idealists. There was little resiliency in such a man, but his courage was undeniable. Needless to say, his flaming spirit left a lasting impression on William.

After graduation William worked for two years as an apprentice in a Providence law office. Upon his return to Newport he found clients eager for his services and soon succeeded in building a thriving law practice. When the idea of marriage entered his mind, he lost no time in choosing a wife. Lucy Ellery, the daughter of a leading Newport lawyer, caught his eye, and he began eager pursuit. Lucy thought him "lively and pleasant in conversation" and offered little resistance to his blandishments. They were married in 1773, and settled down immediately to the job of raising a family. Their first child, a boy, died a few months after birth. Another boy arrived the following year and three years later, a daughter, Anna. William Ellery was two years Anna's junior.

A small woman, Lucy Ellery gave the impression of being taller than she actually was. Though not handsome, she had eyes that were clear and full of life and that looked right through pretense and sham. If she had a fault, it was her rigid adherence to truth, which made it difficult for people of less probity to live up to her exalted standards. This reverence of the truth she had inherited from her father, a man of salty humor but strict ethics.

Lucy's father was William Ellery, the second of that name in the family, and like his father before him, a graduate of Harvard. His marriage to Ann Remington, daughter of Justice Jonathan Remington of the Superior Court of Massachusetts, had joined the Ellery line to the Bradstreets, famous in New England since Anne Bradstreet, the "Tenth Muse Lately Sprung up in America."

In a letter to his namesake, Grandfather Ellery once wrote an unflattering self-estimate which was probably intended as a warning to William to settle quickly upon his goal in life and not to follow his grandfather's youthful example, for William Ellery had left Harvard without a purpose and had gone into business, a profession for which he had little enterprise or skill. He had prospered, however, until increasing difficulties between America and Britain ruined his business. In the very year that the lads of old Nassau were building their bonfire he had been forced to close up shop by the privations of the revenue acts and non-importation agreements. He joined the Sons of Liberty and began the study of law, two enterprises more congenial to his spirit than the crass world of trade.

In the Congress of 1776 Mr. Ellery wrote his name on the Declaration of Independence. His Newport friends gave him the nickname of "Ellery the Signer" and the name stuck. He remained in the Congress until 1779. He was home in Newport when his grandson was born, and from the first the bond between the two was that which ordinarily exists between father and son.

The Channing children were sent early to school because their mother's health was poor. William, so young that he had to be carried by the family colored servant, went from one dame school to another until he was ready to attend the boarding school of Master Robert Rogers, a local pedagogue whose reputation had spread beyond Newport and Rhode Island as well.

A rather formidable man was Master Rogers, with a look of determination in his stubborn chin that made the heart of the stoutest boy quail. If he used the rod unsparingly, he was neither worse nor better in this respect than any of his contemporaries. At Rogers' school William learned his lessons well, if not brilliantly. He learned also to hate flogging, not so much for the bodily pain as for the insult it offered to the spirit. Here too he became acquainted with young Malbone, a celebrated painter in later years, and Washington Allston, one of the cheery Southern lads who had been drawn to Newport by accounts of Master Rogers' school.

According to Allston, William was a generous and open-hearted boy with a frankness and courage that earned him the respect of companions much older than himself—no mean feat among the younger generation where age usually commands great respect, and the lack of it, obeisance. He was the natural leader in games but never took advantage of his position. Whenever there was any doubt about the correctness of his point of view (and this was seldom), he was quick to give way to whoever disagreed with him but in such a way that he suffered no loss of prestige.

William was not considered quick in school. There is a story of his having had difficulty in Latin until an assistant in his father's office took pity on him and said, "Come, come Bill! They say you are a fool, but I know better, bring me your grammar and I will soon teach you Latin." Whoever he was, the good lawyer must have possessed the divine afflatus, because "Bill" read the classics and especially Virgil with great delight in his college years. He also had encouragement and wise instruction from his grandfather, who loved the classics like old vintage wine and never tired of discoursing upon the wisdom of the Ancients.

In the hours not devoted to school work, William enjoyed himself in the million and one pursuits that please the mind and body of an active boy. There were, of course, duties around the house and in the garden to be performed under the watchful eye of his mother, a severe taskmaster; but these took so few hours from the day that there was ample time to clamber about the crates on the wharves and to play pirates among the rocks on the beach.

There was one prohibition, however, that his mother strictly enforced. She forbade her boys to bathe in the sea without supervision, and woe to him who disobeyed her. The combination of warm sun, inviting water, and dusty boy generally proving too much for childish wills, there were often culprits before the Channing bar of justice, but never William. According to his older brother George, William agreed to his mother's proposal to practice swimming on the kitchen table. However free from danger such a method might be, it was singularly unsuccessful in teaching one to swim. William never learned; and although he might glow with virtue because of his mother's wishes, he must have felt unhappy on the many occasions he had to walk home alone from the beach while his brothers and fellow playmates splashed happily in the surf.

The habit of solitary reflection, which was to become so characteristic of his later years, seems to have fastened upon him as a child. He was fond of lonely rambles on the beach; liked to go apart into some beautiful setting with no other playmate than his kite and indulge in reverie and contemplation; and spent more time in solitary thought than with his companions.

On one of these rambles in his father's fields, he found a nest of four young birds. When he discovered them, they had no down and opened their little mouths as if they were hungry. He gave them some crumbs from his pocket and returned every day for weeks to feed them. One morning when they were almost ready to fly, he found their nest covered with blood and the birds cut into quarters. In a nearby tree the mother and father mourned their young. He cried like a baby, imagining that the parents thought him the author of their misery. This made him still more unhappy, and he wanted to tell them that he was not responsible. Unlike most boys, who waste little time sympathizing with the unfortunate, he was so impressed by the incident that he resolved then and there to fight inhumanity wherever and whenever he found it.

Like every resolution he was ever to make, this was a serious promise to himself to live up to a standard of absolute value. Tolerance came naturally to him because his parents and his grandfather were tolerant people and because they had taught him the significance of what Rhode Island had always stood for. He had heard many times of the glorious heritage left by Roger Williams and Anne Hutchinson. Their precepts and example had made the name Rhode Island synonymous with freedom and toleration so that the little people of the world looked to her as a beacon in the darkness. Other colonies in America had professed principles of freedom, but none had left the consciences of men so free. And this freedom, according to Grandfather Ellery, had brought prosperity and progress to the Island.

Before the Revolution and the destruction caused by the British, Newport had been one of New England's leading commercial centers, and an aura of poetry and romance had clung to her ship-filled harbors and brightened her somnolent summer days. Although the population of the town had shrunk to less than five thousand when William was born, more than nine thousand people had lived there in the years before '76. Not even New York had been able to match the volume of her mail. Commerce had made Newport rich, and commerce had attracted strange visitors to her wharves, beaches, and streets.

Rich in the world's goods, she was rich also in the evils of the world's business. Southern planters coming to her wharves to exchange rum for human cargo stopped over at her watering places to leaven the loaf of local corruption, at the same time adding a touch of refinement to local manners; while the seafaring townsfolk, infected by the breezy habits and raffish manners of the world travelers who trod the decks of the ships at anchor in her harbor, went their usual intemperate ways, swearing, drinking, and carousing until the fires of the flesh had paled to ashes.

Amidst this surfeit of wealth and excess there was also poverty; but Newport was no different from other cities, and her people were inclined to accept want as part of the scheme of things in the same way that they accepted the blessings of Nature.

Rhode Island was singularly happy in her relative isolation. Southward she looked to the open sea and to gleaming sails and spired masts. North, east, and west the placid waters of Narragansett Bay laved softly against her shores. Glen and cove called mysteriously to child and man alike. Craggy ledges gave testimony to the fury of the sea but imperiously held against its violence; and the beaches stretching out for miles beside the blue sea beneath ever-changing skies and the white sun made up a landscape of breathtaking beauty. In the mind of the growing child the only yardstick was the pleasure of the moment, and the carefree boy could have only an intimation of the immensity of nature's gifts. But one day the man would realize that nothing on earth had helped to form his character so much as the beauty of his early home.

William's later memories of the early years of Newport were not entirely pleasant. His father, of a really amiable and benevolent disposition, was often too busy to spare time for his son. Lawyer Channing was a strict disciplinarian at home and followed the example of most parents of the period, who believed that children should be kept at a distance. Still there were rare occasions when he unbent enough to tell the boy about old Nassau and of his hopes of one day sending him there. More frequent than these informal talks were the times when William went to court with his father. Too young to appreciate his father's ability as a lawyer, he found it difficult to understand the vehemence of his father's pleading or his indignant responses to an opponent's equivocation. As a result he was sometimes afraid.

One of the few golden moments that William shared with his father occurred when he was ten years old. His father took him to the State convention that adopted the Federal Constitution, where he saw and heard at first hand the exultation of Rhode Island patriots, happy at last to be a part of the union of states.

More than most boys of his age William was keenly aware of the political questions agitating the country. Grandfather Ellery, who had returned to Congress the year after William's birth, had remained there until the boy was seven. A Whig during the revolution, he had become a Federalist after the war, still following the banner of his idol Washington. After his retirement from Congress he returned to Newport, and the intimacy between the man and boy deepened.

Thus it was that the molding of character which the busy father had to forego was left to the grandfather, who printed indelibly on the boy's mind principles to which he himself was heart and soul devoted. In the pursuit of truth, for example, the old man was always more eager for certainty than for amount and variety of results. When the truth refused to give itself up to his search, he did not indulge in conjecture, nor did he expect the imperfect state of things always to produce certainty. His reverence for truth and certainty spread to the boy, who made it such an integral part of his character that more impatient seekers after truth sometimes misunderstood the mature man's habitual reticence for pusillanimity. In his own strong and characteristic man-

ner of expression Grandfather Ellery held that the obligation to up-
hold liberty was just as sacred as that which bound him to his wife and
children. Much of his fervor penetrated to the heart of his grandson,
where it lay smoldering, ready to flame into passion heat whenever the
cause of freedom was in danger of attack.

The boy's father was also a devoted member of the Federalist party
in the days before it became extremely conservative and its interests
grew more and more separate from those of the masses. At the beginning of the French Revolution he shared in the universal hope for
freedom which it inspired. However, with the execution of Louis XVI
his hopes for freedom in France died, and he began to concentrate on
domestic affairs. As a leading lawyer and an earnest supporter of the
Federal party he was frequently asked to play host to eminent men.
Washington dined at his home; and young William, who had never
expected to see the great man face to face, sat entranced throughout
the meal. No other man ever quite measured up to the ideal of Washington created at that moment. John Jay and other noted men of the
political world came to the Channing residence, and William had
many opportunities to listen in on the councils of the mighty. The
world of politics, as a consequence, never ceased to fascinate him, even
though he was seldom able to appreciate the merits of politicians
themselves.

Matching his interest in political matters was his concern for social
evils. Intemperance impressed him as a really great evil. Drunken
sailors stumbling aboard ship and intoxicated townsmen were common
sights in Newport, but the boy's natural feeling of disgust was height-
ened by the great contrast between the sodden victims of demon rum
and the sober persons of his father and grandfather. As for another
evil, which later he would judge the most wicked of all human crimes,
he seems to have been completely ignorant. Since his innate sense of
love for all creatures could scarcely have permitted him to be convinced of injustice on the part of his father and the other people about
him, the only explanation for his failure to recognize the evil of domestic slavery is that he had been taught to believe that slavery was
part of the normal scheme of things.

Slavery was familiar to him, for he had been carried to school as a
tiny child by one of his father's slaves and Negro servants waited on
him at home. His grandfather, like most respectable merchants of Newport, had imported slaves from Africa, and Lawyer Channing never
openly opposed the practice of keeping slaves. He did, however, treat
his own servants affectionately and after the Revolution liberated

them. One of them, Duchess (by her own admission an African princess), had a home of her own to which she often invited the children
of the family whom she served. At such gatherings William learned
that race and color were no bar to affection and honesty.

Not the least significant influence on William's childhood was the
force of religion. The atmosphere of his home was deeply pious, perhaps too much so; for his playmates called him the "Little Minister,"
a rather unbecoming title for a normal growing boy. His Grandfather
Ellery, a student of ecclesiastical history and dogmatic divinity, was
fond of discussing disputed points of theology although he abhorred
sectarianism. He attended the Congregational church regularly but
overcame any impulse he might have had to become a church member.
Harmony among Christians, he believed, would be more readily
achieved if party names were entirely disused.

William's father was a member of the Second Congregational
Church, and Ezra Stiles, grandson of the Puritan poet Edward Taylor,
was the family minister until he was called to the Presidency of Yale.
Stiles, a Yale graduate of the Class of '45, had been licensed to preach
in 1773, but his brilliantly receptive mind was filled with the deism of
the time until he was called to the ministry of the Newport Church
two years after his ordination. However faith was finally won, he became firmly convinced that the reasonableness of religious doctrines
was to be deduced from God's revelations rather than inferred from
man's reason.

During Channing's early youth and young manhood, Stiles exerted
a greater influence on him than any other man, with the possible exception of Grandfather Ellery. The indignation that William felt
whenever he saw any invasion of human rights, he himself attributed
to the example and teaching of his scholarly mentor. No other being,
he declared, excited as much reverence from him while Stiles was still
alive. What stirred him most about the older man was his lack of sectarian spirit. Stiles carried into his religious teaching and practice the
same spirit of liberty which then animated the whole country politically.

He abhorred intolerance and church-tyranny in all its forms. The
impact of this attitude on the impressionable boy was tremendous, because he felt that this was freedom, living and breathing, and sallying
out into the market place.

Another man, in many ways the direct antithesis of Stiles, exerted
considerable influence on the youthful Channing. This was the Reverend Dr. Samuel Hopkins, whose doctrine "Hopkinsianism" was to

become a byword in New England and to have grave repercussions in the religious controversies of the early decades of the coming century. Hopkins, another Yale man, had left New Haven in 1740, just two years before Stiles was to enter.

Along with other students at Yale, Hopkins had been caught up in the ground swell of the Great Awakening. Carried away by evangelical fervor, he sought out the Reverend Jonathan Edwards, whose sermon on "The Trials of the Spirits" has impressed him, to ask permission to study with him. Edwards acceded to his request, and the two spent some four months of intensive soul-searching together.

Hopkins was ordained in 1743 and moved to Great Barrington, where he remained for twenty years. Seven of those years were particularly rich, because he was able to spend time with Edwards, who was laboring nearby among the Stockbridge Indians.

The death of Edwards in 1758 left a void in Hopkins's life that was never filled; but he carried on, editing his idol's works and writing a memoir of him, but most important of all, building on Edward's foundation a distinct and original school of theologic thinking. His doctrine of "willingness to be damned for the sake of Christ," though abhorrent to the mind of a man of the twentieth century, became the badge of "consistent" Calvinists when "a foolish consistency" was the hobgoblin of very serious minds.

Channing's first impressions of Hopkins were unfavorable. Because his own church, the Second Congregational, was closed during his childhood, he accompanied his parents to Hopkins's services. A child, with an average share of the normal child's restlessness, he found little in Hopkins's appearance or message to attract him. Adding to his discomfort was the fact that the church was literally as cold as a barn in winter time. Windows rattled and added their cacophony to the minister's raucous delivery. Hell-fire might prove a palatable diet for the spirit, but it had little effect on shivering bodies. So it was that William was introduced to the gaunt old minister and his stern diet.

But first impressions are not always lasting, and William was to alter radically his opinion of Dr. Hopkins. Hopkins's fiery indictment of the local slave trade had earned him few friends in Newport, which cherished its part in the West Indies traffic. Channing, however, did not forget the old man's benevolence, and in his total assessment of the man it would outweigh the pervasive gloom of his doctrine.

And speaking of the gloom, it must be remembered that the prevailing winds of doctrine in Newport, as in the rest of New England, were Calvinistic, although the specter of the Genevan reformer had

willing to be condemned for christ [handwritten marginal note] already begun to lose its haunting force in the post-Revolutionary world. Though hell-fire and damnation might seem to youngsters like William to partake more of the nature of vaudeville than of Christian preaching, there was yet a kernel of belief in its existence, which needed only the confirmation of parents to germinate into the fruit of belief.

On one of those very rare occasions when Father William could spare some time for the boy, he took him to hear a preacher who had attracted considerable attention in a neighboring town by the force of his evangelism. Impressed by his father's interest in driving some miles to the meeting, young William drank in eagerly what the speaker had to say. And a bitter message it was, though couched in glowing rhetoric. In one sense, it was another harrowing of hell. The depravity of man, his helplessness before evil, and his reliance on the sovereignty of God were so vividly described that there seemed no need for a heaven and certainly no room for any place but hell. The heart of the boy quailed; sad of spirit, he walked from the meeting in the company of his father, and the very heavens seemed filled with the same gloom that lay on his spirit. "Sound doctrine, sir," his father replied to an acquaintance, and the boy said to himself, "It is all *true*." Henceforth, he reflected, all true believers would have to relinquish earthly pursuits to prepare for the day of judgment.

They got into the chaise and began the trip homeward, each lost in his own thoughts, the boy not daring to speak to his father, whose silence he took to be the result of feelings similar to his own. But presently his father began to whistle, and when they reached home, instead of calling the rest of the family to share the terrible knowledge, he calmly sat down to read his newspaper. William was not slow to grasp the explanation for his father's conduct. What he had heard was not true. No! his father did not believe it; people did not believe it. It was *not* true! The sense of relief was gratifying; but it was soon succeeded by a feeling of anger, for he felt he had been imposed upon. He resolved never to be fooled again by fine words.

Thus childhood passed into boyhood, and William grew to have a separate identity in the Channing household. In a family as large as the Channings there was never a lack of companionship, if one were in the mood to receive it. Although, sometimes, life seemed confusing to the childish mind and human destiny bleak and unfathomable, there were still many compensations. Large families were fun, and if mother and father were kept so busy providing for the wants of their children that they had little time to lavish affection upon them, the children themselves could provide the companionship.

There was older brother Francis, for example, whose budding genius would never have chance to flower—Francis, whose mere entrance into a room was like an influx of sunshine and spring breezes through an open door. Five years William's senior, Francis Dana stood in striking contrast to his younger brother. He was tall and lithe where William was small and delicate, but the disparity in years and physical appearance was no impediment to an intimacy rarely enjoyed by brothers. Francis spent many hours with William during their boyhood, and the two of them joined forces later on, when the growing size of the family—seven children in eleven years—demanded that the older children assume responsibility for the younger ones.

Younger than Francis by three years, Anna was the mainstay of the family. Her affection for others was so genuine and contagious that she made everyone feel happier for her presence. The younger girls, Mary and Lucy, were her special charge, but she managed to mother the boys as well. William seldom needed supervision, but the same could not be said of happy-go-lucky Walt and George. These two were full of the Old Nick, and they had more than the usual assortment of boyish escapades and scrapes. Even as small boys they were very close, but the bond between them was firmly cemented when George rescued Walt from drowning in Easton's pond. Contrary to their mother's prohibition, they had gone skating; and the thin ice had crumbled beneath Walt, dropping him into the freezing water. George's quick thinking saved his brother's life, but their homecoming was no occasion for celebration. A hard-and-fast rule had been broken and punishment was swift and certain.

A happy family, the Channings, and a clannish bunch. Separation came hard to them. First Francis went off to Harvard. That was in the fall of 1790, the year of the great Convention, and the year William Channing was made district attorney for the district of Rhode Island. It was also the year grandfather began his long career as customs inspector. Then William was sent to Uncle Henry Channing at New London to prepare for college. The family was beginning to grow up, and in a sense, to break up.

Though he was only twelve and away from home for the first time, William enjoyed being at his uncle's. His Aunt Sarah fell in love with him at the start and mothered him like her own child. Uncle Henry found him bright and receptive to instruction.

According to Ezra Stiles, who knew him as a friend and confidant,

Henry Channing stopped believing in the divinity of Christ early in his ministerial career. When the revivalists swept into New England during the last years of the century, he welcomed their message and became an ardent supporter of the evangelical movement. Under his tutelage William was further emancipated from the Calvinistic tenets which his father's unconcern over the brimstone preaching of the Rhode Island evangelist had led him to question some years earlier.

In the fall of 1793, William was suddenly called home from New London by news of his father's death. The family was stunned by the loss because it was totally unexpected. William's father had been in excellent health, and neither he nor his wife had made any plans for the protection of the family in case of emergency. But the family was made of stern stuff, and they soon took hold of the situation. Lucy was adamant about the boys' continuing their education. She made Francis promise to return to Harvard to finish his degree and sent William back to New London. Soon after his father's funeral, William was busily at work again with Uncle Henry, preparing for college. During the fall and spring, he worked as he had never worked before. In the summer following his fourteenth birthday, he went to Cambridge and took the entrance examinations for Harvard. Shortly afterwards, he received word that he had been accepted for the fall class.

CHAPTER TWO

HARVARD AND THE ENLIGHTENMENT

AUNT SARAH AND Uncle Henry had been like mother and father to William during his stay in New London. They were just like his own family, and their way of living differed little from what he had been accustomed to at home. But when the time came to leave them, he realized that he was about to begin a different kind of life. He knew nothing about Cambridge and Boston, and he was somewhat fearful of what lay ahead. After all, he was only fourteen, shy for his age and completely unexperienced in the ways of fashionable society.

Fortunately, his fears proved groundless. He was cordially welcomed to Cambridge by his Uncle Francis, who took him into his home and heart and put him at ease, so that there was no reason to feel homesick.

Uncle Francis, who had married Elizabeth Ellery, Lucy's sister, was Chief Justice Dana of the Commonwealth of Massachusetts. His home was one of Cambridge's show places. A spacious mansion situated on a hill, it commanded a wide outlook across the valley and meadows of the Charles River, from Mount Vernon on the west with its verdant groves and the green rounded summits of Brighton and Brookline, to the blue hills of Milton on the horizon. What boy wouldn't delight in such a setting! And William had more than the average boy's sense of appreciation for natural beauty. Adding to his sense of security in his new surroundings was the congeniality of the Danas and their friends.

Though Dana House was only a half mile's walk from the College, it was far enough from the campus to keep William from many of the activities of his classmates. In the sense that he was already too reserved and too much of a solitary, this seclusion was not good for him. But the refinement of his uncle's home, the good conversation at table, the meeting with men of position in the community, the hours in the library, and the generally high level of the culture with which he came in contact were more than enough to compensate for his isolation from school affairs. At least they helped him to win a circle of friends from the most distinguished of his class.

Harvard in 1794 bore little resemblance to today's great institution. In the eighteenth century it had become increasingly liberal, though it is true that the students often progressed in the direction of liberalism more rapidly than their instructors. In 1710, for example, a candidate for the bachelor's degree had his name presented to the Overseers only after he had declared his faith in Ames's *Medulla Theologica,* the Westminster Assembly Catechism, the Thirty-nine articles, the doctrine of the trinity, the divinity of Jesus, predestination, special efficacious grace, and the divine right of infant baptism. Twenty years later, the drift toward liberality was scarcely more perceptible. When three candidates for the master's degree at the Commencement of 1739 proposed to take the negative of Calvinist tenets such as "Whether Three Persons in the Godhead are Revealed by the Old Testament," the Overseers insisted on the printed Quaestiones being altered with pen and ink to the affirmative.

But in September of the following year, the celebrated revivalist George Whitefield, speaking in the Cambridge Meeting House, exclaimed about "Godless Harvard." By comparison with its more orthodox neighbor in New Haven, Harvard seemed to Whitefield to be extremely liberal.

When William entered Harvard, undergraduates looked on the tutors as their natural enemies. A student who treated one as a friend was looked down upon as a "fisherman," while the tutors regarded the undergraduates as inmates in a reformatory. The laws of Darwin, though still unformulated, were nevertheless at work, and teacher and student, it seems, were committed by them to a natural antagonism. Harvard had indeed changed in a hundred years; but whether change meant progress depended largely on the view one took toward liberal religious and political views.

There were fewer than two hundred in the student body when William entered, although getting into Harvard was not difficult. Sidney Willard, the son of President Willard of Harvard, declared that "apprehension of the severity of the examination, or what in after times, by an academic figure of speech, was called screwing, or a screw, was what excited the chief dread." Theoretically, the entrance requirements called for a strict examination in Dalzell's *Collectanea Graeca Minora,* the Greek Testament, Vergil, Sallust, and Cicero's Select Orations; a thorough acquaintance with the Greek and Latin Grammars, including prosody; also an ability to translate those languages correctly, and a knowledge of geography and of arithmetic to the rule of three. Actually, however, the examination in grammar covered only the passages translated, and a few lines of English, consisting of forty or fifty words, were given to each, to be translated into Latin.

During the day of the examination, there was considerable confusion to add to the severity of the ordeal. For the more than fifty candidates who had to be tested in the six divisions of the College's work, there were only four tutors to administer the examinations. Because he came from out of town, Channing was one of the lucky few who was given precedence over local scholars from the Boston Latin School. His tutor passed him right through to President Willard for final acceptance, and in his usual brusque fashion the President told him to doff his hat and state his business. William managed the interview successfully, although he was cowed somewhat by the manner of a man whose rule was frequently labelled "quasi-military."

The Reverend Joseph Willard, President of Harvard since 1781, was a sound scholar, of great dignity of manner, but cold and somewhat forbidding in his demeanor. Since his example was followed by his faculty, there was little informality on campus. The President and the professors were never approached except in the most formal way, and upon official occasions, and in the College yard. The three professors, Tappan, Webber, and Pearson, though always courteous and responsive to requests for aid, were nevertheless too reserved to encourage overtures from the students. The supporting cast for these gentlemen of dignity included three youthful tutors, Popkin, Hedge, and Pierce.

Under the tutelage of the bachelor Mr. Popkin, the Class of '98 went through their paces in the Greek. Levi Hedge, a classmate of Francis Dana Channing, assumed the burden of drumming Watt's *Logic,* Locke's *Essay,* and other such tender classics into "the empty Sculls of young Harvards." Pierce, one of four Latin instructors at Harvard during the years of Channing's atendance, was William's personal tutor.

These seven pillars of wisdom ruled over a domain as small physically as it was limited numerically. The Harvard of 1794 consisted of only four red-brick buildings. Harvard Hall (1766) housed the College bell, the chapel, library, commons and most of the classrooms; to its left stood Hollis Hall (1763), a dormitory; to the left of Hollis was Holden Chapel (1741), now used by the Medical School, but which had once housed the General Court of Massachusetts during the hectic days when General Gage was holding Boston down with British troops; to the right of Harvard Hall was Massachusetts Hall (1720), the most ancient of the buildings, used as another dormitory. None of the buildings was particularly attractive. As one witty cynic put it: "The genius of ugliness grinned horribly at the birth of every building belonging to Harvard College."

Amidst these precincts Channing spent four happy years. Not everything at Harvard pleased him, of course. There was the rule regimenting student dress for example. At a meeting of the President and Fellows of Harvard College, April 14, 1797, it was voted that all the undergraduates dress in coats of blue gray or dark blue. No student could appear within college or town limits in a coat of any other color unless he had on a "night gown" or, in stormy or cold weather, an outside garment over his coat. Black gowns were permitted for all public occasions. Silk was forbidden as well as gold or silver lace, cord or edging upon hats, waistcoats, or any other part of student garb. Violations of any of these regulations led to fines ranging from eighty cents to double that figure for each offense. Continual violation was subject to fines and censure from the College Administration.

Long gowns of calico or gingham were worn in summer, and colorless woolen breeches buttoned at the knees and tied or buckled below were the fashion. Half-boots were standard footwear. To distinguish one class from another, students were requested to wear frogs or crows feet worked into their sleeve cuffs, although, if the truth be told, the four classes needed little to set them apart.

Living at Dana House, William managed to escape many of the unpleasant features of the regimen of on-campus students. They were supposed to rise at six in the morning for chapel and retire with the curfew at nine. They lived in dormitories and ate at commons. Breakfast consisted of a tin cup of unsettled coffee, a "size" of biscuit, and a "size" of butter weighing an ounce. Supper was of bread and milk. The main meal came at noon when each student was given the opportunity to load his stomach with a pound of meat, which being boiled on Mondays and Thursdays, caused those days to be nicknamed "Boiling Days." Pewter cans containing cider, which was supplanting the small beer of earlier years, was passed around like loving cups, until they had to be refilled.

Commons was always a problem at Harvard. Before and after William's residence, there was a series of historic rebellions, strikes and walkouts by the students, of which the "Great Butter Rebellion" in 1755 and the "Rotten Cabbage Rebellion" in 1807 were the most celebrated. That conditions were not radically different in the nineties is evidenced by an anecdote of Sidney Willard, President Willard's son. He states that the students who boarded in commons were obliged to go to the kitchen door with their bowls or pitchers for their supper.

Here they received their milk or chocolate and their piece of bread and then returned to their rooms to eat a solitary meal. They often suspected that the milk was diluted by a mixture of a very common colorless, tasteless fluid, which led one sagacious student to put the matter to the test by asking the simple carrier boy why his mother did not mix the milk with warm water instead of cold. "She does," replied the honest youth.

If the students' diet was frugal, their quarters were scarcely more luxurious. A feather bed, a pine bedstead, washstand, table, and desk, a cheap rocking-chair, and two or three plain chairs made up the contents of the average room. The students' rooms—some of the recitation rooms as well—were heated by open wood fires, cared for by poor students who were paid a small sum for this task by the College.

Channing avoided all these trials by living at the luxurious home on the hill. But he could not, of course, avoid rising early to attend chapel or paying fines when he was tardy or absent. Faculty records, however, show he was not often delinquent in such matters, and that he was never guilty of more flagrant offenses.

As a Freshman he preserved a spotless record. He received several small fines for missing prayers and an occasional recitation, but his offenses were due to illness rather than intentional neglect. As for charges of patronizing taverns, intoxication, and gunkeeping, he never succumbed to such temptations, if indeed he ever had any.

Some years after his departure from Harvard, he wrote a description of the state of affairs at the college during his stay as an undergraduate. The picture he painted was most unpleasant. He blamed the French Revolution for having diseased the imagination and unsettled the understanding of students and townspeople. The old foundations of social order and tradition seemed to him to have been shaken, if not actually subverted. The tone of books and conversation struck him as daring and presumptuous. Skepticism abounded and insubordination was rife. The entire moral level of the student body left much to be desired. William himself felt the pressure of these obstacles to right living and thinking, but his natural timidity coupled with an instinctive shrinking from vice and a dread of incurring debts that he couldn't pay proved an effective safeguard against temptation.

Among his fellow students there were some who felt Harvard to be as godless and immoral as he did, but the picture may have been brighter than he made it out. Joseph Story, one of his close friends, considered the students moral, devoted to their studies, and eager to earn distinction. He admitted there were occasional outbreaks against

the Administration, but he saw no reason to consider the students of
his time either more dissipated or unruly than those of other generations. Somewhere in between these very different points of view the
truth would appear to lie. It seems rather unlikely that "the typical
student of the early 1790's was an atheist in religion, an experimen-
talist in morals, a rebel to authority," as one historian of the period
has claimed.

Since the primary function of a university is to inculcate principles
of sound learning in its students—at least it was thought to be *primary*
in Channing's time—some attention should be paid to the order of
studies at Harvard. Though the curriculum was classical, there was
small Latin and less Greek. According to Joseph Story, the number of
textbooks probably did not exceed fifteen. And from reports of Story,
Willard, and Channing, the majority of the courses were textbook
courses, allowing little latitude for either student or teacher. The students were required to memorize the rules in Blair's *Lectures on
Rhetoric* and to recite orally the definitions in Lowth's *English Grammar*. Mathematics, which was not required for admission, proved rough
going for nearly all. Logic was studied in the Sophomore year. In the
Junior and Senior years there were lectures on natural philosophy,
accompanied by experiments. Attendance upon these was voluntary
and there were no examinations. Lectures on astronomy came during
the Senior year, and the two-volume edition of the famous "Geography" by Jedidiah Morse, who would be one of Channing's most
ardent opponents during the "unitarian" controversy some twenty
years later, was used to supplement Euclid's *Elements*.

Not a very diversified curriculum, but there was the College library
to supplement course work. The library contained between twelve
and thirteen thousand volumes. Though described by contemporaries
as "not easily accessible" and "not frequented" by students, the list of
books charged out by Channing during his four years is fairly pre-
tentious.

During his Sophomore year he read, among other things, Sheridan
on Elocution, Leland's Demosthenes, Bacon's Essays, Dryden's Miscellanies, Reid on the Mind, Cicero's Opera, Longinus de Sublimitate,
Middleton's Geography, Shakespeare, Roscommon's Poems, Goldsmith's Rome, Hippocrates' Aphorisms, and Pliny. As a Junior, he
read Brissot's De la Verité, Harris's Treatises, Price's Morals, Don
Quixote, Rousseau's Emile, the Encyclopædia of American Education,
Rousseau du Contrat Sociale, the Pluralité des Mondes, Hutcheson's
Inquiry, Priestley on Necessity, Cibber's Plays, Lillo's works, and Bur-

net's Theory. During his Senior year he borrowed Burnet, Sherlock's sermons, Priestley's Matter and Spirit, The Encyclopædia of American Education, Goldsmith's Animated Nature, Price's Morals, Livy, Hume on Human Nature, Dodsley's Collects, and Shakespeare.

He was no more of the literary dilettante then than he was later. There was always too much to be known for him to waste his time in skimming or reading trashy books. His extra-curricular reading included history, belles lettres, rhetoric, natural science, philosophy, and theology.

History and literature were his favorites. History being to him, as it was later to Carlyle, the biographies of great men, he read avidly books like Leland's *Demosthenes*. In literature he showed a catholic taste, dividing his time between the ancient and modern writers. Of the latter, Bacon, Dryden, and Goldsmith, representing extremes of style and subject matter, pleased him equally well. And he was as enthusiastic as any other Harvard graduate about Shakespeare, who was the rage at Harvard during the nineties. He never lost interest in the drama, though he seldom patronized the theatre, and the sprightly comedies of Colley Cibber and the family tragedies of George Lillo were both to his liking. His taste for Lillo's works is evidence that his later appreciation of writers like Letitia Barbauld, Catherine Sedgwick, Joanna Baillie, and Mary Mitford was fostered at Harvard.

He was particularly interested in everything that promised to improve his speaking and writing ability. He read the works of Longinus, Demosthenes, Sheridan, and Harris so that he might study elocution as an art; and he had easy access to the works of Blair, Campbell and Lord Kames, which were on common reserve lists. He knew Blair by heart, and he was quite familiar with the pleasure-pain calculus of Lord Kames, He could thank Eliphalet Pearson, his Hebrew professor, however, for the simple, lucid style which characterized his mature writing, for there is evidence of a tendency toward ornateness and Latinity in his early college compositions. Professor Pearson's habit of reading compositions aloud and noting with displeasure inflated sentences and flights of rhetoric, tended to discourage "fine" writing, because the object of Pearson's criticism also became the butt of his classmates' ridicule after class. Recitations were always before a group of one's peers, and the ability to speak effectively was certain to win the respect of one's classmates.

William's deepest interest lay in books relating to man's spiritual nature. He carefully studied the works of John Locke, Bishop Berkeley, Thomas Reid, David Hume, Joseph Priestley, and especially

Richard Price. Locke, whose essay on *Human Understanding* had been in use at Harvard since 1742, attracted students of a liberal frame of mind because his psychology, conceiving the mind as *tabula rasa* and discrediting innate ideas—particularly the idea of man's inborn malevolence—had paved the way for a more optimistic reading of the book of man. But Locke's empiricism and sensational psychology repelled William, who found a welcome antidote in the writings of Price. Price's idealism saved him from Locke's sensationalism. According to his own admission, Price's *Morals* and *Four Dissertations* moulded his philosophy into a form it was never to change.

In the *Morals* Price sought to answer some of the great questions inherited from the seventeenth century. He wanted to know whence man derives his ideas of right and wrong, and by what power he is able to distinguish one from the other. His answer was that man possesses the power of *understanding*. Unlike Locke's *understanding*, Price's was a source of new ideas (as was Kant's later). Like sight, which discovers the qualities of visible objects, the understanding, which is the eye of the mind, discovers the qualities of intelligible objects. "It is undeniable," said Price, "that many of our ideas are derived from the INTUITION of the truth, or the discernment of the natures of things by the understanding. This therefore may be the source of our moral ideas."

In Price's idealistic philosophy, pleasure and pain are not to be confused with virtue and vice; they are merely effects or concomitants. Rectitude, to him, was a law as well as a rule. "Rectitude is itself an end, an ultimate end, an end superior to all other ends, governing, directing and limiting them, and whose existence and influence depend on nothing arbitrary. It presides over all. Every appetite and faculty, every instinct and will, and all nature are subjected to it." The demands of the moral law are supreme and ultimate; their fulfillment, in turn, presupposes reason, liberty, and attention. Liberty dominates all our actions: "It is the source and guide of all the actions of the Deity himself, and on it his throne and government are founded. It is an unalterable and indispensable Law. The repeal, suspension, or even relaxation of it, once for a moment, in any part of the universe cannot be conceived without a contradiction. . . . It is, in short, the one authority in nature, the same in all times and in all places; or, in one word, the Divine authority."

Price was also a firm believer in the idea of progress. "There is no end of what is perceivable and discoverable," he said. "There is a proper infinity of ideal objects and verities *possible* to be known; and of systems, worlds and scenes of being, possible to exist. . . . There is no point of *moral* as well as *intellectual* improvement, beyond which we may not go by industry, attention, a due cultivation of our minds, and the help of proper advantages and opportunities." Such improvement would continue even beyond man's existence in his present world.

Price's ideas bear such striking similarity to the dominant passions of Channing's life that one must accept the latter's tribute of his indebtedness to Price, not as eulogistic sentiment, but as a simple statement of truth. Price's doctrine of an innate moral sense, his emphasis on benevolence, his love of liberty coupled with a fearlessness in exposing what he considered to be his country's weaknesses, and his belief in an infinite progress, became the key ideas of Channing's life philosophy.

At Harvard, William also discovered the Edinburgh Enlightenment. Professor Tappan, under whose influence he came, was himself affected by Francis Hutcheson and by moral liberalism in general. In his welcoming address to the freshman class of '94, Tappan had warned the Harvard neophytes that there would be "flattering baits, which folly and vice will here spread to seduce and destroy them"; but he had also encouraged them to control their "affections" rather than to set them aside or extinguish them like the stoics, because they were intended for "the service of God, and the moral perfection and happiness of man."

"Christian patriotism," stated Tappan, "is nothing else than general benevolence embracing, with peculiar sensibility and active energy, that portion of mankind, to which our capacity of usefulness eminently reaches." "Love to God and charity to our neighbor are inseparably united; the one is the sure basis, the other the beautiful superstructure, of universal goodness." Through Professor Tappan and Harvard in general, William discovered Hutcheson and his theory of benevolence and then the other Scottish liberals.

While reading Hutcheson's *Inquiry* one day in his favorite retreat, a clump of willows in the north meadow of the Dana estate, he discovered the doctrine of an innate moral sense and the theory of disinterested benevolence. The effect upon him was similar to that experienced by Jonathan Edwards at the moment of his personal conversion. As William later told a friend, "I longed to die, and felt as if heaven alone could give room for the exercise of such emotions; but when I found I must live, I cast about to do something worthy of these great thoughts. . . ." The glory of the Divine disinterestedness, the privilege of existing in a universe of progressive order and beauty,

and the unlimited possibilities of man's spiritual destiny in a world
ruled by altruism instead of self-love, thrilled the boy.

Hutcheson revealed to him the infinite possibilities in man, but
Adam Ferguson suggested to him that regeneration is a gradual and a
social process. According to Ferguson, a Professor of Philosophy at
Edinburgh, "It should seem . . . to be the happiness of man, to make
his social dispositions the ruling spring of his occupations; to state
himself as a member of a community, for whose general good his heart
may glow with an ardent zeal, to the suppression of those personal
cares which were the foundations of painful anxieties, fear, jealousy
and envy." "Man is born in society, and there he remains." Whatever
progress he makes is due to his own exertion and not to any foreign
agency. Later William discovered a more pleasing combination of
Ferguson's secularism and Hutcheson's benevolence in Price's *Dissertations*. In all of these discoveries, he was guided by the hand of Levi
Hedge, who was devoted to the Scottish school of common sense, of
which Thomas Brown, Thomas Reid, and Dugald Stewart were leading exponents.

Although he was not really gregarious, William was one of four
students in the class of '98 who belonged to four college clubs. His
interest in writing and speaking as well as his scholarship drew him
out into college society and made him eligible in the eyes of fellow
students. Near the close of his Freshman year, he was elected to the
Speaking Club, a group of some twelve to fifteen Sophomores and
Juniors whose principal purpose was improvement in elocution and
oratory. He became the Club's President and also delivered the vale-
dictory address in his Junior year. Shortly afterwards, he was elected
to Phi Beta Kappa. Something similar to Phi Beta Kappa was the
Adelphi Club, consisting principally of those Seniors who expected to
enter the ministry. William joined the Adelphi, although he wrote
Allston that he had no inclination for divinity.

During his Junior year he was also elected to the Hasty-Pudding, a
social club organized at Harvard in 1795 by a group of convivial spirits
who wished to relax and enjoy themselves in informal talks and social
get-togethers. Their meetings were held on Saturday evenings, and
judging by contemporary accounts these weekend sessions were jovial
affairs indeed. The membership was small—some twenty students—and
all took turns in playing host and providing the chief source of pleasure—the hasty pudding. Procured from one of the good housewives
near the College, the steaming porridge was wolfed down around a
cheery wood fire in the students' rooms.

Although William did not have the boarders' incentive to gormandize at these meetings, his walk from Dana House to the campus in the chill evening air stimulated his appetite. The sight of the savory pudding also roused memories of home, because it resembled his Rhode Island favorite "whitepot." He managed to eat his share of the feast and soon began to look forward to Saturday evening as eagerly as the others.

Conviviality had been the primary objective in founding Hasty-Pudding, but its members soon joined more serious motives to their aim of pleasure. Discussions and debates were introduced to provide opportunities for self-improvement as well as enjoyment. The "big event" of the year was the annual celebration in honor of George Washington. In William's Senior year the toasts offered at the Washington celebration reveal the interest Club members had in current politics. George Washington was toasted as "a man brave without temerity, laborious without ambition, generous without prodigality, noble without pride, and virtuous without severity." Less flamboyantly, John Adams was simply styled "President of the United States, the American *Terminus.*" Good Federalists all, the group hoped that Thomas Jefferson might "exercise his elegant literary talents for the benefit of the world, in some retreat, secure from the troubles and dangers of political life."

There was another club at Harvard, which had been started some three years before Channing entered. The Porcellian (or Pig Club) was filled with the "Bloods of Harvard." Their motto, "Dum vivimus vivamus," held little appeal for William so that he never bothered to attend their meetings although they tried hard to entice him. He was no prude, but he could see no reason to waste his time in frivolity.

Participation in the Harvard clubs did wonders for him. The informality and give-and-take of the societies provided a balance to his seriousness and asceticism. They were also valuable supplements to the somewhat thin offerings of the college curriculum.

William did not have a single enemy at Harvard, but it is likewise true that he had few close friends. The details of college days recalled by Daniel White (later Judge White) and by Joseph Story (later Associate Justice Story of the Supreme Court) reveal that they knew Channing well, and the post-collegiate correspondence of Channing, William Shaw, and Arthur Maynard indicates close friendship; but none of these men were as intimate with Channing as Washington Allston, Joseph Tuckerman and Jonathan Phillips.

Washington Allston came up to Harvard two years after William.

He had been at Master Rogers' school for eight years, and the Newport pedagogue had extended himself more than usual for the bright
lad whose boyish sketches gave promise, even at an early age, of future
greatness. Since Allston's rooms were on the way from William's home
to the College, William got into the habit of stopping for a friendly
chat while going to or coming from his lectures. During these informal
talks, the two discussed the days at Newport, doings at the College,
and their plans for the future. Both had grand ideas about the days
ahead. Of the two, perhaps Allston knew better what he wanted. He
was determined to be the first painter in America. William, on the
other hand, vacillated from one plan to another. Though he felt the
expansiveness of the age that lay ahead, he was unable to decide
whether his part would be played in medicine, the law, or the ministry. The two boys did not always agree. On one point, especially, their
views of man conflicted: unlike William, Allston believed that man's
powers were very limited in comparison with the vastness of the world
in which he lived.

Joseph Tuckerman, Jonathan Phillips, and William began a friendship under the elms at Harvard that only death could sever. All three
were little men physically, but all possessed large spirits. Phillips was
the most retiring; for he made little splash in the Harvard pool, and
in later life, seems to have been content to remain behind the scenes,
while his money talked for him in philanthropic enterprises. As a
result of his unhappy home life, Phillips found the college curriculum
unbearable and turned from it to indulge in the speculative thought
of the day.

Channing's dearest friend was Joseph Tuckerman. The two boys
met for the first time while they were taking their entrance examinations, and acquaintanceship soon ripened into friendship. Although
quite different in personality, they found their reading interests strik-
ingly similar. Unlike Channing, however, Tuckerman passed through
his first three years at Harvard as though he were in a dream world.
There seemed to be no direction to his activities: thoughts of the
future were pushed aside for a philosophy of day-to-day living. His
attitude toward most of his studies was disinterest mixed occasionally
with active distaste for subjects like mathematics and natural philosophy. Where literature, and especially English poetry and drama, was
concerned, Joseph experienced the same delight as William. History
and moral philosophy fascinated both and led them into interminable
discussions. More effusive and emotional on the surface than Channing, Tuckerman offered a good antidote to the former's studied

coolness and repression. In the years to come they would work together as a hard-hitting team of philanthropists, the one providing
enthusiasm and verve and the other steadiness of purpose and careful
planning.

Channing had other friends at Harvard, but they belonged to a
different sphere of intimacy. There was Joseph Story, a good friend
of Tuckerman's and William's closest rival for class honors. In years
to come, Story would earn a reputation in the judicial world to rival
Channing's in the ministry. Next to Tuckerman and Story, Arthur
Maynard Walter and William Smith Shaw were William's closest
associates.

Many were the times that these three gathered to talk and while
away the hours discussing future plans and the happenings of the life
about the College. A tap on Walter's window or a cheery halloo was
enough to lure him away from his candle and copybook; and then
the two friends would saunter over to Shaw's if it was spring, or race
madly on the cold winter evenings, their footsteps sounding loud and
staccato on the cobble stone paths that ran alongside the dormitories.
Shaw was always certain to have the fire roaring, and the three would
gather around the mantel eating nuts, smoking cigars, and vying with
one another in heated discussion.

Some years after graduation, Channing singled out from his recollections of undergraduate days these social evenings for special mention. "I was then supremely happy," he declared. "I can still remember
our walks by moonlight,—how we strolled over the common, or took
the solitary road to the Judge's. We leaned on each other's arms for
support; we grew warm in friendly argument; the jarrings which
sometimes prevailed among us only sweetened the concord and harmony which succeeded."

Though he just managed to stretch beyond the five-foot mark, William was rather muscular than slender. In the wrestling matches and
horseplay that were common among the students, he was athletic
enough to hold his own even against heavier and taller opponents.
Allston remarks of his "animal spirits" and tells of occasional unrestrained hilarity, though he confesses William never passed the
bounds of propriety. His laugh was his most distinctive characteristic,
ringing with happiness yet never obstreperous.

The tenor of William's thinking and conduct at Harvard reveals a
gradual awakening to the trend of events round about him. His uncle,
the Judge, who was a keen observer of the contemporary political
scene, often talked to him about the social and economic problems

of the times and guided his reading in these areas. Through these conversations, William also got a glimpse of the fashionable world that lay across the Charles River. The influence of Boston on Cambridge was then very slight, intercourse between the students and the metropolis being infrequent and casual. West-Boston bridge had been completed only a short time, and the road leading to it was new and not well settled. Since walking was the only means of communication and since the inducements to visit in private homes were limited, students were seldom inclined to undergo the unpleasantness of the journey to the city. William was therefore much more fortunate than most of his classmates to have an opportunity of viewing this world, even though it was only through the eyes of his uncle.

Communication between America and Europe was infrequent. With the exception of a few and usually unreliable contacts with the English, there was almost no means of access to any literature and science abroad. Even where English books and periodicals were concerned, there was little more than a semi-annual importation of the most common works, and of these, a few copies of each were all that were available. The most popular of the English magazines was the *Monthly Magazine,* which was read faithfully by only a few of the students like Tuckerman, Story, and Channing. Spring and autumn were highlights in the college year because these were the times when the two packets sailing regularly betwen Boston and London arrived in Boston Harbor with a supply of reading matter.

Despite Harvard's isolation from world culture, influences from abroad insinuated their way into the College halls. Among these, deism, French infidelity, and Federalism were perhaps the most prominent. As America approached the opening of the nineteenth century, serious citizens were deeply troubled by the progress of infidelity and skepticism cloaked under the name of deism.

Deism as a form of rationalism had been hanging on the skirts of Puritanism throughout the last quarter of the seventeenth century, but it was not until the eighteenth that it declared its independence and sought to hasten the intellectual emancipation of New England. In general, it was a kind of lowest common denominator in religion. Following the lead of the "reformers" of the sixteenth century who had substituted for the authority of the Catholic Church individual interpretation of the Scriptures, the deists came to the conclusion that the basis of authority was to be found in reason and in the rational beliefs, common to all men, to which it universally led. As formulated by Lord Herbert of Cherbury, a pioneer in English Deism, the basic credo of the new movement was summed up in five simple axioms: there is one supreme God; He ought to be worshipped; the chief parts of divine worship are virtue and piety; men ought to be sorry for their sins and repent of them; divine goodness dispenses rewards and punishments both in this life and after it.

Later, when Sir Isaac Newton had provided the concept of a harmonious universe working according to immutable laws, deism appropriated the great mathematician's discovery to itself and bolstered its arguments with a divine architect who governed the world by laws as immutable as himself. The sensational psychology of John Locke also became grist for the deistic mill. Though no deist himself, Locke provided, in his *Essay Concerning Human Understanding,* a foundation for the deism of the eighteenth century by giving the movement a philosophic background and additional authority for a hedonistic ethics.

The introduction of English rationalistic works, the cosmic philosophy of Newton and the empirical psychology of Locke together with the appearance of a liberal theological movement and some anti-clerical feeling prepared the way for deistic speculation in the American colonies. Its progress during the provincial period, however, was slow; up to 1776, deism was still an intellectual cult confined to a few individuals in the larger towns. During the Revolution, it became somewhat bolder in tone. The appearance of Tom Paine's *Age of Reason* in 1794 was a signal for an intensive campaign against the force of religion and clerical authority. Paine's deism belonged to the destructive type of free thought which concentrated on attacking such evidences of the Christian religion as miracles.

Among those who sought to save Christianity from such attacks, none were more zealous than the authorities of the American colleges. At Rhode Island College, Queen's College, and Union College, baccalaureate addresses were delivered to impress the graduating classes with the superiority of Christianity over "mere philosophy," as deism was not inaptly called. The authorities at Yale also attempted to save the souls of their students. Lyman Beecher, a Sophomore at New Haven when Channing was a Freshman at Harvard, declares that the majority of the class ahead of him were skeptics. Their favorite nicknames for one another were Voltaire, Rousseau, and D'Alembert. President Timothy Dwight of Yale minced no words in making plain to his students that Voltaire was an atheist and Rousseau a thief, perjurer and fornicator. No good, he declared, could come from a philosophy espoused by men of such *loose* characters! At Princeton, according to contemporary report, pious youths were just as difficult to find as they were on any other college campus.

At Harvard the deism of Paine made such rapid progress that the authorities presented each student with a copy of Watson's *Apology for the Bible,* the standard rebuttal against *The Age of Reason.* But they did not stop there. The French-fed plague of rationalism with its "foul spirit of innovation" was a scourge to be sedulously avoided for many reasons, political as well as religious.

Looked at in one way (and most Federalists chose to see the question in a light most favorable to them) , a France at odds politically with America was also a citadel of atheism plotting to destroy America by undermining its principles of freedom and Christian belief. Daniel White expresses the feeling that was pervasive among his associates at Harvard as follows: "So deeply and so generally had the French *mania* [the name for deism or atheism] seized upon the popular mind in this country, and so susceptible of its fiery influence were the ardent spirits of young men, all alive to freedom of thought, of action, and indulgence, that reason, argument and persuasion had for a time no power against it." Thus "French infidelity" was simply considered deism decked out in the garments of nationalism.

Shortly before graduation, Channing sat among his classmates in the College chapel listening to an address by Professor Tappan. At this time of intense anti-Gallicism, and on the occasion of the approaching departure of another Senior class, Tappan felt obliged to inveigh against deism, particularly of the French brand. His chief target was the "Illuminati," a European association thought to be actively scheming to overthrow civil and religious institutions in America.

Tappan warned his audience against "those wrong and dangerous principles which would seduce them from the principles and practices of sound morality and piety." He was only reinforcing what he had been saying for some time past, for he had issued a warning more than five years before, that "a species of atheistical philosophy, which has of late triumphantly reared its head in Europe, and which affects to be the offspring and the nurse of sound reason, science, and liberty, seems in danger of infecting some of the more sprightly and free-thinking geniuses of America."

Deism and infidelity were especially baneful to Federalists. From 1793 onwards, the Congregational ministers of New England had allied themselves with Federalistic conservatism; and in order to stem the rising tide of democratic ideas, they cast aspersions upon the French Revolution and its principles of liberty and equality. The

Federalist party at this time possessed a large portion of the wealth, the talents, and the influence of the new nation. John Adams, a staunch member of the party, was then President, and a majority of Congress supported all his leading measures. In New England his popularity was almost unbounded, and sustained by a weight of opinion and of members which was without precedent in America. The opposition to his administration was comparatively small, although in the Southern States it was formidable. Party feeling ran exceedingly high. Badges of loyalty to our government and of hatred to France were everywhere worn in New England, and the black cockade was a signal of patriotic devotion to "Adams and liberty."

The contagion of party feeling could not, of course, be kept outside the walls of Harvard. In his Senior year William secured permission from the College authorities to call a meeting of students to discuss the political crisis. At the meeting he spoke so eloquently that his classmates accepted his motion to send a message to President Adams. A committee to draw up the address was appointed, but William was most responsible for the document that was finally sent to the President, who returned a warm reply. Both address and answer were published in the Boston newspapers.

A glance at the contents of the address reveals that William was in complete accord with the sentiments of the party to which William Ellery and William Channing had been devoted. Glowing with patriotism and couched in typical eighteenth-century grandiloquence, William's effort bespoke sincerity and dedication of purpose, even though it was largely descriptive and rhetorical. One passage suffices to characterize its general tone and method: "We have seen a nation in Europe grasping at universal conquest, trampling on the laws of God and nations; systematizing rapine and plunder, destroying foreign governments by the strength of her arms or the pestilence of her embraces. . . . We have seen this same nation violating our neutral rights, spurning our pacific proposals, her piratical citizens sweeping our ships from the seas, and venal presses under her control pouring out torrents of abuse on men who have grown gray in our service. We have seen her ministers in this country insulting our government by a daring, unprecedented, and contemptuous appeal to the people. . . . We have seen this, Sir, and our youthful blood has boiled within us. . . . Our lives are our only property; and we were not the sons of those who sealed our liberties with their blood, if we would not defend with these lives that soil which now affords a peaceful grave to the mouldering bones of our forefathers."

Proud words often come home to haunt their speaker, but William was soon able to show that he had meant every syllable of his address. The occasion was Commencement Day for the Class of '98 and the issue was freedom of speech. The story really begins the previous June. Some of the ardent Federalists among the Class of '97 had severely criticized the Republicans (the adherents of Jefferson) in their farewell remarks; and the uproar that followed had nearly turned the proceedings into an armed camp. After numerous debates the Faculty decided that the only way to avoid a repetition of such partisan strife was to prohibit the introduction of party questions in future addresses. Channing became involved in this issue when he was informed that the highest honor of the graduation program had fallen to him. He had been chosen to give the closing oration on the subject of "The Present Age."

As soon as he learned of the proscription laid down by the Faculty, he hurried to President Willard and declared his unwillingness to speak under any such restrictions. The President was willing to accept his resignation but urged him to reconsider, because he felt the principle involved too trifling to make any fuss about it. But not so Channing or his classmates. They gave him unqualified moral support, one of them who bore the reputation of "radical" going so far as to pen him a note stating that "the government of the College have completed the climax of their despotism. They have obtained an arrêt which from its features I could swear is the offspring of the French Directory. Although they pretend to be friends of American liberty . . . they are *Jacobins,* or at best *pretended patriots.*"

As usually happens in affairs of this kind, rumors began to circulate, which in turn magnified the whole business to the proportions of a local *cause celébre.* The *Columbian Sentinel* printed stories of both sides in the debate, and these brought new partisans into the discussions. Actually the tension built up among students and townspeople was largely wasted energy, because President Willard had acted quickly once he saw that the matter was getting out of hand and was threatening to do harm out of all proportion to its significance. He called Channing in to discuss his desires in the matter and made enough concessions to get William's promise that he would deliver the oration. It was a signal triumph for William and a complete vindication of his view that freedom of expression could be earned if one were willing to stand up for his rights. He posted exultant letters to his brother Francis, his mother, and Uncle Henry about his victory. If they were able to detect a note of pride in what he wrote, they could easily forgive him because they knew what anguish he had gone through.

Commencement Day was a brilliant affair even though the program failed to go on as scheduled. Joseph Story, William's closest competitor for class honors, recited the class poem with fervor and dignity; but Arthur Walter caused an uproar by refusing to take part in the scientific conference that had been scheduled. The other participants did the best they could without him, but Walter was prevented from receiving his degree. The French dialogue, which had been carefully prepared by the honor students in French, had to be cancelled because feeling against the French government was running so high that it was thought inadvisable to risk incurring the public's wrath by speaking in the French tongue. When the time came for the closing oration, everyone was wondering what would happen next. But Channing was unperturbed by the delays and changes in program. Advancing to the speaker's platform, he began firmly but with his characteristic nervous expression to extol the virtues of the age in which he and his audience were living. His message found enthusiastic response from the audience, and when it was finished, his classmates hurried to congratulate him. The fear of his creating dissension and partisan feelings proved groundless, although everyone who heard him was quick to admit that he had spoken eloquently for the cause of freedom and the responsibilities of governing bodies to refrain from hampering the free exchange of ideas. Those who knew him well were not surprised at his method of handling his subject, since his opposition to bias and wrangling was well known.

Few of the graduates were as happy and proud as William, because few of them had worked with such seriousness of purpose and knowledge of the importance of their college experiences. Although he was younger than most of them, he saw more clearly than they that the course of their future actions had already been determined. He had done his best, and his best had been rewarded by academic honors and the friendship of students and Faculty as well.

Harvard had been good to him. He had learned a great deal under her elms. He had learned to cherish knowledge and to respect wisdom in others; he had learned also that great ideas are powerless of themselves to effect revolutions in men's thinking and conduct; that there must be men who are willing to fight for these ideas. He had learned a fuller meaning of the word *liberty* which his grandfather and Ezra Stiles had cherished. He had learned a new insight into the beauties of nature—the pleasure of still autumnal days; he had learned the gift

of a "general, liberal, generous education" and the danger of a special-
ization that makes "but half a man of you." He had *learned!* That
was what was important.

When he attended the chapel exercises on Class Day, he tried to
total mentally what he had gained. As he bade farewell to the professors and the tutors after Chapel, he saw in their smiles evidence of
their pleasure in his learning. And when he left them to join the
happy throng of graduates parading through the halls, he knew by
their hearty congratulations that he had succeeded in winning their
friendship and admiration. And finally when he was surrounded by
family and friends, he realized why he had worked and struggled to
be the first in his class. His sacrifices were forgotten in the pleasure of
knowing that those dearest to him were proud of being a part of his
success.

CHAPTER THREE

AMONG THE VIRGINIANS

ALTHOUGH HE JOINED the "Minister's Club," as the Adelphi was popularly called, at the end of his Junior year, Channing had really had no intention of preparing for a ministerial career. Purely social reasons lay behind his choice. Toward the end of the final year, his attitude changed, and he became actively interested in things religious. As he himself put it, "the prevalence of infidelity imported from France led me to inquire into the evidences of Christianity, and then *I found for what I* was made." God's ministry was the answer. Although his decision seems precipitous, it actually was not, because his secular reading provides clear proof of his steady withdrawal from more worldly pursuits and a gradual reawakening to spiritual things.

Once the die was cast, he was quick to share the news with his friends. Some of them were surprised because they had expected him to follow in the footsteps of his father and older brother; but those who knew him best took the announcement as a matter of course. From long experience they knew how his mind worked, and they were willing to accept his decision as right and final.

When the time came for them to go their separate ways, they parted cheerfully although a close observer might have detected a suspicion of moisture in the eyes of several. Joe Tuckerman was going to Dedham to study divinity with Thomas Thacher. Phillips was off to Europe, and Bill Shaw was ready to take over his duties as private secretary to President John Adams. Joe Story was eager to return to Salem and the law. By comparison, William felt unsettled because his immediate plans called simply for his return to Newport and a summer of relaxation. He had a definite goal in mind, but he was still in the dark concerning the way to achieve it. However, he was too optimistic to worry long about the future, and he returned to Newport in a cheerful frame of mind.

Back home, his family and friends gave him a cordial welcome. Over the preceding four years he had been home only during college recesses and summer vacations. Visits had to be paid and repaid, and they kept him busy for several weeks. Once the excitement of renewing

34

acquaintance with old friends and places had died down, he settled back to enjoy himself. The days flew by too fast to count. August came and went and he was beginning to grow restless. At first it had been pleasant to relax and think only of the moment, but as summer began to shade into autumn, idleness began to pall and his contentment changed to a feeling of sadness.

He sought out the beach where he had spent so many happy moments as a boy, but even there he found it difficult to overcome his spiritual malaise. Still the towering crags and roaring waves had a power to heal his spirit. Filled with awe and delight he gave himself up ecstatically to the sea and the sky. As he wrote to Bill Shaw, "I am either born to heaven on 'rapture's Wing of Fire,' or else I am plunged into the depths of despair." Old Eliphalet Pearson would have retched at this gushy and naked expression of sentimentality, but a youngster of eighteen could be forgiven even such unrestrained emotion as this. To all but his intimate friends Channing seemed to be calm and standoffish, but beneath the surface he was surcharged with emotion that required constant control. Hardly a moment would pass in his life when he would not have to guard against excessive feelings and an over-display of sentiment.

The real cause of William's trouble was simply the let-down that follows naturally after any decided change in environment. His most perplexing problem was the question of getting a job. His conscience wouldn't let him depend any longer on his mother, and he was independent enough to want to start supporting himself. He wrote to Uncle Henry in New London about his plans to get work and told him that he hoped heaven would soon smile on his exertions.

A few weeks later, heaven, in the guise of a young gentleman from Virginia, did smile. He met David Randolph of Richmond, who was spending the summer in Newport. Randolph invited him to return to Richmond with him as a tutor for his children. William accepted immediately. In October he set forth with Mr. Randolph for the journey southward.

Richmond society was a revelation. What a change from the reserved and formal society of New England to the fashionable environment of Richmond! His employer was United States Marshal for Virginia, and the most celebrated men of the South visited in his home. John Marshall, who was then Chief Justice of the United States Supreme Court, was a frequent caller, and equally famous people were often to be found chatting and drinking on the Randolph veranda. The social whirl of Richmond was somewhat of an eye opener, but William was not completely abashed by the refinement of manners. The years that he had spent in the Dana mansion now stood him in good stead, and his rough corners were soon rubbed smooth.

He was especially captivated by Virginia manners. He wrote his brother Francis that the men called each other by their Christian names and conversed with a familiarity and frankness of boys at play. He told Bill Shaw that he had to blush for his own people when he compared the selfish prudence of the Yankees with the generous confidence of the Virginians. He admitted that he found great vices among his Southern acquaintances but also that their virtues were more than a match for their failings. The one thing that impressed him most about them was their disinterested attitude toward money. As he put it, their patriotism was not tied to their purse strings.

In his travels about Richmond and the surrounding plantations he used his entré into Southern society to full advantage. Keeping his eyes and ears open he drank in every bit of information that came his way. His humanitarianism, already awakened by his grandfather and further stimulated by his reading in the "School of Sensibility," found ample scope for application in his study of slavery. Since the slave quarters in the neighboring plantations were open for inspection, he had excellent opportunities to study the social conditions of the Negroes on the Randolph estate. Whenever he could, he distributed rations in the slave huts and talked freely with the domestic servants in the house. On one occasion the Randolphs put him in charge while they were away on a visit. The experience left an indelible impression upon him of the Negroes' utter wretchedness.

But the Negroes didn't get all of his sympathy. He realized that the whites were also suffering from the slave system. The problem of slavery was not a simple one, he soon decided, and tried to seek out the causes for what he considered to be an unmitigated evil. The moral sentiment of the community was not corrupt, that was easy to see. Many Southerners abhorred slavery. Many also agreed wholeheartedly with Thomas Jefferson's views of the subject. But moral sentiment and the effort of even a brilliant and respected man like Jefferson were not enough to overcome the economic obstacles that abolition or emancipation presented. The very year William was born Jefferson had come within the proverbial hair's breadth of securing gradual emancipation of the slaves in Virginia. At the present time the importation of slaves was prohibited in all the states except North Carolina. Even there efforts to hamper the slave traffic were meeting with success. In the North emancipation was making rapid headway,

and many Southerners were hoping that the South would soon follow
suit.

But despite these encouraging signs, he could see that slavery continued to flourish and that the condition of the Negroes remained relatively unchanged. What possible solution to the problem could there be? He heard many answers, but none without flaws. Southerners like the Randolphs were so eager to be quit of slavery that they even flirted with the idea of leaving their beloved South. But only momentarily, for they realized that running away was no answer.

Despite his youth and inexperience William was not fooled into believing that the planters were the greatest sufferers from slavery. Although he was firmly convinced that slavery was degrading to white as well as black, he was more certain that slavery was an evil because it struck at God in the slave. On this point he was indignant. Nature, he was sure, had never made such a distinction. When one man was forced to substitute his will for that of another he became a mere machine. This was what he would later call the moral argument against slavery, and as far as he was concerned it was the basis upon which all other claims against slavery must be laid. Slavery was a "waste" system as far as economics went, but he was more upset over the spiritual enslavement it fostered than the economic hardships it created.

Politically he was in an environment even more alien to his native New England than the world of social intercourse. Newport and Cambridge were strictly Federalistic; Virginia was Jeffersonian. Born and raised in places sacred to the memory of "Saint George" and among people devoted to the cause of Adams and the Constitution he was now in the center of America's domestic Jacobins. The change in political climate was greater even than the difference between the wintry blasts of Maine and the zephyrs of Virginia, but it was a change that he needed. Federalism was only one side of the political coin, and his vision of reforming and instructing a vicious and ignorant world required a whole view of the universe.

After he had been in Virginia about nine months, he felt free enough to write his friends about the change in his political opinions. He was still quite firm about his opposition to Jacobin principles, but his attitude toward France had softened considerably.

Even more serious was his backsliding in the matter of a standing army. The XYZ fiasco had led John Adams to recall Ambassador Gerry from France and to begin preparations for strengthening our national defenses. The existing army could not be depended upon for this purpose because it already had its hands full policing the frontier. Adams and his advisors decided, therefore, that the standing army should be increased.

At this point Channing wrote to Shaw, who was in close contact with the President, in unequivocal terms: "You may call me Jacobin, if you please, but I am *not* for enlarging our *standing army*. I wish there was nothing of the kind. . . . I am opposed to standing armies on account of their *moral effects*. The activity of war leaves the soldier little time to corrupt himself. But an army in time of peace is the hotbed of vice. . . . A soldier *by profession* is too apt to forget that he is a citizen."

Worse than this he wrote shortly afterwards, "I blush when I think of the Alien and Sedition Acts. They have only served to show the weakness of government." The four laws passed by the Federalists in June and July of 1798 were intended to keep from American shores undesirable foreigners, particularly the type that was virulent in its abuse of American institutions, and also to punish those persons who were found guilty of conspiring against the government and its officers. As so often happens, the laws served only to arouse considerable indignation. When the question of their appeal came up in Congress, John Marshall was the only Federalist to vote for repeal. His argument, that the laws were "calculated to create unnecessarily, discontents and jealousies at a time when our very existence, as a nation, may depend on our union," undid, as far as Federalists were concerned, all the good he had achieved in the XYZ affair. But his firm stand won William's admiration.

Notwithstanding these chinks in his political armor, William's Federalism was still tolerably sound. The day was still far off when his liberalism would merit for him the name of "locofoco." He was still happy to find "odium . . . everywhere attached to the name of Jacobin" and he relied "implicitly on the firmness and independence of the president" to frustrate the machinations of the French. He wished "France to fall" but he did not want England "to rise on her ruins."

Despite his opposition to "the foul impurities of French principles," he was dreaming dreams of social improvement which had been projected by radical French thinkers and their English followers and friends. When he had been with the Randolphs a year, he decided to undertake a systematic course of reading. He gave himself three years in which to accomplish his purpose. His first love, history, engaged his deepest attention. By reading the biographies of monarchs such as Henry VII, George III, and Louis XIV, he proposed to familiarize himself with the modern world. He read Hume but found that "he does not throw light enough on the rest of Europe." He wondered whether he must "wade through Gibbon to get acquainted with the Empire" and finally decided to postpone the "Decline" until he began a course of ecclesiastical history.

"I shall now read history very differently from what I used to do," he declared. "I shall read it as a politician and a moralist. I shall found my opinions of government on what I see to be the effects of different systems and not on idle speculation."

Above all his other readings, he cherished Ferguson's "Civil Society." To another member of the Scottish school, William Robertson, who, together with Hume and Gibbon made up the great triumvirate of eighteenth-century English historians, he gave credit for being put in "a right direction in historical matters." Robertson taught him the value of broad views of human affairs and led him to look for the steady causes and tendencies at work among nations.

From the Scotch historians he turned to Rousseau. He had read *Emile* in college and now *Eloise* attracted him. "What a writer!" he exclaimed. "Rousseau is the only French author I have ever read, who knows the way to the heart." From Jean Jacques he was drawn to William Godwin, an adherent of the Frenchman's revolutionary ideas. He was particularly impressed by *Caleb Williams,* although Godwin's *Political Justice* was also a favorite. He could not agree with Godwin's mechanistic conception of the universe or with his reliance upon reason to the exclusion of man's emotional nature, but he did seize upon Godwin's idea that all "human inventions are capable of perpetual improvement." It made him melancholy to reflect that Rousseau and Godwin and Godwin's wife, Mary Woolstonecraft, were all deists. The latter's *Rights of Woman* impressed him as being a "masculine" performance; but he could not recommend her views on marriage, although he was surprisingly liberal, for the time, in his judgment of her irregular unions with Gilbert Imlay and Godwin.

His forays among the "perfectibilitarians" brought him by a straight line to a vision of a perfect society. To those of his acquaintances who had watched his concern for humanity develop, such a result was by no means unpredictable. Nor was he, in those millennial days of the late nineties, when revolution here and abroad had opened up vistas of man "sceptreless, free, and uncircumscribed," more enthusiastic than many another young idealist. To those young men who were reading such contemporary novels of purpose as *Desmond, Hermsprong,* and *Hugh Trevor* and who were familiar with the school of "sensible" philosophers, dreams of human reformation came naturally. William's mind like theirs was fertile breeding ground for communistic schemes.

Writing to Shaw in the spring of 1799, he outlined his views of how man should be enfranchised. Avarice was the greatest obstacle to human progress, he declared. The only way to eliminate it was to establish a community of property. Convinced that virtue and benevolence were natural to man, he blamed selfishness and greed upon the false ideas of superiority of the body over the mind and the separation of individual interest from that of the community as a whole. The only sane solution lay in educating men to understand that the powers and dignity of their minds were unlimited.

It is easy to see how Rousseau and Godwin had added their mite to the store of knowledge he had secured from Hutcheson, Ferguson, and Price. It should also be noted that he had already struck the characteristic note of his later writing and preaching. It is *mind, mind* that requires our care, he says. The real wants of men are but few and can easily be supplied, but the dignity of their nature and the happiness of others require improvement in science and virtue.

To achieve this improvement he sketched, in his letters to Shaw and Arthur Walter, a scheme for a fraternal organization that would have as its goal the foundation of human happiness. The particulars are lacking, but there are several hints that he was considering joining himself, as a minister, to a group of Scotch emigrants whose fundamental principle was common property. His friends thought him crazy, and spoke laughingly of his grandiose ideas.

Arthur Walter, pretending with mock seriousness to accept his scheme, proposed to carry out the "imaginary republic of Coleridge and Southey, and a community of goods, in the backwoods, or, better far, in some South-sea island." But Walter, whose enthusiasm was more restrained than Channing's, also asked, "Will you make yourself miserable, because you cannot reach the rainbow from the hill?" He went on to remind Channing, "In heaven you will find the scope you seek for progression in virtue; but here the mind partakes of the clay which incloses it. . . ." Here Walter had hit on a tendency in Channing's thinking that was as much a liability as it was an asset, for while it lent strength to his aspiration, his penchant for overlooking the clay in man would always subtract from the practicality of his plans for man's improvement.

Walter was not the only one to criticize William's blind spot. Francis Channing reminded him of Plato and Socrates and of their utopian projects, then added, "My brother advances with noble ardor to a vast-er enterprise. . . . To make all men happy, by making all virtuous, in his glorious project. I adore it, thou moral Archimedes! But where wilt thou stand to move the mental world?" For the moment, William could only rest on his theoretical knowledge.

His days in Virginia were not entirely spent in social visits among the gentry or in airy speculation about the millennium, for he had not forgotten why he had come in the first place. His purpose was really two-fold. He wished to prepare himself for the ministry and support himself while he was doing it. The latter purpose took up most of his energies, though he found himself with ample time for study. Accord-ing to his letters, the task of educating the twelve youngsters who were put in his charge took up only his mornings. The afternoons and eve-nings were his own. Although he departed from current teaching prac-tice by refusing to use the lash on his pupils, he thought of himself later on as having been too strict a disciplinarian. Such self-criticism smacks more of over-scrupulous modesty than of accuracy, for cruelty was not in his makeup. He knew that the learning process could not go on if the pupil was lacking in interest, and he relied upon his own en-thusiasm to stimulate his charges.

However wise he may have been in dealing with the Randolph chil-dren and their friends, he was badly in error where his own education was involved. In a spirit of foolish asceticism, or perhaps stoicism, he labored at his studies until the early morning hours in a small out-building which he had chosen for its privacy. Without proper clothing (he spent his money on books instead of an overcoat and was too proud to write home for help) and frequently forgetful of mealtimes, he kept a lonely vigil with his books that was interrupted only by his duties as a tutor. Not content with this he played the Spartan by sleep-ing on the bare floor. His body was strong, but it could not stand up forever under this kind of punishment. That he managed to bear up at all is evidence that, for him at least, there was something to his the-ory of mind over matter.

For his idea that care should be expended entirely on the mind lay behind his peculiar behavior. This was his way of subduing the flesh and elevating the mind. Had he paid closer attention to the golden-mean philosophy expounded in the Grecian and Roman histories he was reading, he could have saved himself life-long physical misery. The irony of the situation was that he defeated the very purpose he was trying to achieve. Instead of curbing his animal nature, he made him-self so frail and weak that he became prey to every idle fancy that entered his mind. At night when he left his reading from sheer exhaustion, he fell into an uneasy slumber broken by bad dreams and near-hallucinations. In the daytime he was often plagued with indigestion, so that his infrequent meals nauseated instead of nourishing him.

When he finally realized how foolish he had been, the damage had already been done. He soon discovered that his body could not be depended upon to carry him through long periods of physical exertion. This upset him, but he was dismayed to discover that when he was physically ill, his mind had a tendency to wander and his imagination to inflame his passions. He confessed to his friend Shaw, "I sit down with Goldsmith or Rogers in my hand, and shed tears—at what? At fictitious misery; at tales of imaginary woe."

Shortly thereafter, an incident occurred that made him realize that there was no moral merit in merely feeling. He had lent a friend a sonnet of Southey which had wrung tears from him. When she told him she thought it "pretty," he realized that his friend, whom he admits "was goodness itself," lacked the degree of feeling that he himself possessed. The light had dawned: there was no correlation between benevolence and feeling. Many people who were lacking in benevolence possessed a super-abundance of emotion and vice versa. "It is true," he said, "that I sit in my study and shed tears over human misery. I weep over a novel. I weep over a tale of human woe. But do I ever relieve the distressed? Have I ever lightened the load of affliction?" Even as he phrased these questions, he could feel that his mind was becoming disburdened of a dark cloud of error. Virtue did not consist in mere feeling. Virtue really meant "acting from a sense of duty."

This "sense of duty" was to become the foundation of his entire ethical system, and his preaching would consist of little else than an attempt to hammer home his belief in its significance. Time and time again, he would define it in his sermons, but his definitions would simply be synonyms of the "innate moral sense" of the Shaftesbury-Hutcheson-Price school of thought. He had not really discovered something new; but he had realized for the first time the full implications of what had hitherto been only a beautiful theory to him. Only now did he realize that "disinterested benevolence" was not a phrase to be read but a way of life to be followed.

In the meantime, while the process of self-discovery and of learning about the external world was going on, he was concentrating more and more upon religion and upon preparing himself for the ministry. Turning away from the "Gallican" criticism of Christianity he found in his reading and in the society around him, he went to the Scriptures to seek out the will of God. There he found truths that made him feel as though he had never, until that moment, known the meaning of the term *Christian*. His thoughts became fastened on the world to come, and he lost sight for a time of his social ideals in the contemplation of immortality. With the same enthusiasm that he had adopted eighteenth-century benevolence and political liberalism, he now welcomed Christian *caritas*. After much perplexity and doubt, he made the jump of faith and accepted the providential mission and miraculous character of Christ, although he was too scrupulous to accept any doctrines, religious or otherwise, until he had applied such tests as lay within his power.

In the main he depended upon the Bible for his evidence. As he told his friend, the Reverend Joseph McKean, he had not "applied to any commentators or to any authors except the Apostles themselves." The Scriptures were to him, as they were to all orthodox Calvinists, "the only source of divine knowledge," and he became accustomed to judge every action by the standard of Scriptural morality. Where sectarian doctrines were concerned, he had already cultivated a caution in committing himself that was to become habitual during his ministry.

The effects of this intense dedication to God's word coupled with his complete disdain for material comforts finally brought about what he described to his Uncle Henry as "that *change of heart* which is necessary to constitute a Christian." He spoke of his "conversion" and declared that his sentiments and affection had been completely redirect- *God* ed. No longer was mere morality a desirable goal. He had submerged himself in God, and love of the Creator had become his only desire. Mankind was to be loved only because they were children of God. To seal his new-found covenant, he penned an act of self-consecration, laying bare past offenses and promising sincerely to seek God's love and justice.

He had come to Virginia filled with political enthusiasm and believing that pure morality, or "disinterested benevolence," was sufficient to secure human happiness and to open up the way to unlimited progress. Now his political liberalism had deepened into religious faith, and his secular morality had received a large infusion of religious piety. As a matter of fact, his sense of piety was, in kind and degree, not very dissimilar from that of Jonathan Edwards. In time, however, piety in the Edwardian sense would gradually disappear from his ethical code, and he would come to love mankind more because of the dynamic potential of human goodness than because of the static concept of man as a child of God. In reality, what would happen would be *change in view of religion*

a complete reversal of his youthful concept of religion. William Channing, tutor in the Randolph family, might think of religion's being rooted in love of God; Dr. Channing, the minister of the Federal Street Congregation in Boston, would preach the "worship of goodness"—of love of man flowering into the love of God. In a sense, this change would represent in little what had already happened at large in the religious circles of New England—piety would gradually turn into moralism.

After he had been with the Randolphs for a year and a half, his health grew so bad that he needed complete rest and quiet. Since Newport was the best place for him, he asked the Randolphs to release him. They agreed, and he left Richmond in July in a leaky coal sloop manned by a drunken captain and crew. The trip was uneventful except for the haphazard seamanship of the ship's captain, and William arrived in Newport none the worse for wear. But his family could scarcely recognize the pallid invalid who greeted them at the dock. Gone was the smiling and vigorous youngster who had left them less than two years before, and in his place stood an old-young man who was a stranger. Had they fully comprehended the changes in him, they would have felt even more dismayed, for he was mentally and spiritually as far removed from the boy who had charmed their hearts with his gay banter as one could be and still not lose his identity altogether.

CHAPTER FOUR

NEWPORT AND CAMBRIDGE

News of Channing's return soon reached his friends at Cambridge, and letters began to arrive from former classmates. His first visitor from Harvard was Washington Allston, who hurried down to Newport as soon as graduation was over. Since William's departure from Harvard, their contact with each other had been restricted to infrequent letters. As a result, both were brimful of things to talk about.

When he got over the shock of seeing William so gaunt and pale, Allston began to question him eagerly about Richmond and his experiences there. Channing talked freely about his new-found ideas, and in turn queried Allston about his plans to become America's "first painter." Allston told him that he had decided to study abroad and was hoping to be admitted to the Royal Academy in London. His enthusiasm was infectious, and William was cheered to think that the future lay bright before his friend. When Allston left for Charleston in December, their boyhood acquaintance had ripened into firm friendship.

While William was convalescing from his illness he kept busy by tutoring young Randolph, who had returned with him from Richmond, and Edward Tyrrel, the baby of the Channing family. Francis had returned to Cambridge to establish himself as a lawyer, so William was left in the position of paterfamilias. Although the responsibility was heavy for a lad of twenty, William was equal to it. He had succeeded in gaining the mastery over self that is so necessary if one is to exercise supervision over others. Within a short time his mother began to call him "Father" William because he reminded her so much of the husband whom she had lost.

Besides his tutoring, he undertook to supervise the studies of his sisters, Anna, Mary, and Lucy. Though more inclined to serious talk, he could at times descend from Mount Olympus to forget himself in a game of draughts or to wander along the beach with one or all of the girls.

For the most part, however, he shunned society. Believing that retirement "made less work for repentance," he avoided companionship in order to seek a purer spirituality. Once again he was forgetting moderation and inviting trouble for himself. He drew up a list of suggestions for self-discipline. Heading his list was an injunction to cultivate an active spirit of Christian charity. He urged himself to remember that "I have lost that day in which I have done no good to a fellow man," and resolved to search for wretchedness so that he might "communicate the last of his store." Religion, he reminded himself, must never be represented as gloomy or hopeless. Charity demanded he respect all sects no matter how he might differ with their views, but he noted that "it will sometimes be necessary to change the tone of approbation and pity to that of denial." Such occasions, he concluded, required deliberate action and firm adherence to whatever decisions might be reached.

His program was ambitious but there was nothing theoretical about it. Putting it down on paper was hardly necessary, for he had seldom deviated from it; and the future would increase the intensity of his devotion to its principles. It was as much a history of his past as it was an outline for times to come.

Although his days were filled with a variety of tasks, there was never a moment when his whole energy was not devoted to preparation for the ministry. His time was passed in study either at the Redwood Library, only a few minutes' walk from the Channing residence, or at the beach, by now his second home. In the quiet precincts of the library he spent day after day and sometimes week after week without interruption from a single visitor. When he grew tired of his peaceful study, he took himself to the beach, where the roar of the surf and the brilliant sunshine combined to restore his energies and stimulate him to further exertion.

If these two favorite haunts were influential in shaping his mind, there was a third and even stronger force acting upon him. This was the friendship of the seventy-year-old Samuel Hopkins. William had never really become acquainted with the old gentleman until now, although the sight of the ungainly figure of Hopkins was one that he had not forgotten through the four years at Harvard and the months in Richmond. First impressions are supposed to be lasting, but a visit or two quickly dispelled the fear and reserve built up in childhood. Soon he began to look forward with increasing eagerness to his visits to the gambrel-roofed parsonage of Dr. Hopkins, which was situated on the next street below William's home.

Young Channing became attached to Dr. Hopkins chiefly because of the latter's theory of disinterestedness. On one occasion when Hopkins received a hundred-dollar bill for a copyright, he donated the entire amount to a missionary collection, although he could have put it to excellent use by satisfying any of a dozen personal needs. The fact that Hopkins not only preached but practiced his theory was a source of great satisfaction to William, who believed that words without action meant little. Hopkins's perfect honesty and his love of honesty in others also attracted William despite his horror of Hopkins's religious views.

"His views of the Divine agency and sovereignty were utterly irreconcilable with human freedom," he once wrote. "Still in forming his religious opinions, he was superior to human authority; he broke away from human creeds; he interpreted God's word for himself; he revered reason, the oracle of God within him. . . . He maintained that all holiness, all moral excellence, consists in benevolence, or disinterested devotion to the greatest good; that this is the character of God; that love is the only principle of the divine administration. He taught that sin was introduced into the creation, and is to be everlastingly punished, because evil is necessary to the highest good. . . . Other Calvinists were willing that their neighbors should be predestined to everlasting misery for the glory of God. This noble-minded man demanded a more generous and impartial virtue, and maintained that we should consent to our own perdition, should be willing ourselves to be condemned, if the greatest good of the universe, and the manifestation of the divine perfections should so require. True virtue, as he taught, was an entire surrender of personal interest to the benevolent purposes of God."

Hopkins was a stern man and his system contained a number of paradoxes. Although he accepted the most severe form of predestination, he rejected the doctrines of total depravity and election. Instead he believed and taught that Christ suffered equally for all mankind. Such amelioration of Calvinistic beliefs was most acceptable to William, and he did not fail in later years to give Hopkins full credit for "mitigating the harsh features" of the Genevan system; but it was the idea of benevolence that really thrilled him. For the first time, the image of it had become clear and distinct in his mind and soul. Francis Hutcheson had developed, Richard Price had enlarged, and Samuel Hopkins had printed the finished picture that now lay before him. One day Hopkins's "triumphant humanitarianism" would become transformed into Channing's idea of "diffusive charity"; the sovereignty of God would be superseded by his "paternity" and Calvinism would be beset by Unitarianism, "the half-way house to infidelity."

For the moment William was only a student of theology, and the task of winnowing the tares of falsehood from the wheat of truth was more than enough to keep him preoccupied. As Dr. Hopkins facetiously remarked to him after a "guest" appearance in the pulpit of Hopkins's church, "The *hat* is not made yet." He was referring to theology as a progressive science and comparing the different stages of it to the successive processes of making a hat. The beaver was to be born, then to be killed, and then the felt to be made, etc. Having explained the similitude, he added, "The hat is not made, and I hope you will help to finish it."

Hopkins never lived to see his hope fulfilled, but it is unlikely that he ever doubted Channing's ability to succeed where he had failed. In his "Farewell to the World," he wrote of the people of Newport, "They have appeared more dissolute, vicious, erroneous and ignorant, than people in general are in other parts of New England"; there is every reason to believe, therefore, that he felt Channing would have a far better opportunity than he had had to harvest the seed of piety in the hearts of Newport citizens.

In December, 1801, William received an award that he had scarcely dared to hope for: he was appointed a Regent at Harvard. Leaving Newport, he arrived in Cambridge in January, 1802, to assume his new duties. The office of Regent was little more than a sinecure. Daniel White, William's friend from Hasty-Pudding days, remembers that President Willard had recommended the establishment of the office "to afford an eligible situation for some worthy student in divinity, who might be induced by it to pursue his studies at Cambridge." The duties involved were far from onerous. In addition to occupying a room in one of the halls and preserving order in the rooms in his entry, William was charged with the keeping of certain records that had formerly been assigned to the college Butler. To assist him in the performance of his duties, he was allowed the service of a Freshman.

That he was thankful for his new position goes without saying, because it provided him with the financial support he so badly needed and enabled him to use the resources of the Harvard Library. Moreover, though he was once again separated from his family, he was now reunited with Francis and could easily renew his friendship with former college chums. In a sense, however, he was a stranger in a familiar land, because he had been conspicuously absent at commencement the summer before, when nearly two thirds of his graduating class had received the degree of master of arts.

In Harvard Yard once again, William buckled down to the serious

study of divinity. Both the Reverend Joseph Willard and the Reverend
David Tappan were available for consultation. As an undergraduate,
William had come under Tappan's benign influence so that it was only
natural now for him to seek advice from the man whom such critics as
George Cabot, Fisher Ames, and Judge Lowell considered one of the
best preachers of the day. He seldom consulted Willard, whose wooden
face and strong nasal intonation were not conducive to private discussion. Although Professor Tappan was considered a "moderate Calvinist" (to many people, this phrase was a contradiction in terms), he
came as near to being impartial in his theological views as it is possible
to be and still have any views at all. Instead of indoctrinating students
with his ideas, he urged them to judge for themselves. William, who
had learned already to appreciate the value of self-reliance and toleration, warmed immediately to Tappan, and when his ordination drew
near, showed his affection by having Tappan preach his ordination
sermon.

Although William kept no record of the studies he followed in his
preparation for the ministry, his reading had to be confined largely to
English writers in divinity, since the new era of scientific theology
ushered in by German scholars had scarcely dawned; and in America,
especially, several decades would have to pass before any appreciable
influence from Germany could be discerned.

In general he thought English theology of little worth. He considered the established church "the grave of intellect" and "a dozing
place to minds which anywhere else would have signalized themselves."
Even so he admitted there were "powerful thinkers" in the English
system, and he made up a list of books and authors whom he could
recommend.

The list was headed by Butler's *Analogy,* "one of the noblest productions of the mind," and Butler's *Sermons,* "among the finest ethical discussions." Then followed Lardner and Paley on the "evidences" of
Christianity; Campbell and Farmer on miracles; Priestley's "Letters to
a Philosophical Unbeliever"; Watson's answers to Paine and Gibbon;
Locke's "Reasonableness of Christianity"; Edwards on the "Will" and
Samuel Clarke as counter-blast; Law's "Theory of Religion"; and
Hartley's "Observations on Man," "on the whole an admirable work"
but "disfigured . . . by a gross mechanical philosophy of the mind." He
almost blushed to acknowledge it, but he had to confess that he had
not read either Hooker, Cudworth, or Chillingworth. There was more
to his list, but enough has been said to show that here, as everywhere,
he reacted against materialistic, necessitarian, or utilitarian views and

tended to accept only broad views of Christianity that were in "harmony with human nature, and with the great laws of the universe, as we understand them," and that tend "to secure the true perfection of the individual and the race."

Of the writers most frequently mentioned (i.e., in addition to Hutcheson, Ferguson, and Price), Joseph Butler and William Law were most prominent. Butler's sermons "Upon Human Nature," he regarded as unsurpassed in English for clear, full, condensed thought. Law appealed to his sympathies by a piety and earnest longing for spiritual perfection that came near to being mysticism. His interest in these two authors, so unlike in most ways and representing divergent currents of mind in the intellectual climate of the Enlightenment, is further evidence of his capacity for entertaining the claims of both the rationalists and the intuitionists. Like his pupil and successor, Ralph Waldo Emerson, he possessed a dualism reminiscent of the early Puritans in America, who were able not only to persevere in their study of Ramean logic but had time also to seek out God's "wonder-working providences." Both men, and their ancestors as well, realized that the mind is mighty, but they knew too that the heart also "hath its reasons."

As he studied, William wrote down the ideas that came into his mind. Writing, as he often told his friends, was a witness to his study habits, the best means he knew of making clear his own thoughts. He would note new suggestions, place contradictory views side by side, set down general statements, then qualify them by particulars. Begun in his student days, this habit of thinking with pen in hand became second nature to the busy minister. Books, pockets, desk—all were constantly littered with slips of paper on which were written ideas that were deemed significant at the time of reading. This eclectic method proved invaluable when his works were sought for publication, because it made the task of organization somewhat easier. It appears likely also that it was responsible for the derivative quality of much of his thinking as well as his frequent failure to effect smooth transitions between sentences, paragraphs, and larger units of writing.

The habit of self-examination begun in Newport was continued at Harvard. His journal entries during this period reveal the rigorous standards to which he was attempting to hold himself. He was aware that he read too much and reflected too little and resolved to reverse the procedure by concentrating first on primary sources of knowledge and then resorting to the various commentaries. Like Milton, he had come to the conclusion that "Fame is no plant that grows on mortal soil," and he reminded himself that his object in life was to do good to the world by promoting the cause of religion. Humility seemed to him most desirable in studying the Scriptures, because he was afraid of being led astray by human systems. He prayed for the simplicity of a child that he might avoid narrowness of sentiment and determined to concentrate on a few important truths rather than to become lost in the chaos of universal knowledge that had hitherto distracted him.

Most evident among his self-admonition is the new tone of humility. Though never entirely lacking in his nature, it had now become almost child-like. Noteworthy also was the change of emphasis in his studies. For the time being at least, he had pushed secular knowledge into the background so that he could concentrate on the Bible. Already he had begun to lay the foundation for the criticisms that were to label him a man of narrow scope and limited depth. It would appear, however, that he felt he had no choice in the matter. Man can do only so much, and the improvement of the heart struck him as being infinitely more important than the enlargement of the understanding. If breadth of knowledge were a deterrent to virtue, what course was left to the aspirant to goodness? It was as simple as that; once the problem was analyzed, the solution became obvious.

Though never fully checked, William's struggle for self-improvement was seriously hampered by ill health. Mental depression induced by physical debility brought on mental inactivity. He lost interest in his studies and, like Enceladus, groaned under a mountain of doubt and sluggishness. Realizing the harm in such attitudinizing, he turned to his brother Francis for help. Together, they strolled among the woods of Mount Auburn or about the shores of neighboring ponds, until the combination of friendly conversation and natural surroundings elevated William's spirits and enabled him once again to see the world in proper perspective.

As he neared the end of his studies, he joined the First Church in Cambridge, at that time under the charge of Dr. Abiel Holmes, a Yale graduate but "liberal—for a Connecticut man." Dr. Holmes was a handsome, kindly man, whose marriage to Sally Wendell little more than a year before William joined his congregation had caused many a female breast to sigh with disappointment; his Calvinism, though it might seem horrendously wicked one day to his son Oliver, was scholarly rather than militant. Soon after his union with the First Church, William drew up some articles of faith. Though strongly Hopkinsian, the articles reveal an Arian view of Christ. That is to say, he considered

Christ neither God nor man, nor God and man, but a being who was *sui generis,* and pre-existent.

In the autumn of 1802 he appeared before the Cambridge Association to present a sermon which he hoped would gain him a license to preach. Though specific proof is wanting, the odds are in favor of his having preached on the text, "Silver and gold have I none, but such as I have give I thee." This passage from the *Acts* of the Apostles (III, 6) was his usual point of departure in his early sermons, and understandably so, since it enabled him to discuss his favorite subject, benevolence.

After he had delivered his sermon, one member of the Association, the Reverend Charles Stearns of Lincoln, questioned him. On the surface, the question was innocent enough! Did Channing believe God to be the author of sin? Actually, the query was not as innocent as it sounded because the subject was the cause of considerable debate between the Hopkinsians and their more orthodox brethren. In asking the question, Stearns, himself an Arminian or perhaps a Unitarian, although the latter term had not yet come into usage, must have been prompted by the rumors concerning Channing's supposed adherence to Hopkins's particular brand of divinity to inquire where William stood in the controversy. William managed to satisfy his curiosity and his sermon was accepted by the Association. Though still unordained he was now a licensed preacher.

Using his silver-and-gold text he began to speak in pulpits in and about Cambridge. He preached in Medford for the Reverend Dr. Osgood; and Osgood, a man of outspoken character, praised his eloquence and sincerity. Others were also favorably impressed by his manner, and it was not long until churches in Boston were noticing him. He preached at the Federal Street Society and was well received. Crowded audiences attended his sermon in Brattle Street Church and were delighted with his presentation. That was early in December. Both Boston churches wanted him to consider settlement, but he was not ready for such a decision. Tired and spent by the strain of preaching in different places and before strange audiences, he returned to Newport about the middle of December to rest and think.

But the rest and quiet were hard to find. When Dr. Patten, minister of the Second Congregational Church, invited him to give the monthly lecture, he could not refuse. The news of his sermon was soon noised about; and he was greeted by a large and enthusiastic audience. His text was still the same verse from the Acts. A few quotations from it reveal that he was already preaching the doctrine of love that would forever constitute the essence of his religion. "All Christian morals," he said, "may be reduced to one word, love. God is love, Christ is love. The gospel is an exhibition of love, and its end is to transform men into love." Urging patience and kindness in dealings with one's fellow man, he went on to say, "Perhaps Christ, when on earth, won the hearts of publicans and sinners more by his gentle manners and offices of kindness, when he ate and drank with them, than by exhibiting his miracles." He concluded simply, "Men generally need sympathy more than silver and gold."

Whenever or wherever he preached, he had an attentive listener and enthusiastic supporter in Grandfather Ellery. "You cannot conceive," wrote the old man to his son, "what satisfaction it gives me to see my grandson walking in the truth with so much steadiness, and with so much eloquence and wisdom dispensing the light of the gospel. If he lives, he will be a burning and shining light." William was enjoying every day of his visit in Newport; but neither praise nor pleasure was sufficient to blind him to the fact that he must soon come to a decision concerning his immediate future.

Two weeks after he arrived in Newport, he had received a written "call" from the Deacon of the Federal Street Society. The invitation was most flattering, but equally inviting was a similar request from the Brattle Street Congregation. Fortunately, he was able to reach a decision quickly, because Dr. Thacher, whom he was being asked to assist at Brattle Street, died, leaving the full responsibility of a large parish to whoever would accept the Society's call. He knew he was not physically able to accept such a task, and he informed the Brattle Street elders that he must decline their request. Soon afterwards he decided to accept the post in Federal Street left vacant by John Popkin, which paid twenty-five dollars a Sunday and included a free house and wood. The salary was not great, but it compared favorably with that of any other minister in town; and the requirements of the congregation were within his powers.

Once his mind was made up, William came to Boston to confer with the Committee of the Federal Street Society. The conference evidently was satisfactory to both, for on February 12, 1803, he wrote to the Committee accepting the invitation to settle with them as their minister. Then he determined to build up his strength for the tasks that lay ahead of him. Very opportunely for him, Stephen Higginson, Jr., a wealthy Boston philanthropist, invited him to share his Brookline home. The Higginsons, in many ways like the Randolphs of Richmond, were more than kind and he found every convenience for study and relaxation at his disposal.

In May he wrote to his Uncle Henry, telling him of his acceptance of the Federal Street post. His primary purpose in writing, however, was to tell his uncle that May 18 had been proposed as the day for his ordination and that he wanted him to preach the sermon. "In this most solemn act," he wrote, "I wish you to bear a part. You have had no little share in conducting me to the choice of the sacred profession. I ask, I need, your advice, direction, and encouragement. No one will feel half the interest you do in my welfare; no other person will bring so much affection to the performance of this part of the solemnity. . . . I think that from your lips I shall receive the deepest impression of the awful magnitude of my duty as a minister of Christ."

May 18 came but William was not ordained. Shortly after, however, his friends and the parishioners of Federal Street received the following missive:

> Honored and beloved: the providence of God having preserved us in peace and unity during our destitute state, and having led us to the choice of William E. Channing, and him to accept of our united invitation, we therefore request your presence and assistance by your pastor and delegates on Wednesday, the first day of June, next, to join with other churches in solemnly separating him to the work of the ministry with us. We ask your prayers for him and for us, that he may come to us in the fullness of the blessing of the gospel of peace.

On Wednesday, the first of June, 1803, the ordination finally took place. Abiel Holmes gave the introductory prayer; Dr. Osgood offered the prayer of consecration; Henry Channing delivered the charge; and Joseph Tuckerman gave the right hand of fellowship. David Tappan delivered the ordination sermon in place of Henry Channing. Speaking thoughts that might easily have come from William himself, the Reverend Tappan made a stirring plea for non-sectarianism in religion.

"It ill becomes ministers of Christ," he declared, "to rend asunder his mystical body by substituting the narrow zeal of a party in the room of that comprehensive spirit which unites man to God and one another. It ill becomes them to contend even for truth in a manner unfavorable to Christian love and its practical fruits; for such contention injures both the moral credit and moral influence of the truth; it disfigures and endangers the Gospel Church even by those very doctrines, which, rightly entertained, constitute her principal strength and beauty. It is by speaking the truth in love, and by carrying it out in a holy temper and practice, that Christians are to grow up into a compact, flourishing, and glorious community."

George Ticknor, then a lad of twelve and a complete stranger to Channing, attended the services with his father, a member of the ordaining council. Recalling the occasion later, he wrote, "I have still no recollection of anything in the services of the day, till they were about to be concluded. Then the pale, spiritual-looking young man, whose consecration I had witnessed without really understanding its purport, rose and announced the closing hymn. My attention was immediately fastened on him; and particularly on his visible emotion when he came to the last stanza:

> My tongue repeats her vows,
> Peace to this sacred house!
> For here my friends and brethren dwell;
> And since my glorious God
> Makes thee his blest abode,
> My soul shall ever love thee well.

His looks, the tones of his trembling voice, and the devout air with which he repeated rather than read these lines, are still present to me whenever the scene comes up in my thoughts." Ticknor remembered also how sad he had felt because the young man's feeble appearance seemed to augur an early death.

For William the day was one of triumph, but he was all humility before the thought of the responsibility that he had undertaken. "Who am I?" he thought. "What are my powers? How little am I able to answer expectation!" Awed by the magnitude of his duties, he was nevertheless reassured by his faith in God's love. With prayer to sustain him and the thought of God's mercy always before him, he would do his best to perform the Almighty's will.

CHAPTER FIVE

A NEW ERA OF PREACHING

For the first few months after his settlement Channing was too preoccupied with his own personal problems to give much thought to the world around him. He continued to live with the Higginson family, but finally, not wishing to impose longer on their hospitality, he went to board with one of his parishioners until a parish house could be prepared.

According to reports from the family with whom he stayed, he was completely absorbed in his own contemplations. Society was distasteful to him: he spoke only when spoken to; ate hastily; lived mostly in his study, declining invitations from friends who wished to draw him forth from his seclusion; and seemed happiest when alone. His old enemy was upon him again—the habit of brooding in solitude over a problem that greatly concerned him.

Though never the recluse that Nathaniel Hawthorne later became, Channing was guilty, on a much lesser scale, of the same heinous fault for which Hawthorne's creation, Ethan Brand, had searched so unsuccessfully. Unlike Brand, who discovered too late for his personal salvation that the unpardonable sin was "the sin of an intellect that triumphed over the sense of brotherhood with man and reverence for God, and sacrificed everything to its own mighty claims," William, whose moral nature was more highly developed, realized in time that his "speculations about the origin of moral feelings, etc., cannot justify a practical neglect of them." But the struggle for control over himself was not easily won, and final victory eluded him until he had been in the ministry for quite some time.

Most of his troubles were due to an over-refined conscientiousness that would never permit him to be satisfied that he was sufficiently worthy or well prepared to carry on God's work. Continually vacillating between skepticism and complete credulity, he found himself unable to find the mean.

In a letter to his uncle, his feeling of inadequacy is plain to be seen. "I have no right," he confesses, "to complain of the trials of my ministry. They are small, compared with what thousands of my brethren are called to endure. I can complain of nothing but myself. Every day teaches me more of my weakness and corruption, and yet I seem to grow no better. I hope my hearers are more profited by my discourses than I am, or I shall do little good."

To most people it might seem that he was over-scrupulous. But that was only part of the answer. While it was true that he could not countenance the more somber features of Calvinism, he had still not thrown off completely the attraction of that system. Calvinism might go overboard on the side of man's depravity, but he was convinced that he and all other men were sinful by nature. Even though he himself had had little actual experience of sin, he had inherited a strong sense of personal guilt. More accurately perhaps, his association with Hopkins, an inveterate searcher after personal faults, had aroused a latent scrupulosity in him. Whatever the cause, the effect of his self-depreciation was to make him morbid in his thinking and gloomy in his preaching.

Finally, when his sense of weakness had become so strong that he was no longer able to bear it alone, he told his brother that he was resolved to quit the ministry. Francis didn't comprehend the problem fully, but he was wise enough to appeal to his brother's rational nature. It was obvious, he said, that William had not given himself or the ministry a fair trial. A few months were no test of his worthiness. Common sense should have told him that. Moreover, he strongly suspected that of all professions, the ministry had the greatest power to make its members feel humble before the magnitude of their duties and responsibilities. William saw the justice in these remarks and went home with a new sense of purpose. He was far from being completely cured, but he would never again be tempted to despair.

In the fall he arrived at a decision that he and Francis had discussed many times. Long ago, both had agreed that one of them should remain unmarried at least ten years so that their mother might be assured of support for herself and her younger children. Since he now had a fixed, certain income and Francis was still trying to get a toehold in his profession, he released Francis from his part in the agreement and accepted the full responsibility for taking care of the Channing family. He wrote his mother that he had a parsonage he could not occupy and fuel he could not burn; if she would come to live with him, she would save him much waste and trouble. Not long afterward mother, brothers, and sisters were gathered under the same roof. Much of Lucy Channing's burden was lightened, and William was no longer homesick.

William's beginning salary of $1,200 was certainly not munificent but it seemed to him "the potentiality of growing rich beyond the dreams of avarice." Once his responsibility to his family was ended, he would even insist that the Committee of his church should decrease it, and not once, but numerous times. For the present, he turned over the lion's share of his salary to the family and lived very frugally on the remainder. Whatever extra fees he received for weddings or other special functions, he gave to Anna, Mary, or little Lucy.

As much afraid as ever of self-indulgence, he took the smallest room in the house for his study. His bedroom, a cold, cheerless, and almost bare cell which he shared with a younger brother, was located in the attic. Such behavior seemed pure foolishness to his family, but they could not distract him from his ascetic purpose. Only when sickness made it necessary would he lighten the Spartan routine. He still had his sense of humor, however, for he could laugh at himself, as an anecdote related by one of his brothers will show. After a particularly bitter night in his arctic sleeping quarters, he awoke, and turning to his brother, who was cringing beneath the counterpane, commented "If my bed were my country, I should be somewhat like Bonaparte; I have no control except over the part I occupy; the instant I move, frost takes possession."

In his dress, he practiced a similar simplicity, buying the most inexpensive garments and wearing them until only his neatness saved him from open reproach by relatives and friends. The reason for such self-denial was, of course, his natural humility, but the extreme nature of his self-abnegation can be explained only in terms of his recently acquired sense of unworthiness, which led him to do penance for what seem only fancied faults.

He tried to take part in the friendly groups that were drawn to his fireside by his mother's naturally vivacious temperament, but he found it impossible to unbend and to leave off his studious habits. His social unease was regrettable because it created a well of reserve that most people found difficult to penetrate. Striving to reach perfection *per saltum*, he was forgetting his own dictum that the ascent to goodness is gradual and was neglecting the social side of his nature in his haste to improve the spiritual.

From the beginning his preaching proved successful. According to Dr. John Kirkland, later one of Harvard's most distinguished presidents, but then an outstanding exponent of the mellifluous pulpit oratory that Edward Everett eventually carried to perfection, Channing and Joseph Buckminster, who followed William into the ministry by two years, introduced a new era in preaching. When Channing entered the ministry he proceeded, simply but cogently, to unfold his beliefs with an earnestness and sincerity that could not fail to impress his listeners. Believing man infinitely perfectible and possessing a moral faculty capable of being unfolded, much as the intellectual capacities are capable of development, he preached virtue as the true end of religion and government. All men, he declared, must be made aware of their duties and obligations to each other, to their community, and to the nation. It was his duty to assist them in developing and directing their highest faculties.

Soon after his installation in Federal Street, he began to attract to his sermons many former parishioners who had drifted away under the luke-warm ministrations of his predecessor, Reverend Popkin. Members of other congregations, attracted by the force of his ethical message and by the power and grace of his pulpit addresses, also came to listen. When it became his turn to preach the Thursday lecture in Chauncy Place, the usually thin audience became a crowd, because the range of his thought and the simplicity of his style were gratifying to men and women accustomed either to evangelical ranting or lackluster dogmatizing. Perhaps the chief novelty in his preaching was the directness with which he brought his Christian principles to bear upon actual life. He saw, and made others see, that life was no mere round of play, but a magnificent scene for glorifying God and for educating the human spirit.

In his journals he listed the goal he had set for himself: "My great end is the promotion of the moral and religious interests of mankind, the cause of virtue, the gospel." To attain this end, he proposed to devote all his actions—his exercise, relaxation, visits, prayers—to the accomplishment of moral improvement. He hoped for a revival of religion in politics and labored to get away from the habit of reading sermons so that his congregation might be more impressed by the spontaneity of his message. He told his people that he could do little without their cooperation. His limited resources were a handicap, but he did what he could by lending books, encouraging study groups, and discussing whatever problems his parishioners chose to bring him.

At the time he began his ministry, it was customary for ministers to spend most of their time making the rounds of their parishes and keeping up their social contacts. Since little time was then left for study, the quality of most sermons was poor. He was determined to revise this procedure. For one thing, he knew health would not permit a heavy schedule of social visits; for another, he felt his people did not need conversational pablum as much as soul-stirring messages to arouse them from their mental and moral stupor. To provide such stimulus, he felt that he must spend long hours in study and meditation. This practice he followed so faithfully that his people, both young and old, were most favorably impressed by the intimacy with which, in his sermons, he dealt with matters-of-fact of every-day living at the same time that he reached above the world of things to explain the glory of God's word.

From the very first a man of the New Testament, he preached lovingly on its texts. Before men could believe and choose the gospel, he was convinced they must be "new-born, have a new heart, a new principle . . . a change by the spirit into a meek, submissive, self-renouncing, self-abhorring, benevolent state of soul." In order to assist in this rebirth, he desired to preach "striking, rather than melting sermons." Knowing how feeble were any efforts he might make in behalf of the salvation of others because "God alone can soften my people," he spent hours in prayer. When he did visit his parishioners, he spoke plainly on religion and attended strictly to the wants of those whom he visited. He held periodical prayer-meetings and meetings for conversation and religious instruction, alternating them to keep interest alive. To the sick he was a faithful friend, never failing to heed their requests and usually bringing them much needed consolation. On one occasion, however, when he was attending the bedside of a dying parishioner, he was so overcome that he burst into tears; at another time he was forced to leave the room to conceal his feelings. But usually he greeted the sick and bereaved with a calm air and a cheerful smile that brought them some measure of peace.

His parish duties did not take all of his time, however. He enjoyed the interludes when he could chat with Joseph Tuckerman, who came down occasionally from Chelsea to visit; and he made a point of keeping abreast of the Harvard scene by quizzing his younger brother Edward, who had just entered as a freshman. As they compared their first impressions, they found their reactions were pretty much alike: commons was still commons—and still bad; courses of study had changed but slightly; and the faculty showed only the effects of another ten years of trying to win undergraduates to an appreciation of the finer things in life.

He was also enjoying his role as a silent partner to Dan Cupid. Through his friendship with the Higginson family, he had managed to bring Francis into the circle of Susan Higginson's acquaintances, and love was doing the rest. When Francis and Susan announced their engagement, he was as happy as the two lovers, because of his small part in bringing them together.

When the first number of *The Monthly Anthology* appeared, he was listed as a contributor. To anyone familiar with the sentiments and style of his sermons, his short moral fable entitled "The Guest" was easily recognizable, although its narrative form showed him in a new guise. Stylistically barren because it lacked the flesh-and-blood detail of sound narrative, "The Guest" was also too obviously didactic to win readers by its artistic merits alone. Still it showed evidences of a certain sensitivity to the requirements of plot that might have developed into an effective story technique with more practice. Around the friendship of two young men who are sincerely devoted to each other, he had attempted to weave a story illustrating the theme that truth is so essential to human dignity that he who deviates from it in the slightest way not only lessens his self-esteem but also incurs the contempt of his friends. The finished product left nothing to be desired in so far as the theme was concerned, because it was clear as crystal, and the basic situation of a friendship destroyed by good intentions was sound; but his characters were so flat and lifeless that the total effect was one of serious preaching rather than delightful teaching. Perhaps he thought so himself because he never tried again to repeat this venture.

In addition to "The Guest" several other bits by Channing were offered to readers of this first volume of the new magazine. In language reminiscent of Carlyle he anticipated the clothes philosophy of that writer's *Sartor Resartus* by remarking that "dress, like the countenance, is an expression of the soul."

On the subject of eloquence, he had considerable to say. From his earliest college days, the subject had intrigued him, and he had tried at various times to formulate a definition of it. As a newly ordained minister, he had become increasingly aware of the importance eloquence played in winning the attention of an audience; and he had grown somewhat dissatisfied with the eighteenth-century standards of "harmony" that had pleased him during his undergraduate days. Basically, however, his conception of eloquence was still the grand style of Longinus and Demosthenes, those favorites of his college reading.

Eloquence, he wrote for *The Anthology,* "belongs only to towering souls, impressed with vast and strong conceptions, and glowing with great and generous emotions. . . . If we desire eloquence, let us then enlarge the mind and invigorate the virtuous sentiments of the heart." As evidence of his rebellion against the lack of variety that had resulted from the eighteenth-century principle of uniformity, there was his plea for unity in variety. Though couched in the rhetoric of Blair—the urbane style composed of balanced constructions and antithetical ideas is typical of the Scottish rhetorician—his argument was for freedom and ease in composition:

> There is often in works of taste and eloquence, a uniform tedious elegance, more disgusting than coarseness and barbarity. An easy, unbalanced, unlabored style should form the ground of composition. This will give relief and prominence to the most important parts, and produce an agreeable variety. We love to travel through plains, and the eye naturally reposes now on the verdure of the fields, and now on the soft blue of heaven. Dazzling objects soon fatigue and overpower us. In the same manner, simple truth, in a plain perspicuous style, with familiar illustrations, should form the substance of a discourse, and all that is melting, magnificent, and solemnizing, should be introduced by natural transition from this easy course. Composition should indeed be always rich in thought. By simple truth we mean not stale repetition and bareness of sentiment. There is nothing to gratify us in a desert level of sand, but we delight in the fertile well-watered plain.
>
> Eloquent composition should resemble nature. Here should be rugged force, there flowing melody, here solemn gloom, there cheerful sunshine, in one part the wildness of the storm and of the uncultivated waste, in another the charms of order, and the mildness of the evening sky.

"The fertile well-watered plain" was a far cry from the towering fastnesses and perilous depths of *sturm und drang* romanticism; but such phrases as "rugged force," "wildness of the storm," and "uncultivated wastes" represent a decided advance on the school of Goldsmith. To put it another way—one could almost be certain that Channing would echo the sentiments of Joseph Buckminster, a defender in the beginning number of the *Anthology* of the merits of Gray against the arguments of John Gardiner, a supporter of Pope. Without a doubt, he was moving forward æsthetically as well as theologically from the positions into which his heritage and education had led him, to take his stand among the advance guard of American thinkers.

If these early attempts at literary composition are to be fairly judged, it must be admitted that they do not reveal talent awaiting only further expression to develop into genius. They were neither better nor worse than the other contributions printed in *The Anthology*. More ambitious attempts would not be made until many years later, when a more mature and more polished style, the result of writing and delivering hundreds of sermons and public addresses, would earn acclaim for the famous "Dr. Channing."

Although the period immediately preceding Channing's settlement

has been labelled "the dryest in the history of the American pulpit," it
was not simply by contrast with the prevailing tone of such preaching
that his sermons made a fine initial impression. Whether he was standing behind the simple, unadorned pulpit in his own small meeting-
house, or preaching in an "exchange" pulpit, he became for many in
his audience a living example of his theory that great objects make
great minds. Believing in its corollary, that a minister should preach
only upon great themes, he chose God, eternity, the kingdom of Christ,
the perfection of the world, the *summum bonum* as his subjects.

One of these subjects—the perfection of the world—was a special
favorite. The whole creation appeared to him to be a great field in
which an infinitely varied display of love was laid before man's gaze.
This love, "the harmonizing principle which reduced to unity and
simplicity the vast diversity of nature," fills the soul of the Christian;
only he can hear the music of the spheres—"the music of the suns and
planets joining their melody in praise to their benignant creator."

Closely allied in his mind with this idea was that of the harmony of
holiness. The Christian, he said, must not trust in any single virtue;
for if his religion is genuine, it will draw in its train the whole of
moral excellence. Particular actions are to be approved only where
they evince a general conformity of heart to the love of God. Tender-
ness to man and submission to God are demanded by the principle of
impartial benevolence, the harmonious exercise of which constitutes
the soul of religion.

Just as Channing's emphasis on world harmony revealed his affinity
with the school of eighteenth-century benevolence, so his expressions
of political theory proved him still a child of the Enlightenment. Like
the Congregational ministers of Massachusetts who had thoroughly
threshed out in their pulpits, long before the American Revolution,
the major political issues over which that struggle was waged, Channing also believed in keeping the duties of citizens and the responsibilities of government before his parishioners. An extract from his
notes, written sometime during his first year in the ministry, is typical
of his political theorizing and also indicative of his close adherence to
John Locke's philosophy of government:

> It is right that every *individual* should be secured in all enjoyments
> which consist with *general* enjoyment. An individual in a state of nature
> would suffer a wrong, if made to experience any unnecessary harm or
> privation. Thus, before all compact, it appears that individuals have a
> right to appropriate the useful objects of the world; and social compact
> is necessary only to establish certain rules or principles according to which
> those objects may be appropriated to general advantage. These rules form

what we term the rights of man; they grow out of the eternal moral truth, which is the fountain of all right, that the *greatest good* should be promoted.

Justice, which he always considered the other side of the coin *mercy*, was defined as a respect for property and the rights of man. But any form of justice unconnected with benevolence was not worth possessing. Only "if the institution of property originates in the general good, if the right of property be nothing more than the right of the individual to enjoy all which is consistent with general good," is justice "in truth *one* with benevolence." If we are to judge by the actions of men, then there is all too little of this kind of justice. "We carry our own shame on our foreheads. Most of our civil institutions grow out of our corruptions. We cannot live without mutual dependence, and yet we are forced to hedge each other round, to bind and shackle each other, to institute inquiries, and to watch with anxious caution lest we should abuse each other's necessities, and take advantage of trust to betray it."

The just man, he concluded, "appeals from the laws of the land to the dictates of conscience. . . . He considers that laws do not create right, that there are eternal principles of truth and rectitude to which all civil laws must be reduced as their standard; and to the principle written by God on the heart, and confirmed in the Holy Scriptures, he refers all his actions which relate to the property of others." In this statement, although Channing was echoing the idealism of Richard Price, he was also anticipating Theodore Parker's arguments that the experience of mankind should be revised by trying its teachings by the nature of mankind; that ethics should be tested by conscience; science by reason; and the creeds of churches and the constitutions of states by the constitution of the universe.

In his work of bringing a new kind of preaching to the people of Boston, Channing was not left long to labor alone. On January 30, 1805, Joseph Stephens Buckminster was ordained and installed as pastor by the Brattle Street Society. Some four years younger than Channing, young Buckminster had nevertheless arrived sooner at a more liberal theology. Six months before his ordination his father had written to him as follows: "If the Committee of Brattle Street, or of any other Church, should apply to you with the view of hearing you in order to propose a *settlement,* I advise you, as an honest man, (and this you seem desirous to be,) to tell them plainly that you do not believe in the proper Deity and Divinity of Christ, nor in his vicarious satisfaction and atonement for the sins of men, and I presume they will trouble you no more." A month later the Reverend Joseph Buckminster, with sorrowful heart, addressed his son in even more serious vein: "My Unhappy Son,—If you are fixed and settled in the sentiment that Jesus Christ is not a Divine person, nor any thing more than a created messenger of God, and that the business of his coming into the world was only to publish truth, and to attest the truth that he published with his blood, and give hope and confirmation of a resurrection, but not to make atonement and satisfaction for sin, and if there is no hope of your having different views upon these points, it is best for you to think of some other profession than the ministry; you had better be a porter on the wharf than a preacher with such views."

While he lived, Buckminster outshone Channing in the Boston firmament. A dramatic preacher and an able scholar, he quickly became a favorite in the intellectual and literary circles of the city. At the meetings of the *Anthology* Society, of which he was a charter member, his literary taste and judgment quickly became the delight of his companions; and his pen was constantly engaged in reviewing and writing for the Society's magazine. The skill of his reading voice was especially remarkable. Very early in his short, meteoric career, he possessed the gift of creating a strong emotional bond between himself and his audience. Not until Channing was near the zenith of his fame was he able to achieve the same degree of success.

But the man who has been called "the founder of literary Boston" was not destined to retain his laurels for long. Buckminster suffered from epilepsy, and it was growing rapidly worse. From Paris in 1806, where he was traveling for his health, he wrote to Channing, then laid low by an attack of dyspepsia: "Before this reaches you, you will be restored, I trust, to your people. . . . I am sometimes ashamed of myself, when I think that I am here in Paris in perfect idleness, while you are sinking under the labors of your ministry. But God grant that we may be able to congratulate each other next summer, upon meeting, as I hope we shall in health, and taught by our suffering to cherish more carefully than ever this inestimable gift of our Maker, and not to draw upon it too fast, so that we may use it longer and more sacredly in the service of our people and for the interests of truth." His hopes were in vain. He and William would be reunited, but death was stalking and getting closer all the time.

CHAPTER SIX

A DARKLING PLAIN

A SHORT TIME BEFORE Buckminster sailed for Europe in 1806 and while he was still abroad, several happenings of some significance occurred in Boston and vicinity.

In nearby Salem, Joseph Story had just taken one of his first great strides up the judicial ladder by becoming a member of the Massachusetts Legislature. Since his arrival in Salem, he had been plagued by the political conservatives who infested that community. "It has been frequently asserted," he declared, "that my political views are Jacobinical. This I utterly deny. . . . Yet I must also declare, that I have never for a moment believed Mr. Jefferson to be an enemy of his country, nor to my mind has his conduct ever been substantially *proved criminal* in any degree." Such an unbiased attitude was difficult for the Federalists to understand; but Story's worth was known to his constituents, and his career could not be hindered for long.

Down in New London the Reverend Henry Channing was having his troubles. For some time now he had doubted orthodox views of the trinity, although he had not protested publicly against them. In 1805, however, he openly espoused the cause of the Reverend John Sherman, an avowed anti-Trinitarian. His action led to his dismissal by his own congregation. After twenty years of service, a church council had found him sufficiently deficient in orthodox beliefs to relieve him of his duties. In Connecticut, tolerance of heresy was narrower than in Massachusetts, but events of the next few years would prove tolerance far from an excess quantity in the Bay State also.

When Henry Channing received his dismissal from the good people of New London, the course of American Congregationalism was far from placid. This was particularly true in Boston, where the word *heresy* was as naturally attached to the name of the city as the phrase *baked beans* would be in a later age. Schism was in the air and manifestos were flying back and forth.

To begin with, there were three fairly distinct parties in the established Congregational order of Massachusetts. In the center were the moderates: men like Abiel Holmes, David Tappan, and Joseph Buck-

minster of Portsmouth, who were only slightly influenced either by the
new-light doctrines of Jonathan Edwards on the right or by the liberalism of left-wingers like John Kirkland and William Bentley, the fabu-
lous Salem diarist.

To the right was the party of "consistent" Calvinists, until his death
in 1803 led by Samuel Hopkins, who left his followers with the badge
of his name and a set of principles that demanded man's submission to
God's absolute sovereignty.

On the left wing were the liberals, by far the smallest of the three
groups, and strong only in Boston and the surrounding towns. For the
most part Harvard-trained, this group took Calvinism seriously and
deliberately rejected it. Among their number were William Emerson,
Joseph Tuckerman, young Buckminster, and many other good friends
of Channing. Channing, however, was still not a member of any of the
groups just mentioned. He had rejected the main doctrines of Calvinism and was certainly unorthodox in his Christology, but traces of
Samuel Hopkins's influence still lingered in his theological make-up,
although he had little sympathy for Hopkins's followers. When he had
fully clarified his views, he would seek his proper place among the
liberals; but that time had not yet arrived.

As far as the growing tensions among the three parties were concerned, events came to a climax in 1805. The most significant occur-
rences were the establishment of an argumentative periodical by the
orthodox and the affair known as the Harvard Controversy.

In June, some four months before the liberals founded the *Anthology* Society, the first issue of the *Panoplist* appeared. The difference between the Preface of *The Monthly Anthology* and the statement of purpose in the *Panoplist* was the "difference between two religious cultures." Where the former was liberal and literary (its editor,
William Emerson, had borrowed from Addison to state the aims of the
new magazine as attending "Theatres, Museums, Assemblies, Balls, etc.
and whatever polite diversions the town may furnish . . ."), the latter
was definite and sectarian. Jedidiah Morse, the moving spirit behind
the *Panoplist,* was trying desperately to guard the citadel of orthodoxy
against encroachment by such liberals as Buckminster, John Kirkland,
and William Emerson, and was ready to do battle with any and all
persons whom he considered guilty of contaminating the pure stream
of evangelical teaching.

The definite aim of the *Panoplist,* according to its statement of purpose, was "pure truth, flowing from the sacred fountain of the scriptures; nothing of the Shibboleth of a sect; nothing to recommend one

denomination of Christians, or to throw odium on another; nothing of the acrimony of contending parties against those, who differ from them; but pure, genuine Christianity, in which all the followers of the Lamb, who are looking for the mercy of the Lord Jesus Christ unto eternal life, can unite with pleasure, as in one great common cause." However, it adopted from its very inception a belligerent attitude. In its book reviews, reprints of sermons, and miscellaneous reports, there was only praise for "revivals in religion" among the orthodox and only condemnation of "irreligious tendencies" among the liberals. Morse was aching for a showdown, and the issue of the Harvard Controversy gave him an excellent opportunity.

When the Reverend David Tappan died in August, 1803, the Hollis Professorship of Divinity at Harvard became vacant. The problem of choosing a successor to the kindly old minister would have been relatively simple had not the smaller issue been complicated by the larger problem of conflicting views between the liberals and the orthodox. For some time the trend of growing liberalism at Harvard had been the cause of considerable dismay to the orthodox leaders, and conservative stalwarts like Morse were afraid that "corruption" at Harvard would undermine the cause of true religion. Morse and his friends had been instrumental in installing Tappan in the Harvard Professorship, and only Dr. John Clark of Boston, one of the overseers, had opposed their choice. But the strength of the liberals had increased a hundredfold during Tappan's twenty years at Harvard, and Morse knew there would be a struggle before Tappan's successor was appointed.

The two leading candidates for the Hollis Professorship were the Reverend Henry Ware, Sr. of Hingham and the Reverend Jesse Appleton of Hampton. The liberals supported Ware and the conservatives favored Appleton. According to Sidney Willard, Appleton was a "practical and very serious teacher, acceptable to the orthodox, and . . . to many who widely differed from them in speculation." Of him, the elder Buckminster wrote his son, who was then debating the "call" from Brattle Street: "If I were as much of a Hopkinsian on some points, as you, my son, are upon others, I should be glad they had thought of Mr. Appleton for Cambridge. I think there is no man so likely to render calm and to keep quiet the two opposite parties, and to preserve Cambridge from becoming the arena of theological discord." But Joseph's father was wrong on two counts: Joseph was certainly no Hopkinsian, and Jesse Appleton was not the man for the opening at Harvard—at least the liberals thought not, and theirs was the winning side.

Henry Ware, against whom charges of Arminianism and Unitarianism were leveled by the orthodox, was capably defended by his supporters, among whom was Judge Francis Dana, Channing's uncle. In
answer to the charge of Ware's being a Unitarian, his friends replied
that "he had never professed the sentiment imputed to him, and to
mention such a thing was 'a calumny.' " For a time the keen sense of
rivalry between the two factions led the members of the Harvard Corporation to postpone a decision, but Ware finally was elected on February 7. His appointment was confirmed by the Overseers a week later,
and he was inaugurated. For Jedidiah Morse it was only the beginning
of things. A true heresy-hunter, he would not stop until he had stirred
up a much greater storm in the next decade, a tempest that would
embroil Channing.

While the din of controversy was resounding through the halls of
Harvard, the Channing family was busily preparing for Francis's approaching marriage. He and Susan Higginson were married on November 30, 1806, at Trinity Church. No one had the slightest premonition
on that happy day that their happiness would be contained in a brief
four years together. Certainly Channing, whose slender figure and pale
countenance contrasted sharply with the glowing strength of his handsome brother, had no thought of Francis's early death. He was as happy
as the bride and groom themselves. For once he had put off his usual
gravity and entered into the celebration with full heart. In response to
his brother's gratitude for bringing him and Susan together and making their early marriage possible by his act of self-sacrifice, Channing
replied that he was pleased to be cast in the role of Cupid, but he was
sure he hadn't a sacrificial bone in his body.

Channing's joy over the marriage of his brother changed quickly to
sorrow when he was informed of the death of Arthur Maynard Walter.
The premature decease of this bright young man was a serious blow to
Boston's literary aspirations. No one had been more zealous than he to
surmount the ramparts of Boston ignorance. He had played a leading
role in setting up *The Anthology,* and he and William Shaw ("Athenaeum Shaw") , more than anyone else, were responsible for laying the
foundations of the Anthology Reading-Room and Library. Walter did
not live to see his friends incorporated as "The Proprietors of the Boston Athenaeum," but his spirit must have hovered over the tiny group
who were instrumental in establishing this Boston landmark. Although
never open to the general public, it remained, for almost half a century, the only library in Boston. During that period the Channings,

Emersons, Lowells, and countless other members of the best families found the Athenaeum a cultural must.

In the same year that the Athenaeum came into being, Harvard was the scene of one of its most uproarious student rebellions. As one might guess, Commons was again the center of the difficulty. The affair has come down in history as the "Rotten Cabbage Rebellion," which title should be sufficient description of its proximate cause. Both Edward Tyrrell, who was a Senior, and Walter, a Junior, were active participants, and both were prevented from being allowed to graduate in course. When they brought the news home, they were a bit dubious about their reception, but if they expected a reprimand from Lucy Channing or William, they were disappointed. In the Channing household it was customary for everyone to fight his own battles as long as the contest was fair. William knew the lengths to which student ardor could go, but he was also well aware of the great provocations emanating from the Harvard Buttery. The entire matter was discreetly forgotten.

It was difficult in the first years of Channing's ministry for those on either side of the widening breach in Congregationalism to call him one of their own. Both orthodox and liberals exchanged freely with him; and if the truth were told the former were the more friendly. Apologists of Channing would often insist that his religious thought was all of a piece from first to last; but if his early sermons were not formally Calvinistic, they were frankly evangelical. A fine example of this kind of preaching was the sermon which he delivered at the ordination of John Codman.

When John Codman was graduated from Harvard in 1802, he went to study theology with Henry Ware, who was then pastor at Hingham. But Ware, whose views were characterized not long afterwards as Unitarian, certainly did not attempt to seduce young John from Orthodoxy, or if he did, was unsuccessful, because Codman's review of William Cooper's "Four Sermons on Predestination" appeared in the *Panoplist* (June, 1805) instead of in *The Anthology*.

Channing's connection with Codman had come about quite naturally. It was his practice to dine on every Saturday with the Codman family, where he became acquainted with John, whom he always regarded with esteem and affection. Although in after years their views of Christian doctrine placed them in widely different camps, their mutual friendship and regard never were interrupted. When Codman went abroad in 1805 to study theology in Scotland, his mind became filled with doubts similar to those Channing had only recently experienced.

Attempting to relieve Codman's anxiety, William wrote him the following note of consolation: "It is good to doubt and to fear, when our minds instead of sinking into despondency, are excited by painful uncertainty to self-examination, to careful inquiry into the nature of true religion, as exhibited in the Scriptures, and to humble fervent prayer. I believe, my friend, we are apt to expose ourselves to much needless pain, by forming loose and value opinions of our characters; by condemning ourselves on account of something which we cannot define. I am here speaking of my own experience, rather than yours. I have often felt gloom overspreading my mind, without being able to tell on what account I felt it."

But unlike Channing, Codman ended in orthodox certainty. When he was invited in October, 1808, to become the pastor of the Second Church in Dorchester, he wrote the following letter to the Church and Parish:

> As *Arian* and *Socinian* errors have of late years crept into some of our churches, I think it my duty to declare to that Church of Christ, of whom I have the pastoral charge, that I believe *the Father, Son* and *Holy Ghost, to be the one living and true God;* and that my faith, in general, is comfortable to the *Assembly's Catechism,* and to the *Confession of Faith* drawn up by the Elders and Messengers of the Congregational Churches in the year 1680, and recommended to the Churches by the General Court of Massachusetts.
>
> With regard to the discipline of the Church, I shall be guided by that excellent *Platform of Church Discipline,* drawn up at Cambridge.

These views were acceptable to the Second Church and shortly afterwards Channing received from him an invitation to preach the ordination sermon. As a member of the Brattle Street Church, Codman would normally have asked Joseph Buckminster, his own minister; he chose Channing because by his own testimony the latter was more in accord with his views. Channing accepted because Codman was his friend and also because he saw an excellent opportunity to make known his views of what constituted a good minister and, by so doing, perhaps ease some of the tension among the various Congregational factions.

Taking as his text Paul's exhortation to Timothy, "Be Instant in Season, Out of Season," he spoke on the subject of the "Importance of a Zealous and Affectionate Performance of Ministerial Duties." If we are to be good ministers, he told his colleagues, we must not "confine ourselves to a cold, mechanical round of what we call our duties, and to feel that we have done enough when we have done what is claimed and expected." No, we must "press forward in the path of duty, undismayed by the opposition, unabashed by the ridicule of the world." But public zeal alone is not enough; the good minister must also labor unceasingly in private to improve himself mentally and spiritually, for "a minister can impart to his people only what he has himself received. . . . He should never be contented with his present attainments, never imagine that he has learned all which God has revealed, never say that he has formed his system, and has nothing to do but to preach it. Divine truth is infinite and can never be exhausted. The wisest of us are but children; our views are very dim and narrow; and even where we discern the truth, how faint is its practical impression."

The good minister should let men see that "he has come, not to dazzle them with the studied ornaments of rhetoric, . . . but to fix their solicitous attention on the concerns of eternity." This purpose can be achieved without frenzy or tumult, for it is "in the still small voice we may discern the language of the heart." True ministerial eloquence does not consist in rules—rules are only useful to teach us what to avoid—true eloquence is the expression of a heart that is filled with the love of God.

As another solemn incitement to earnestness, a minister should always consider the dangerous circumstances of his people. To whom is he sent to preach? To men of upright hearts? With a look of fearful apprehension and in a tone of voice that indicated a deep conviction of sin, Channing proceeded to paint a picture of human depravity that confronts the minister:

> He is called to guide a wandering flock through a thorny rugged wilderness, beset with snares and beasts of prey. . . . He is sent to a world of sinners, in whose hearts lurk idolatry, sensuality, pride and every corruption. He is sent to many who are bound in fetters of iron and are perishing with the most loathsome diseases. He is indeed sent with balm for their wound, with light and hope and consolation. But there are those, and sometimes not a few, who turn away from the proffered aid. . . . He sees immoral beings, committed to his care, advancing with rapid steps to the brink of an abyss, from which they are never to arise, and can he be unconcerned? Can he read of that fire which is never quenched, of that worm which never dies, and yet see without emotion fellow-beings, with whom he sustains the tenderest connections, hastening forward to this indescribable ruin?

These last utterances reveal that the orthodox Codman had made no mistake in choosing his ordination speaker. Here was a Jonathan

Edwards without Edwards's poetic fire, it is true—but with the same technique of drawing the fearful sinner so close to the abyss and the "fire which is never quenched" that the resulting tension would cause him to repent and seek holiness. But just as imprecatory sermons were exceptions rather than the rule in Edwards's preaching, so Channing resorted less and less frequently to the methods of his Codman sermon, although they were remarkably successful as one may gather from a letter which young Henry Ware, just beginning his study of theology at Phillips Academy, Exeter, wrote to his father. "I have been reading a few sermons," said Henry, "but none, indeed none that I ever read, struck me so much as Mr. Channing's at the ordination of Mr. Codman. . . . It must be a treasure to young ministers and ought to stop effectually the cold sermonizing of your rationalists who maintain the strange contradictions of religion without feeling."

Religion without feeling—the phrase was just as contradictory to Channing as it was to young Ware. He knew that the deists and freethinkers had made the error of cultivating the mind at the expense of the heart; he was resolved not to make the same mistake. As early as 1805 he had written in his journal, "Religion is the rectification of the soul; it is inward health; it is the direction of affection to the most interesting objects. It consists of feelings and disposition which include every thing generous, distinterested, sympathetic, and pure." These were the teachings he had learned from Hutcheson and Price. But though he might prize the affections, he was careful also not to confound the love of God with the "ravings of enthusiasm," for he had the typical eighteenth-century aversion to religious fanaticism; and part of his cultural inheritance from Charles Chauncey and other critics of the Great Awakening was a dislike of "raised affections."

The fullest record of Channing's mental and spiritual development during the early years at Federal Street was kept religiously in his private journal, which reveals an amazingly close agreement between his private thoughts and his pulpit utterances. Never guilty of believing one thing but saying the opposite, he displayed in his self-examination the same ascetic temper and solemn spirit manifest in his sermons. There were scattered evidences, however, that he was beginning to draw closer in his theology to the high moral aspirations for which he later became so famous.

If the idea of God's paternity had not yet usurped the concept of Divine Sovereignty in his mind, it was beginning to seem very attractive. No character could bring God so near to men as that of a Father, he declared. "I fear we have learnt insensibly to view him as possessing only a general benevolence . . . a benevolence neither very strong nor ardent, not descending to individuals, and not essential to the felicity of the Divine nature . . . but I do not perceive that we dishonor God by believing that his creation is a real source of felicity to him, that he finds a real happiness in doing good, and in viewing with complacence obedient, virtuous, and happy children."

Such an argument was pure anthropomorphism, but Channing saw nothing specious in comparing divine and human perfection. He was still not prepared to equate the two, but he was working steadily toward the idea of "essential sameness" which would set his theology apart from the views expressed by Protestant and Catholic theologians alike. By so doing he was reprimanding if ever so gently, New England Calvinism. Similarly, his views on the atonement represented a defection from the traditional doctrine. "Mercy," he said, "is an essential attribute of God, not an affection produced in him by a foreign cause. His blessings are free, and bestowed from a real interest in his creatures—not purchased from him, and bestowed by another on those whose welfare he disregards." Although Channing used the Edwardian terminology in speaking of a "new birth" for all those persons who had fallen away from God, he regarded regeneration as a gradual or progressive change rather than a sudden spiritual experience. Knowing man's nature to be sinful, he nevertheless believed that this sinfulness might be mitigated from the very beginnings of infancy, provided the atmosphere of the home environment was Christian. In this respect he was anticipating the doctrine of Christian nurture that was to gain much popularity in the years after his death.

When Channing wrote or spoke of Christ, his emphasis was on the moral grandeur rather than upon any special qualities of the Saviour. That human nature was glorified in Jesus was a recurrent note in his journal, which would seem to indicate that he was not always a strict logician and that his conception of Christ was Arian rather than Socinian. Perhaps it is closer to the truth to say that his remarks concerning Christ were so confusing and contradictory that almost any member of any sect might lay claim to some part of his Christology.

In one place he defines the incarnate Saviour as "man as he was before the fall, man restored, raised from his ruins, man in the true glory of his nature, man such as God designed." In another, Christ becomes "the Son of God in a peculiar sense, the temple of the Divinity, the brightest image of his glory. In seeing him we see the Father." Finally as "Lord and Sovereign of the whole human race," he was appointed by God the Father to recover the world to piety.

The logic of language declared all three characters—man, Son of
God, Sovereign of the human race—could not be synonymous. What
then can one think of Channing's bewildering shift in points of view?
Simply that he was in a quandary: he had to make Christ a little less
than God but yet a lot higher than man. Preferring really to leave
the problem unresolved, he resorted to loose analogies and fuzzy description to cloak his indecision. The result was a kind of indefinite,
unphilosophical sort of Arianism.

But there was one characteristic of Christ concerning which Channing never wavered—that was His simplicity. "He was simple and
familiar," he wrote. "He did not, like the ancient teacher, affect a
distance from the multitude, and reserve his mysteries, incomprehensible by vulgar mind, for select disciples. He addressed all men with
one voice, with the same doctrines, promises, and admonition. . . ."
In this same quality of simplicity Channing also found the peculiar
excellence of Christ's gospel. "It is a plain, perspicuous religion,"
he wrote, "and suited to the comprehension and wants of all classes
of society." Here he was saying nothing new; he was only enunciating
a principle which had been widespread in the circle of eighteenth-
century rationalism, particularly among the deists. It is not to be
wondered at, therefore, that he was labeled a deist by critics of his
famous Baltimore Sermon and the New York Sermon of 1826. But
his appeal to the *consensus gentium* was accompanied by a belief in
revelation and miracles, which separated him, as if by a deep gulf,
from the deists and free thinkers.

Because from the very first his preaching had attracted new members to Federal Street, it soon became obvious that the old Meeting
House, then in its sixty-fifth year, was no longer adequate to house
the growing Congregation. By a unanimous vote, the Society decided
to replace the wooden structure with a more handsome edifice of brick.
Charles Bulfinch, the celebrated Boston architect, was called in to design a new church. Plans were submitted and approved, and Channing
laid the cornerstone on April 11, 1809. Six months later he and his
congregation assisted in dedication ceremonies. On November 23,
1809, Bostonians were invited to visit the newest temple on Boston
Acropolis. The occasion was not without a certain elegance and classic
grace, as the following lines from the *Columbian Centinel* of the previous day indicate:

> Crowned with new grace, with towering height sublime
> Like a fair phoenix rising in its prime,—

'Mid circling domes in humbler grandeur spread,
This sacred temple rears its matchless head;
Whose spire majestic, piercing through the air,
Lifts its proud point to heaven, and glitters there.

A humble servant of God had commenced his career in the humblest of the houses of God. Now he was beginning to rise in the hierarchy of Boston divines and to exert the influence that would one day lead a wise critic to announce that in Boston "the popular area of religion was whatever this eminent divine held."

CHAPTER SEVEN

LAUGHTER FRAUGHT WITH PAIN

JUST A YEAR PRIOR to the cornerstone ceremonies at Federal Street, Washington Allston had set sail from Italy to return to an America from which he had been absent for seven years.

They had been seven fat years of golden friendships and accomplishments. From London, where he had soaked in all that the English masters could teach him, he had journeyed to Italy and the Eternal City; there with the poet Coleridge, "the fountain of whose mind was never dry," he explored the sacred hills and learned "never to judge of any work of art by its defects"; in the company of Washington Irving—not yet a writer, but still in his own way as interested in literature as Coleridge—he had rambled among the mazes of the brooding city, trying to drink in the mystery of its past. Here where the present seemed an interloper, he had found the inspiration to create his own work and the courage to return home. He had learned his art from the living tradition of the studios and from the great creators and masters of the language. He knew the importance of drawing and of form, but more importantly he had discovered color, the key to whatever success he would ever earn.

Upon his arrival in Boston, he set up a studio in Court Street, a short distance from Faneuil Hall and a few minutes' walk from Channing's home. He found a warm welcome at the Channings, especially from William and Anna. No longer the demure young miss Allston had known during the infrequent visits of his college days, Anna—or Ann, as she preferred to be called—was now a mature woman of thirty with a sweetness and charm that immediately captivated the young painter. His visits grew more and more frequent, and no one was the least surprised when Ann announced her engagement. The marriage took place a year later.

During the three years that Allston was located in Boston, he spent considerable time painting portraits, most of which were of his new family. Allston's intimacy with the Channings stimulated him to do some of his finest work. In the painting of Lucy Channing he caught the sturdy independence and inflexible integrity that were so characteristic of William's mother. The portrait of William himself, however, was much more impressive. As a modern critic would one day remark, "The intense, delicate head seems to float like a luminous apparition within the shadows. The effect is gained almost entirely by light. The color is of the simplest: black coat and white stock, warm flesh tone and dull-red background." Allston was particularly successful in capturing the inner spirit of his friend. On the broad brow and in the brilliant eyes there is the mark of the scholar, but the faintest suggestion of a smile lurks about the mobile lips and relieves the countenance of severity.

At about the same time that Allston painted William, he did a portrait of Francis Dana. Handsome where William was not, Francis might easily have been taken for a matinée idol, except that his face revealed a strength of character and an exuberance of spirit that are so often wanting in such popular figures.

Sadly enough, however, sitting for Allston was one of Francis's final acts. During the spring of 1810, while on a business trip to Vermont, he caught a cold which affected his lungs and rapidly developed into consumption. Hoping to get relief, he went to Newport for the summer but to no avail. In the autumn he decided on a sea voyage, the last recourse for tubercular persons. His wife, Susan; his cousin, Mary Gibbs; and his brother-in-law, John Higginson, accompanied him. But it was too late. En route to Rio de Janeiro on the ship *Liberty* he died on November 8, leaving Susan to face the problem of supporting a family of three small children.

Alone on a strange ship and confronted by a long voyage that gave little promise of being less hazardous than the first month of it had been, Susan, who was distraught by shock and grief, entertained gloomy thoughts of being destroyed by the savage sea. She wrote home to her family, "If I should never return,—and often I feel as if I never should,—tell William that I give my son to him. He must bring him up as his own, and make him as much like himself as possible."

Her fears proved groundless, however; and when she returned to Boston the following May, she found a ready welcome and a certain measure of peace in the Channing home on Berry Street. Restless and unable to forget her loss, she tried to imitate William's calm acceptance of the fact of death, but the poignancy of her grief was not easily dulled. Channing's modestly prevented any overt demonstration of friendship, but he did find numerous ways to help, both financially and spiritually. In the long years that followed Francis's death—Susan never remarried—Channing assumed a father's responsibilities toward his nephew and was perhaps the chief agent in shaping his character. ⬆

Two events affected Channing deeply in the years 1811-1812. The installation of his former pupil, Samuel Cooper Thacher, as minister of the New South Church in Boston, filled him with joy and hope; the death of Joseph Buckminster left him melancholy and full of regret. Following his graduation from Harvard in 1804, young Thacher had read theology under Channing's supervision. A brilliant student, full of literary promise and a thorough liberal, Thacher earned William's confidence immediately; and their association quickly ripened into friendship. Thacher, who was also an intimate friend of Buckminster, had accompanied the latter on his voyage to Europe in 1806. Upon his return to Boston the next year, he was appointed Librarian at Harvard, where he was able to continue his theological studies as well as his connection with *The Monthly Anthology*. Finally the opportunity for which he had been praying and studying came. He was called to replace the distinguished Reverend Dr. Kirkland, who had given up his pastorate at the New South Church to accept the Presidency of Harvard. Channing gave him the right hand of fellowship at his ordination, and the next day, recorded in his journal his reactions to the solemn occasion.

Actually, the journal entries represent a kind of written examination of conscience. Channing wondered whether he had been "a faithful diligent minister, inquiring for every means of doing good to my people, and devoted most sincerely to their improvement." He was fearful that he and his fellows might only be going through the motions of doing God's work and "not desirous enough to see fruits from our labors." Giving thanks that heaven had seen fit to bestow upon him the blessing of Thacher's friendship, he noted that "the purity of his character and life, and his devotion to his profession, render him peculiarly important to us at this time."

While Channing and Thacher were absent from Boston for reasons of health (Thacher had already been touched by the omnipresent scourge of consumption), word reached them of the death of Buckminster. Both were deeply shocked. Channing especially felt the loss. It seemed to him as though God were trying to even the lists in the contest between His forces and the powers of evil.

As soon as he returned to Boston, he spoke to the Brattle Street congregation. "My own heart sunk [sic] within me, when I heard the painful tidings of his death," he exclaimed. "I felt for the loss I had experienced as an individual; but this sorrow was faint, compared with my painful sense of the heavy loss which our churches had experienced."

Later he wrote a friend, "People here, as you know, are attached to religious institutions not so much by a sense of the value of religion as by their love of their minister; and I fear that their zeal will grow cold, when their ministers are removed. I wish that there were more attachment to the truth, and less to the man who delivers it. The loss of Dr. Buckminster appears to me irreparable. I know no man who united so many gifts from nature, so many acquisitions from study, and such power of rendering religion interesting to all classes of society, especially to the improved, the polished, the fashionable."

Because they had been his closest friends, the Buckminster family naturally turned to Channing and Thacher for editorial assistance when they decided to published some of Joseph's sermons. George Ticknor, into whose hands Buckminster's papers had come, recalls that Channing gave a great deal of time to the task. According to him, Channing's first interest was in seeing justice done to Buckminster's reputation. He was guided by a rule of selectivity that said "Beware of publishing too much!" The best of a man's writings, he claimed, should be fastidiously selected for the press. Care should be taken "lest the best be lost and fail of their effect by being surrounded with much that wants interest and will not be read." His editorial policy proved very successful because the published "Sermons" was popularly acclaimed.

Buckminster's writings were by no means voluminous—there simply hadn't been time to write much—and there was a remarkable evenness in the flow of his thought; but still the scope of his work was broad for a man of his calling, and his genius was more literary than religious. His Phi Beta Kappa Address of 1809, entitled "The Dangers and Duties of Men of Letters," represents the most forward thinking of his day concerning the role of the man of letters. To the young scholars of Harvard, he had prophesied: "You, my young friends, are destined to witness the dawn of our Augustan age, and to contribute to its glory. . . . The men of letters who are to direct our taste, mould our genius, and inspire our emulation,— the men, in fact, whose writings are to be the depositories of our national greatness,—have not shown themselves to the world. But, if we are not mistaken in the signs of the times, the genius of our literature begins to show symptoms of vigor, and to meditate a bolder flight, and the generation which is to succeed us will be formed on better models, and leave a brighter track." Channing undoubtedly never forgot those words, for his own remarks on literature some twenty years later contained essentially the same line of argument.

There is a kind of profit-and-loss accounting connected with everything that happens in time and space. Although Channing sincerely regretted the death of Buckminster, it was actually he who benefited most from it. Shortly before he died, Buckminster had been chosen to give the first lectures on Biblical Criticism at Harvard. In preparation for his new duties, he had sent to Germany, which was becoming famous for its scientific Biblical exegesis, for books to supplement his already excellent library of some three thousand volumes. When they arrived, he had secreted himself in his study until death had entered and found him out, leaving the precious volumes for someone else to come and unveil their secrets. As fate would have it, Channing was the fortunate one.

No less than Buckminster, Channing was interested not only in extending the circulation of the Bible but also in promoting a rational interpretation of it. In 1811 he had addressed the first anniversary convocation of the Bible Society of Massachusetts, and the following year had become Chairman of its Executive Committee. It was expected that he should be asked to take the lectureship left vacant by his friend. He accepted the appointment, purchased at auction a large number of Buckminster's books, ordered others from abroad, and began to prepare diligently for the forthcoming lectures. Unfortunately his health was not up to such strenuous activity and he found himself bound in conscience to resign.

What positive effects might have resulted from his being able to continue, he could only speculate about. Certainly a first-hand acquaintance with German philosophy would not have changed his basic mind-set: the pattern of his thinking was pretty well determined, and he did not need to go to German thinkers for the doctrine of ideas. As for his becoming a thorough scholar like his successor, Andrews Norton, that was highly improbable, both because he feared that scholarship might lead to over-cultivating one's understanding at the expense of one's feelings, and also because he possessed a mind that was essentially synthetic rather than analytic, eclectic rather than original, intuitive rather than critical. Moreover, with his intuitive reach beyond the limits of Biblical truth, he could never have become, like Norton, a defender of the status quo. Scriptural commentaries he did read, and he recommended them freely to others; but in the last analysis he sought for proof of the excellence of Christianity in the actions of men.

As the first decade of his ministry drew to a close, he directed his attention more and more to what he considered an extremely critical state of national affairs. In 1810 on the occasion of a Public Fast, he delivered a sermon on the military despotism of France. His youthful animosity towards that country had not abated in the least while his attitude towards Napoleon was extreme to the point of violence. Straining every nerve to awaken Bostonians to the dangers to which they, as well as France, were exposed by Bonaparte's ambition, he chided them for their apathy towards the plight of other nations.

"There is a still stranger insensibility to our own dangers," he warned. "We seem determined to believe that this storm will spend all its force at a distance. The idea, that *we* are marked out as victims of this all-destroying despotism, *that our turn is to come and perhaps is near,*—this idea strikes on most minds as a fiction." But, he insisted, "France is not a common nation. She lusts for war, and her leader seeks world domination. Religion, virtue, and liberty wither under her power, and she breathes an air polluted with infidelity, impiety, and atheism."

Channing's attitude is understandable. From his early youth, he had been deeply interested in the political scene. He had shared with his grandfather and father an attachment to liberty under constitutional limits; like them he had expected great things from the French Revolution. When revulsion against the excesses of the new French government finally came, it was all the more extreme because of his former idealism. At first he had watched with high hopes the "armed apostle of democracy"; but when he saw Napoleon destroy smaller and defenseless states to build an empire, he recoiled in horror. By so doing, he was simply living up to his standard of Christian benevolence and showing his Federalistic colors.

Two years after he had given his fast-day sermon, New England faced another political crisis. It was June, 1812, and war had been declared against Great Britain. "Mr. Madison's War," as it was popularly known in Massachusetts, held no allure for the majority of Bay State citizens, who regarded England not as a traditional enemy but as the "world's last hope" against the scourge of Napoleon. Those who favored the war were from the West and South, and they were working through the organization of the Republican party.

Opposition to their plans naturally was strongest in Federalist New England. When the states were requested to place militia at the disposal of the national government, Massachusetts refused on the ground that it would be unconstitutional. Her citizens assumed very little of the burden of the war loan, and her commercial interests fought every attempt to make them support the war effort. Bay Staters had long memories, and thoughts of the Embargo of 1807-1809 and the languishing commerce that resulted from it still rankled. To express his disapproval, Governor Strong of Massachusetts appointed a day of fasting and prayer. In Charlestown, the Reverend Jedidiah Morse thundered that the war was "punishment for our national sins," while Channing, just a few miles away, was calmly saying, "I am unable to justify the war in which we have engaged."

Channing's view on war were one and the same from first to last. He considered it a patriotic duty to denounce an unjust war, but he never stopped to check his point of view with popular sentiment. In 1812 a majority of Americans were of one mind with him, but it was a case of pure coincidence rather than cause and effect. There would be other wars and rumors of war and the people would vacillate, but not he. All wars were horrible, he believed, but a just war was possible. The conscientious Christian must examine all claims carefully before passing judgment.

Channing did not deny that Britain had provoked the United States, but he did believe that war as a method of retaliation was out of proportion to the magnitude of the offense that had been offered. He was mainly concerned, however, about the evils that would ensue from the conflict. He uttered the common plaint that "war is a death-blow to our commerce," but—and it is likely that some of his more affluent listeners winced at this point—he also declared, "loss of property is a small evil attending this war,—its effect on our *character* cannot be calculated." His conclusion, on the other hand, was designed to bring forth a unanimous endorsement from his listeners: he reminded them to consider who was leagued with them against Mother England.

"When I view my country," he said, "taking part with the oppressor against that nation which has alone arrested his proud career of victory,—which is now spreading her shield over desolated Portugal and Spain,—which is the chief hope of the civilized world,—I blush,—I mourn. . . . Let our government know that we deem alliance with France the worst of evils, threatening at once our morals, our liberty, and our religion."

Less than a month later he delivered another sermon as a kind of sequel to his fast-day address. President Madison had appointed a day of "Humiliation and Prayer" to mark the declaration of war, and Channing took the opportunity to express with greater precision sentiments that he had not had time to explore in the earlier utterance. He was interested primarily in clarifying the relationship between the citizen and his government, he said, "as the foundation of the social edifice—the great security for social happiness. . . . Disaffection towards a government, which is administered with a view to the general welfare, is a great crime; and such opposition, even to a bad government, as infuses into subjects a restless temper, an unwillingness to yield to wholesome and necessary restraint, deserves no better name."

But this is not to say that rulers are never to be opposed. Subjects have rights as well as duties. "Government is instituted for one and a single end,—the benefit of the governed; the protection, peace, and welfare of society; and when it is perverted to other objects, to purposes of avarice, ambition, or party spirit, we are authorized and even bound to make such opposition, as it suited to restore it to its proper end, to render it as pure as the imperfection of our nature and state will admit." No man, he declared, should be immune to public scrutiny. "Rulers, when they leave the common walks of life, leave none of their imperfections behind them." On the contrary, power often has a tendency "to corrupt" and "to harden the heart against the claims and sufferings of mankind."

Although Channing was willing to grant a people's right to use force to overthrow an unjust government, he expressed, with his usual caution, the limitations surrounding such a power. "It becomes us to rejoice," he said, ". . . that we live under a constitution, one great design of which is—to prevent the necessity of appealing to force—to give the people an opportunity of removing, without violence, those rulers from whom they suffer, or apprehend an invasion of rights." This is one of the principal advantages of a republic over a despotism. A republic, he went on to say, rests upon two fundamental rights—the rights of suffrage and freedom of speech. Of these, freedom of opinion, of speech, and of the press is the very soul of republican institutions—the safeguard of all other rights.

In comparison with his more mature declarations concerning freedom, Channing's remarks suffer; yet he pulled no punches in his attack upon cowardly Americans who would resort to the most violent means to muzzle opposition to governmental policy. He was incensed by recent attempts to silence editors of obstructionist newspapers; and his eyes flashed with indignation as he declared: "We have seen a savage populace excited and let loose on men, whose crime consisted in bearing testimony against the present war; and let loose, not merely to waste their property, but to shed their blood, to tear them from the refuge which the magistrate had afforded, to slaughter them with every circumstance of cruelty and ignorance. I do not intend to describe that night of horror, to show to you citizens, who had fought the battles of their country, beaten to the earth, trodden under foot, mangled, dishonoured!—What ought to alarm us even more than this dreadful scene is, the disposition which has never been discovered to extenuate these atrocities, to speak of this bloody outrage as a mode of punishment, irregular indeed, yet mitigated by the guilt of those who presumed to arraign their rulers."

His reticence concerning the "night of horror" was due not to any sense of false delicacy but rather to the knowledge that his listeners were thoroughly acquainted with the events to which he had reference. Only two weeks before, the citizens of Boston had been warned by the city fathers to be prepared at a moment's notice to suppress any kind of disorder. The cause for such anxiety was the recent riot in Baltimore, one of those atrocities which, though infrequent, bring the average American up short when he realizes such things can happen in the United States.

The train of events leading up to the "Baltimore Massacre" had been set in motion by the policy of a man named Jacob Wagner, editor-in-chief of *The Federal Republican* and a bitter opponent of James Madison and "his" war. An extremist among the Federalists, Wagner waged an unceasing attack upon Madison and his measures, scrupling at nothing, even slander, in his eagerness to win. Before war was declared, he had been allowed to carry on unmolested; but after June 18, the city of Baltimore shared in the feeling that was common in the South and West, that opposition to the war amounted to treason, and should not be tolerated.

Wagner's immunity was short-lived. On June 22, four days after hostilities had commenced, a well-organized mob took possession of his printing office, and in the presence of prominent citizens and the mayor (who did nothing except deprecate their action), destroyed it completely. Nothing daunted, Wagner moved to Georgetown and resumed publication.

Meanwhile, some of his Baltimore associates, who were not disposed to allow a mob to dictate to them, circulated copies of the *Republican* together with a rumor that they were being printed at a certain Baltimore address. Under the leadership of General Henry Lee, a distinguished Revolutionary War hero and a former governor of his State, a group of some twenty Federalists fortified the house from which the newspaper had supposedly issued and waited for an attack. They did not have to wait long. A mob soon gathered and broke open the door, whereupon the small garrison fired, dropping some of their assailants to the ground. A pitched battle was in prospect, when the mayor arrived with a squadron of cavalry and persuaded the beleaguered Federalists to submit to the civil authorities.

While the mob howled and uttered threats, Lee and his companions were marched off to jail. That night the mob entered the jail and seized the prisoners. A few escaped, but the rest were severely beaten. All night and until noon the next day, eight of the victims lay unconscious on the prison steps, while the mob, which would not permit their removal, tortured them to determine whether they were dead. When the rioters finally permitted the bodies to be removed, one was dead, General Lee was severely crippled, and the others were seriously injured.

Perhaps no other incident did so much harm to the Republican cause as this flagrant example of mob violence. It provided excellent ammunition for the New England clergy who were, almost to a man, opposed to the war. Channing, however, was more disinterested in his motives than the majority of his colleagues. Although he was opposed to the war and considered it harmful, he was much more alarmed by an attitude of mind that could condone such an act as the Baltimore riot.

"The cry has been," he said, "that war is declared, and all opposition should therefore be hushed. A sentiment more unworthy of a free country can hardly be propagated." War more than any other measure of a government should be subject to free discussion by the people. But he was careful to point out that freedom of speech is not license to say whatever one pleases. "Nothing," he insisted, "is to be spoken or written but the *truth*, and truth is so to be expressed, that the bad passions of the community shall not be called forth, or at least shall not be unnecessarily excited."

The usual rejoinder to such high-minded idealism is that it calls for angels rather than men. Channing was not unaware of this. In fact, he would have been more surprised by a complete acceptance of his views than by opposition. Contrary to what many of his critics were to say about him, he was no facile optimist, self-blinded by wishful thinking. Humanity in its present state was synonymous with imperfection. He knew this, and he told his people so; but—and this was important—it need not remain so. The millennium was a long way off, but the thing to do now was to begin thinking about it. Truth, once embraced, could mean the beginning of man's emancipation from his faulty human nature.

The restraint which Channing exercised in commenting upon the beginning of the war, though markedly different from the usually intemperate reaction of his fellows-in-opposition, did not mean any less distaste for it. Like many another American, he followed with jaundiced eye the staggering progress of the American forces during the two years following the declaration of hostilities. Fortunately for the infant nation not yet out of its swaddling state, Britain was so preoccupied with European affairs that not even the magnificent blunders and grand inefficiency of her puny opponents were sufficient to earn defeat for them. In 1814, when a climax seemed probable, good tidings reached Massachusetts. Bonaparte had fallen, and there was unbounded exultation in the hearts of men like Channing, who regarded the little Emperor as an atrocious tyrant.

On June 8, 1814, a number of prominent citizens of Boston and Massachusetts gathered at the home of the Honorable William Phillips, the Lieutenant Governor, to draw up plans for a celebration to commemorate God's goodness in overthrowing the despot. George Cabot, Harrison Gray Otis, John Lowell, and Channing were named to make the necessary arrangements. A sermon was called for and Channing elected. One week later, the Stone Chapel was jammed with an enthusiastic group of Bostonians, whose pent-up joy was only awaiting release by the speaker before them. They were not disappointed. Giving full vent to personal feelings which were in complete accord with the emotions of his listeners, Channing painted the degradation resulting from despotic government. Then he reminded the people of the apprehension that had filled the entire Christian world when Napoleon's destructive career was in the ascendant and asked them to contrast that dismal prospect with the glorious vision of peace now before them.

God's will in bringing this about seemed so plain to Channing that he begged his hearers to hold fast their confidence in God and never to despair of human nature no matter how dark the future might appear. He considered the fall of Bonaparte an augury of a new era, and he believed that men were at last to be permitted "to anticipate the long lost and long desired blessing of general and permanent peace." When he concluded with the words, "The oppressor is fallen and the world is free," his audience burst forth with cheers that reverberated from every surface of the King's Chapel.

His joy, however, was tempered by the sober reflection that the United States and Great Britain were still at war. Many of his friends were so worried over the dire economic straits into which New England had been driven by high taxes and a war-enfeebled commerce that they were even thinking of urging secession from the Union. But this was unthinkable to Channing. Furthermore he was sustained by a firm trust in a benevolent Deity, who orders all things for the best; somehow he knew the conflict would be resolved, but in God's own time.

Certainly his proposal of marriage to his cousin Ruth Gibbs indicated his confidence in the country's future in general, and in his own career in particular. He had loved her for many years and had waited patiently while he fulfilled his promise to Francis; he would not have urged her to share his fortunes unless he had been certain of his ability to make her happy. Now his obligations were nicely taken care of. What had once been a large household had now dwindled down to his mother, his younger sister Mary, and himself.

The charmed circle had been broken first by Francis's death. Then Allston had swept Ann away to England. Sister Lucy had married young William Russell and had gone to New York City. Edward Tyrrell was now on his own as a young lawyer. Just the year before, he and George Ticknor had been admitted to the Massachusetts bar, and at the moment he was also working with his cousin, Richard Henry Dana, Judge Francis's son, and several others to start a new literary magazine. Walter was now Dr. Channing and was already attracting attention as a rising young obstetrician.

Before he proposed, Channing had carefully considered the responsibilities involved in taking such a step. Although this premeditation seems unromantic, it really was not. He was no throwback to an age when women were selected as mates on the basis of what they might bring by way of breeding or dowry to enhance the reputation or financial status of their husbands. By this time, caution and thoughtfulness were second nature with him. Besides, he looked at marriage as an indissoluble bond that endured throughout eternity. How could he afford then to let this "most solemn engagement of life be an act of rashness and unreflecting passion?"

Marriage and the family were, as he saw them, the bulwarks of society against the forces of social disintegration. Through them he expected men to work toward the perfection inherent in human nature. But marriage was not a simple *affaire de coeur:* not a matter of passion or animal attraction. On the contrary, he believed it was instituted for a noble end. Its purpose was "to awaken the heart, to exercise and strengthen its sensibilities and charities, to train it to the perfection of social virtue, to confer the highest enjoyments of friendship, to secure to each party the benefit of the other's strength, intelligence, and virtues, and to unite both in forming useful and virtuous members for the community." The formality of such a statement did not preclude love in marriage. "Man is made for love," he would insist time and time again. The word *love* as used in this sense meant, of course, the highest form of disinterested benevolence; but love between man and woman was God's own way of providing for the propagation of the species and insuring man's future greatness. That was why He had sanctified the marriage contract.

Channing's views concerning marriage had evolved from personal family experiences and his relations with people whom he had known both as friends and parishioners. In his own family he had seen how his father and mother had complemented each other to make a happy home and a successful marriage. William Channing's patience had been an admirable balance for Lucy Ellery's impulsive temper, and she in turn had been a tower of strength to him. His Uncle Henry and Aunt Sarah had taught him how love could bless and crown a marriage with fulfillment. Judge Francis Dana and his wife Sophia had set him a fine example of social compatibility when he lived with them in Cambridge, and the Randolphs had been models of how to live graciously and charitably within the marriage bond. The family circle at the Higginsons had been full of mutual confidence and strong friendships; and Susan Higginson had made the brief years of Francis Channing's life fruitful and happy. With this wealth of family associations to guide him, he was well prepared to plan a happy married life of his own.

What of Channing's bride-to-be? As a childhood schoolmate, Ruth Gibbs had often brought a smile to William's lips with her capricious ways and elfin tricks. A first cousin of William—her mother, a sister of William's father, had married the wealthy George Gibbs, one of Newport's leading merchants—Ruth was often in his company at family get-togethers. Later, after William's father had died, and the family fortunes of the Channings stood in ever sharper contrast with the Gibbs's, William's Aunt Mary had increased her solicitations to Lucy Channing to share some of the blessings provided by the Gibbs's fortune; but Lucy's independence had never permitted her to accept anything that was not strictly within the bounds of friendship. The two families, however, were always close to each other, and the children had been like brothers and sisters until William went away to Harvard.

During the years away from home he had often thought of Ruth and wondered whether she still remembered him. The best evidence of what she meant to his adolescent heart is his own testimony concerning the episode of his reading Francis Hutcheson under the willows on the Dana Estate. When Hutcheson's *Inquiry* had revealed to him an entirely new vision of a perfectible world, he looked around for someone to bring about the millennium immediately. As he later explained it, "My enthusiasm at that age, being then but fifteen, turning strongly to the female sex, I considered that they were the powers which ruled the world, and that, if they would bestow their favor on the right cause only, and never be diverted by caprice, all would be fitly arranged, and triumph was sure." Sitting down at his desk, he had then written in true knightly fashion to the Lady Ruth for assistance; but when he had finished, his courage, born of the moments of elation following his vision of a world remade, had oozed away; and he could not send the letter.

Following the years at Harvard and Richmond, Channing had seen Ruth only occasionally in Newport and Boston. But these meetings were sufficient to prove how much she meant to him. He didn't tell her of his love because he couldn't marry until his promise to Francis was kept, and he didn't think it fair to ask Ruth to wait that long. Furthermore, he was only too well aware of the discrepancy in financial status between Ruth's family and his own. Finally when her persistent refusal of all other suitors made it plain that her regard for him was more than cousinly, he overcame his scruples and proposed.

On July 21, 1814, they were married by the Reverend Dr. Gardner at the Gibbs's home on Mount Vernon Street. Their honeymoon was spent at Oakland, the Gibbs's country-seat in Portsmouth, only a few miles from Newport.

After the newly-weds returned from Oakland, they took up their life in the Berry Street parsonage with Channing's mother and sister. It was September, and the people of Boston were apprehensive of an invasion by the enemy. Only a few weeks earlier the British had occupied Washington, burned the White House, the department buildings, and the Capitol. At such a moment, Channing felt obliged to do what he could to strengthen the spirits of his parishioners. Accordingly just a week after the American naval victory over the British fleet on Lake Champlain, which had helped to quiet the fears of Bostonians, he delivered a sermon on the obligations of citizens in times of political crisis.

In his opening remarks he defended the right of the religious instructor to deal with political matters. He needed no convincing himself, but he was probably on the defensive because of a bitter attack that had followed his address at the Stone Chapel earlier in the year. Only a short time before, a certain "Messala" had published in Boston an acrimonious diatribe accusing him of perverting the proper functions of his pulpit. "When a clergyman converts the pulpit, which should be consecrated to 'the healing voice of Christian Charity,' into a theatre for political lectures; when he consents to become the instrument of a party, to exasperate the bitterness of faction, and mingles in the fury of party collision, he is disrobed of the sanctity of his calling, and we have a right to consider and treat him as a common political brawler," wrote his anonymous critic.

Channing had undoubtedly been touched by the sting in these remarks, although he knew in his conscience that the charges of partisanship were unfounded. Whoever he was, Messala was pro-French and therefore anti-English. As he viewed the situation, "The conquest of France has left the arms of Britain unemployed, and we know it to be her intention to exert her whole force to wreak her resentments, even to the last letter of vengeance on us." In the light of subsequent events, Channing could scarcely deny the logic of these remarks (the English, it would seem, were already prepared to enter Boston harbor) ; but he knew no unbiased observer would charge him with jumbling together "in his turbulent imagination the abolition of Christianity by Robespierre, and its re-establishmnt by Napoleon." That was hitting below the belt, and he would not dignify his attacker with an answer. He responded only to the extent of telling his congregation, "You will not . . . consider me as leaving the province of a religious teacher, if I speak to you of the dangers and claims of our country, if I address you as citizens, and attempt to point out your duties at the present solemn period."

There was nothing new in his sermon. On several previous occasions he had spoken about the war, and now he was simply trying to bolster morale by repeating his principles. His chief reminder was trust in God. "If God be for us," he said, "no matter who is against us. . . . God is still 'wonderful in counsel and excellent in working'; and if he wills to deliver us, we cannot be subdued."

Anticipating that the congregation might wonder how they could gain God's favor, he repeated what he had said many times before: "He is a moral governor, the friend of the righteous, the punisher of the wicked; and in proportion as piety, uprightness, temperance, and Christian virtue prevail among us, in that proportion we are assured of his favor and protection." Although he abhorred war and had decried this one, Channing was not then prepared to condemn a purely

defensive war. His early training, historical studies, and liberal principles were then such that he himself would have fought side by side
with his people to defend his country or city against an invader. He
urged them to pray to God for assistance in their need, but he also
counselled them to defend their homes.

While he and his bride were following his advice to "read together
the same books, view together the same scenes of nature, enjoy the
same society," the Massachusetts legislature was issuing an invitation
to the other New England states to send delegates to Hartford to
confer upon "their public grievances and concerns" and to take measures, if necessary, to call a convention of all the states to overhaul
the Federal Constitution. In December, twenty-six delegates from
Massachusetts, Connecticut and Rhode Island did meet at Hartford.
Ardent Federalists led by Pickering and John Lowell were hoping for
constitutional revisions to protect New England interests; or, if that
should fail, that New England would make a separate peace. Unfortunately for the extremists, a conservative group led by the politically indolent George Cabot gained control.

After a secret session, the convention recommended some seven
amendments to the Constitution and suggested several ways to safeguard the New England interests. There was a strong hint, also, that,
if these recommendations went unheeded, the possible objective of a
second convention might be secession.

While a committee to lay these views before federal authorities was
on its way to Washington, news of Stonewall Jackson's victory at New
Orleans and of peace negotiations in Europe made its mission
ridiculous. Federalist faces became fire-red and the Republicans were
jubilant, because they could cloak their inefficiency in carrying on the
war by accusing New England of treason.

Though still a Federalist, Channing thought that everything except
essential principles should be sacrificed to preserve the Union. His
considered review of the actions of his Federalist friends during the
war is contained in an article written for the *Christian Examiner* some
fifteen years after the treaty of war. While he found much to praise in
Federalism, he admitted that the "party in some respect [had] failed
of its duty to the cause of the Union and of freedom." Its failure, however, was due not to treachery but to despondency, "the rock on which
Federalism split." Similarly, though he greatly admired George Cabot,
he was obliged to confess that "He wanted a just faith in man's capacity of freedom, at least in that degree of it which our institutions

suppose. . . . He had too much wisdom of experience. He wanted what may be called the wisdom of hope."

Immediately after news of the Treaty of Ghent arrived in Boston, Channing preached a sermon, which he later repeated on the day of thanksgiving for peace. "Thank God!" he exclaimed. "The Union of these States will at least be prolonged. The day which is to witness the dissolution of our political fabric is at least deferred." Urging harmony and a policy of charitable forgiving, he declared, "Nothing now is wanting but an impartial administration of the government, and a spirit of mutual forbearance among our citizens, to fulfill the bright anticipations which patriots of better days cherished for this favored people."

He was not alone in his optimism for the future. Most Americans emerged from the struggle exultant rather than humbled. The picture of a nation in near-collapse—its Capitol in ruin, the states fighting one another, and the national credit bankrupt—was one that everyone wished to erase from his memory. Sectionalism had given way at least momentarily to a spirit of national pride. As Albert Gallatin, a bitter opponent of the war but a major figure in getting the peace treaty signed, saw the situation, "The war has renewed and reinstated the national feelings and character which the Revolution had given, and which were daily lessened. The people have now more general objects of attachment with which their pride and political opinions are connected. They are more American; they feel and act more as a nation."

As a matter of fact, Gallatin's analysis did not go beyond a surface interpretation. There had really been no genuine triumph of nationalism over sectionalism. Men's opinions were still divided on the nature of the union and the theory of secession was by no means dead. It would continue to crop up whenever a particular group felt itself mistreated in the national family, until a far greater crisis than that which America had recently gone through would settle the question once and for all.

On the other hand, if many Americans were inclined to boast about a new era in the nation's history, they had some justification for their claims, exaggerated though they might seem to foreign travelers. For the first time in twenty years—since Channing had entered Harvard as a callow boy—Americans could direct their attention away from Europe and devote their energies to domestic problems. President Madison, after his re-election in 1812, was so eager to smooth over sectional differences that his message to Congress in 1815 was definitely conciliatory to New England Federalists. The "Era of Good Feeling"—

that picturesque misnomer of the *Columbian Centinel*—had not quite arrived, but events seemed leading up to halcyon days ahead.

If the year 1815 marked a clear divergence between Europe and the United States, it also stood for a separation between the old and new in Channing's life. The year began with a happy husband leaving the unpretentious house that he had lived in for ten years, and in which he had shared many precious moments with his intimate family, to go with his wife to the spacious home of his mother-in-law, who wished them to have the opportunity to begin their married life under the most favorable circumstances.

Before the year was half over, one who had always shunned the public gaze and who looked upon religious controversy as directly opposed to God's wishes was forced to come out of his relative obscurity to defend the liberal party of the Congregationalists against what appeared to him to be an unwarranted and vicious attack from the orthodox forces of Jedidiah Morse and his cohorts.

In more ways than one, the preliminary chapters of Channing's life had been completed. The time had now come for him to break through the barriers of provincialism. In the circles of religion and social justice for years to come, his name—famous or infamous—would be public property, and his words would pass for the currency of liberalism wherever they were preached.

CHAPTER EIGHT

LOOKING BACKWARD

CHANNING'S AVERSION TO controversy was deeply rooted. By nature and experience he was inclined to avoid disputation—and never more strongly than when the dispute was sectarian in nature. Still there was a hard core of resistance within him toward any kind of intolerance, and he was never one to back away from a contest in which he knew the right and believed it to be on his side.

For some time he had been aware of growing tensions within the religious circles centering around Boston and Cambridge, and he had given careful thought to the lines of force leading up to the present situation. As he looked back over the two centuries of ecclesiastical history that spanned the distance between the coming of the Pilgrims and his settlement in Boston, he could see that the course of religion had been anything but a straight line of development. Tortuous, perhaps, would be a more suitable word to describe the convolutions through which it had passed.

He could remember distinctly the hours Grandfather Ellery had spent telling him about the Puritans and their dream of a theocracy. The "Saints," as they were known, had brought to New England a rigid orthodoxy. They held, as did John Calvin, the classic "Five Points" established at the Synod of Dort, but their beliefs were also conditioned by their humanistic English background and by their controversy with the Church of England. Certainly their "Foederall" theology was more than a mere duplication of Calvin's *Institutes*. When England proved inhospitable to their vision of the city of God, they had sought out America to try their Utopian experiment; and here in New England they had welded together church and state in a bond that still endured. At least it did in Massachusetts, although Channing could already see signs that the union was growing steadily weaker.

He had always admired the founding fathers as men, but their policy of repressing religious dissent on the grounds that the safety of both Church and State required it was one he could not accept. As a matter of cold logic, he was aware that the Puritans could not afford to tolerate Ann Hutchinson and her antinomian "heresy" if they were to survive as theocrats. But exclusiveness in religion was always to be deplored. Still Massachusetts's loss had been Rhode Island's gain.

As a matter of fact, the Puritans couldn't stem even the tide of internal resistance to their system. Twenty-five years after Ann Hutchinson's dismissal, the Half-Way Covenant had been instituted to provide a way into the church for second and third generations of New Englanders. By then a majority of the first generation of "Saints" had passed away, and the towns were beginning to fill up with scores of their children and grandchildren, many of whom were either non-regenerate or non-churched or both. How could the church be maintained if it were to be made up of regenerate members only? Channing was forced to admit the Half-Way Covenant had afforded only a partial solution. Unregenerate members of the church (baptized children of regenerate parents) were entitled to transmit church membership to their children, but as unregenerate members they could neither receive communion nor take part in church elections. The "half-way" members were little affected by this concession, and Channing could recall from his own youth the controversies that still lingered in the wake of the half-and-half solution.

Once the church doors were opened even only part way to the unregenerate, other compromises were demanded as a matter of course. Jonathan Edwards's grandfather, Solomon Stoddard, was the most influential exponent of one of these compromises. Stoddard, who believed that the Lord's Supper was meant to be a "converting ordinance," urged permission for the unregenerate to partake of it in the hope that they might be converted. Here was a far cry from the unconditioned covenant of grace that the "Saints" had preached. Conservatives like Increase Mather had attacked Stoddard vigorously, but he was successful in disseminating his ideas fairly widely in western Massachusetts. As a result increasing emphasis began to be placed upon human agency in the regeneration process. Thus the way was prepared for the "heresy" of Arminianism.

Stoddard made converts in Boston as well as in his own stronghold of Northampton. The Brattle Street Church, which had invited Channing to settle with it after his ordination, had been established in 1699 by the Brattles, who were ardent supporters of Increase Mather until they declared that they would follow Stoddard's example of doing away with the public relation of a religious experience as a qualification for full communion. Baptism, they declared, would be administered to any child sponsored by a professing Christian. The Brattles were important people, and their defiance of tradition was a slap in the face to Mather as well as an indication of deep-rooted opposition to Old Calvinism.

As the eighteenth century opened, then, there had been numerous indications that a softening process had been going on within New England Calvinism almost from the beginning. From the perspective of Channing's time, it was easy to see that as soon as the people had found a breathing spell from the labors of subduing a rebellious wilderness, and after they had been forced time and time again by the exigencies of a harsh pioneer and colonial life to devise all kinds of makeshift arrangements simply to exist, their utter dependence upon a Divine Sovereign whose Will was law had been supplanted by a spirit of self-reliance. It was as though the theocracy had been doomed from the very start. The conditions of life in a wilderness were exactly those most likely to draw out and develop the individualism inherent in Puritan theology, and this had led ultimately to a reliance upon self and a disregard for theocratic ordinances.

The conservatives in Massachusetts had not given way to the liberal forces without a battle. In 1705 the Mathers submitted a plan to the Congregationalists to create a stricter church government and to provide new controls to keep the Church and ministry in the narrow path of orthodoxy. In effect, the *Proposals,* as the plan was named, called for regional organizations in eastern Massachusetts similar to the Stoddardean groups in the western part of the State. The Mathers's plan had fallen through, however. John Wise of Ipswich riddled the arguments for association, and Harvard went over to the Leveretts, the Brattles and the Colemans. Increase and his son lived on into the twenties; but they died—beaten men, leaving the victory to Solomon Stoddard and his forces in the west and the Harvard liberals in the east. Others among the conservatives had left the field of battle to fight on a new front in Connecticut. The establishment of Yale College gave evidence of their desire not to give up the contest.

The course of the debate between the two factions of Congregationalism in the eighteenth century could be clearly traced in the annual Convention Sermons. Channing had read enough of them to know that neither side was able to secure much of an advantage over the other. If the conservatives defended their views one year, the liberals were certain to get an opportunity to answer the next and vice versa.

In 1722 the Sermon had been delivered by the redoubtable Cotton Mather. His remarks indicated that laxity in belief in the doctrine of the Trinity had already become noticeable. Entreating "that a Glorious CHRIST may never, *Never!* be forgotten," he had warned against the loss of faith that would result from "such books as have been very much in vogue among us; books whereof it may be complained *Nomen Christi non est ibi.*" He was undoubtedly referring to the writings of such Englishmen as Thomas Emlyn and Dr. Samuel Clarke, standard fare for divinity students by the time Channing was preparing for the ministry.

Four years later when the Reverend William Williams of Hatfield had preached the Annual Sermon, he too emphasized the importance of setting forth "the glory of Christ in the wonderfulness of his person, natures, offices and benefits." Williams's concern was due mainly to the immigration of English and Irish Presbyterians who had left their native lands rather than submit to the policies of "Subscription" established in Great Britain to overcome doctrinal laxity, chiefly in the matter of the Trinity. He might easily have had in mind such a group as that which settled three years later in Long Lane and before whose descendants Channing now stood as minister.

This same Reverend Mr. Williams was an uncle by marriage of Jonathan Edwards and the head of a clan with whom Edwards had waged, and eventually lost, a bitter feud. According to Edwards, the issue in dispute was doctrinal laxity—or, more explicitly, Arminianism. But what had he meant by Arminianism?

After the Synod of Dort in 1619 and its condemnation of Jacobus Arminius for deviating from orthodox doctrine concerning the enslavement of man's will, the term *Arminian* became a smear word among Protestant nations, and all efforts to increase human responsibility by giving the natural will power to act in some degree by itself were condemned as Arminianism. Arminius himself had not asked for much—only a small share for man in the process of cooperating with the Divine Will—but his remonstrance against the strictures of Calvinism was enough to shock the orthodox believers of his native Holland and to provoke a civil war between them and his followers.

Not long after the assembly at Dort Arminianism came to England. Contacts between English and Dutch theologians were made by men like John Hales, James I's representative at the Synod; and many Church of England divines, Archbishop Laud among them, came over to the Arminian side. Immediately the cry of heresy was raised by English Puritans, whose strict Calvinism could not abide the more tolerant views of the Dutch theologian. Laudian Anglicans, however, found it much more consonant with reason to believe that God had

not created man to damn him than to accept the supralapsarian doctrine that divine decrees determine alike the acts and destinies of man.
The early popularity of Arminianism among the ministers of the
Church of England naturally led New England from the very beginning to associate it with the prelacy from which the founding fathers
had fled, so that next to Antinomianism and Quakerism, it was considered the greatest of heresies.

The same year that Reverend Williams deprecated disinterest in
the second person of the Trinity, Cotton Mather had boasted there
was not a single Arminian in New England, yet in 1734 Jonathan Edwards was preaching views of man's abominable condition and of his
lack of righteousness before God, which seem to indicate that he
believed the churches needed rescuing from the danger of this very
heresy. Had the encyclopedic Mather been a bad observer, or had conditions changed so radically in the intervening years? The answer to
both questions was "No."

Edwards's charges of Arminianism against such loyal Puritans as
John Barnard; his cousins, Israel and Elisha Williams; and Charles
Chauncy had involved a broader definition of the term *Arminianism*
than Mather was accustomed to. To Edwards, England and New England were as one country, and the core of England was its essential
Protestantism. Consequently, he was disturbed that not only had almost all Anglican divines become Arminians, "but Arminianism has
greatly prevailed among the Dissenters, and has spread greatly in New
England, as well as Old." Whether they knew it or not, he had declared to those against whom he was pressing the Arminian charge,
heresy from abroad, which had in turn spawned a new domestic
variety, had so tainted them that they had ceased to believe what they
confessed. Professing to believe in depravity, election, and the other
tenets of their grandfathers, they were, as a matter of fact, only mouth-
ing words. Teaching that the will of man is enslaved, they were acting
as though the will of the unregenerate were capable of being wooed
and coaxed to goodness—as though it were a self-determining power.

Edwards had been right in pointing out the disparity between belief
and practice, Channing realized, but how wrong he had been in insist-
ing that men were incapable of perfecting themselves! Channing
wished now that he had learned more about Edwards from Samuel
Hopkins. He had come to regret more and more since Hopkins's death
his failure to query Edward's disciple about his relationship with the
great theologian.

Shortly before Hopkins had gone to Northampton to study with

Edwards, the Great Awakening had reached New England. An American counterpart of what was called Pietism in Germany and Methodism in England, the Awakening presented to New Englanders for the first time the idea of group salvation and public conversion. Sinners were urged to make open confessions of their sins, and private soul-searching gave way to public spectacle. The old order of wrestling alone with God and then reporting to the congregation to swear to its covenant had changed into public demonstration.

Hopkins had told Channing that Edwards saw some worth in the revivals, as these mass meetings were called, but he had also deplored their excesses. Itinerant preachers like the Englishman George Whitefield, and local exhorters and exhibitionists, like John Davenport, had given them their unqualified support, while Charles Chauncy and his followers wholeheartedly disapproved.

In the seventeenth century it had been agreed that conversion might take place in various ways—either quickly or slowly—but always from within and in private. In the eighteenth century, however, the revivalists had narrowed the range of experience and established a stereotyped pattern of external conversion attended by unusual effects.

John Davenport, a rabid revivalist, preached a doctrine of direct inspiration from God and argued that human learning was a clog to the free workings of the spirit. Chauncy, on the other hand, rejected the religious-experience idea completely. For him, behavior—not emotionalism—was the only sign of conversion. Speaking of the regenerate man, he had once declared, "The beauty of holiness appeals to him above all else, and sin now appears an awfully evil and bitter thing." When it was remarked to him that some persons might be sanctified from childhood and thus inherit the kingdom without any agony of soul, he remarked dryly, "This, I doubt not, is sometimes the Case, and might oftener be so, if Parents were more generally faithful in the religious Education of their children. . . ."

Like Chauncy, Channing had always rebelled at the "enthusiasm" inherent in revivalism. He could recall his own disenchantment as a boy with hell-fire declamations, and his memories of his own conversions—first at Harvard and later in Richmond—carried no echo of the heroics of the "sawdust trail." If anything, his experiences had been more akin to that of the seventeenth-century "Saints." Chauncy's Puritan forbears had taught him to beware of Antinomians and Quakers, and he was just as wary of God-intoxication when preached by a George Whitefield, a Gilbert Tennent, or a John Davenport as he was of Antinomianism or Quakerism. For him, as well as for Channing, the Bible was the rule by which "enthusiasm" was to be judged, and reason must rule over the affections and passions.

Although Channing was probably unaware of it, a basic difference in the psychology of Chauncy and Edwards accounted for their different judgment of the Awakening. Chauncy espoused the outmoded "faculty" psychology of the Middle Ages, whereas Edwards taught a dynamic system in which the mind of man worked as a unit. Chauncy naturally distrusted revivalistic practices, which seemed to him to by-pass human reason in order to get directly at the emotions.

Edwards, on the other hand, believing that the emotions were neither good nor bad in themselves, could and did make use of them in his work. His *Sinners in the Hands of an Angry God* (1741), delivered without any of the showmanship or spell-binding methods of ranters like Davenport or roarers like Whitefield, showed how effective his method of salvation could be. Edwards's personal conduct as well as his exposition of a new theory of religious affections indicated that he was just as far removed from the extremists among the New Lights (as the revivalists were known) as he was from Chauncy and his Arminian followers.

Looking back over nearly three-quarters of a century, Channing realized that the Great Awakening had been perhaps the first really critical point along the line of New England's religious development. By 1745, when the pent-up energy that had made it possible was expended, the unity of the Congregational Church had been shattered and a cleavage established that was only now beginning to come to a definite conclusion.

Before the lid had blown off New England, the Congregationalists had been one large family—not always united or happy together, it is true, but willing to live and let live; after the excitement of the Awakening had died down the family was hopelessly divided. On one side were the Calvinists, themselves separated into the Old Lights and the New Lights.

The former, rejecting the progressive psychology of Jonathan Edwards, had attempted to keep the substance as well as the form of their grandfathers' religion alive in a world completely alien to the philosophy of the "Saints." The latter, led by Edwards, who had learned from Newton and Locke the value of the New Science and the New Philosophy, had prepared to withstand all assaults against their Calvinism now that their leader had placed a sound eighteenth-century foundation under it. Both of these groups were fundamentally opposed to Chauncy's followers who had fought the Awakening to a standstill. A neat pattern—this new alignment of forces—but it was the result of circumstances rather than of any planned effort. It had continued disintegrating ever since.

After the first furor of revivalism had passed, New England thinkers had awakened to the fact that they were confronted by the Enlightenment in an advanced stage of development. Reason had been enthroned on the continent and in England for some time; now a number of its streams of influence had begun to pour into the whole of New England, where hitherto they had only seeped, by one devious way or another, into certain isolated spots. Several of these influences had become important formative influences in Arminianism.

For one thing, Biblical scholarship began to claim first attention from rational thinkers like Chauncy and Jonathan Mayhew. Disdaining "human creeds" and the orthodox confessions of faith, the Arminians were driven to the Bible for ammunition against their opponents. John Taylor's *Paraphrase with Notes on the Epistle to the Romans* (1745) was typical of the kind of study they relished. Another influence was the Arminianism in England. By 1700, this doctrine had become so widespread that Calvinists were a minority in the Church of England. Rational theologians like Lord Falkland, William Chillingworth, and John Hales were all Arminians. Anglican divines like Daniel Whitby and Thomas Stackhouse were well known in New England, and Mayhew had direct contacts with English dissenters.

Simultaneous with Arminianism and often connected with it was antitrinitarianism. In the 1690's the Church of England was disrupted by controversies over the Trinity, and a flood of antitrinitarian books and pamphlets had resulted. Published in England early in the eighteenth century, such representative volumes as Whitby's *Discourse on the Five Points* (1710) and Emlyn's *Humble Inquiry* (1703) were occasionally read in their original editions in this country; but by 1750 American editions made them available to large numbers of readers. By the time Channing had entered Harvard, antitrinitarian books were no novelty in the College Library.

The struggle of the Christian rationalists in England against deism had also had its repercussions on this side of the Atlantic. Although New England liberals read the sermons of Tillotson, Locke's *Reasonableness of Christianity,* and Clarke's *Lectures,* they had rejected the writings of the deists. Reason was the standard measurement for both groups, but the Christian rationalists offered a far more wholesome program than their opponents, because they still clung to a belief in miracles and prophecies. Channing had read the rationalists as a college student and later when he was studying for the ministry, but deism had never had any appeal for him because of its attempts to undermine revelation. He had, however, looked with favor on the movement away from creeds.

The growing aversion to creeds and confessions in England had behind it a long history in the religion of dissent. In New England, antipathy to creeds came more slowly; but once it had arrived, it firmly entrenched itself. Jonathan Mayhew, perhaps the most popular exponent of the rational theology expounded by Chauncy, was violently opposed to creed-making and its resultant conflicts. "If these *faith-makers*," he said, "are so compassionate as *only to give their brethren to the devil* for not submitting to doctrines and decrees, even this has some tendency to intimidate them." The substance of Christian duty for Mayhew and many others like him consisted in the love of God and one's neighbor and in the practice of morality rather than in a belief in any creed. Reverend William Balch of Bradford asserted, "Morality is the Height of Christianity"; and Lemuel Briant of Braintree reiterated his sentiments in the *Absurdity and Blasphemy of Depretiating Moral Virtue* (1749). Channing's grandfather had taken a similar position and had steadfastly refused to join a church or espouse a particular creed.

In the 50's the Arminians had dropped all pretenses of being orthodox and had begun to condemn Calvinism by name and attack what they considered its dangerous tendencies. In particular they opposed the doctrine of original sin. They did not deny that Adam had sinned or that men were actually sinners, but they did refuse to accept the doctrines of the imputed guilt of Adam and total depravity.

According to the Calvinists, Adam was both the natural and moral head of all mankind. All men were *in* him (as branches in a tree) in a relative and moral sense, since he was their appointed head and representative. Even the "Chain of Being" was dragged into the discussion. Adam, it was said, could have communicated only his kind of rank; therefore all men must have received from him the original sin.

None of these arguments held water for the Arminians. Guilt to them was a personal matter, and the individual could not be held responsible for the sins of his father, even if the parent were Father Adam himself. As the Reverend John Bass of Ashford put it: "representing our Nature as exceeding Corrupt and Wicked as soon as formed, odious to GOD'S Holiness and under his Wrath and Curse; has, so far as I can see a natural Tendency to fill the Mind with the most gloomy Apprehension of the Author of our Being, to damp our

Spirits, to turn away our Hearts from Him; and, in a Word, to the Destruction of all Religion." Channing's attitude was identical, and he would find occasion in the near future to use this moral argument against Calvinism in precisely the same way as Bass had used it.

Jonathan Edwards's *Freedom of the Will* had been a high water mark in the theological controversies of the mid-eighteenth century. Channing had been impressed as an undergraduate by the logical consistency of Edwards's treatise, but his lack of faith in its initial premises had made it easy for him to accept the conventional defense of Samuel Clarke which was always given to students as refutation of Edwards's doctrine of necessity. And so it had been when Edwards first advanced his arguments against the Arminians. Few among them had been won over by his argument. Instead they concentrated on attacking his *The Great Christian Doctrine of Original Sin*. They charged him with making God the author of sin, but he had been content to return the compliment by proving that free-will no more solved the authorship of sin than pre-destination. Samuel Hopkins had not taken the Arminian criticism so lightly, Channing remembered. *His Sin, Through Divine Interposition, an Advantage to the Universe* had been an obvious attempt to lighten God's responsibility in the matter.

But the Arminians had little sympathy for either position. Instead of trying to pierce the Edwardian defenses, they had gone on to relieve man from the bondage of election, original sin, and total depravity by conceding to him the powers of a rational moral agent. By the time Channing's father had graduated from Princeton, man's moral freedom had become a well-accepted notion in New England, and Channing himself had grown up in an atmosphere where the doctrine of "moral necessity" was seldom a matter for even academic discussion.

Despite the continual recession from the high point of Edwards's defense of the Puritan way, from the middle of the eighteenth century on, the questions of natural vs. revealed religion, justification, regeneration, atonement, benevolence, etc. continued to receive considerable attention from the Arminians in New England and from their opponents as well.

To begin with, there was the big question of man's reason and how it was to be used in determining truth and God's will. The Puritans had believed that man's reason was darkened and made unworthy of reliance through Adam's fall. The will of God, therefore, was made known by special revelations to the prophets and by the teaching of Christ, and a complete record of these revelations was to be found in

Holy Scripture. Everything necessary to salvation was contained there-in. The real problem was this: How was it to be interpreted?

The Puritans had agreed that the Scripture provided the rule for its own interpretation: Obscure passages were to be read by the light of those which were more clear. Holy Writ was to be accepted by faith, yet no violence was to be done to reason. Reason actually proved the necessity for faith and endorsed it with convincing testimony. When the Enlightenment began to make its influence felt upon New England, English supernatural rationalism stemming from Newtonian physics and Lockean psychology had provided a rich source for the new rationalism of the Arminians; and a shift in emphasis began to appear. More and more the test of reason began to be applied to revelation, private and Scriptural.

Reason, it had been urged by English uniformitarians, was the same in all men; but Arminians like Chauncy and Mayhew argued that there was a diversity of mental powers. "Our intellectual faculties," said Mayhew, "were given us to improve; they rust for want of use; but are brightened by exercise." This idea had developed into an insistence upon man's natural capacity for infinite enlargement of the personality and growth of character, a point of view with which Channing was in full accord. Charles Chauncy's statement that "all intelligent moral beings, in all worlds, are continually going on, while they suitably employ and improve their original faculties, from one degree of attainment to another . . ." had lost none of its attractiveness for Channing although his friends frequently reminded him that he was over-sanguine in his hopes for mankind.

From Chauncy's time on, reason had become so closely identified with religion that it was difficult to distinguish the two. Natural religion, or "that which unassisted reason can discover and prove," was still to be differentiated from revealed religion, or anything that God had made known to man through immediate inspiration or prophecy; but the distinction between the two was already showing signs of becoming blurred. Twenty years later, the definition of natural religion had become so broadened that it included all of revealed religion. Thus the Dudleian lecturer in 1779, the Reverend Gad Hitchcock, told Harvard undergraduates: "Natural religion is not so properly defined to be that, which mankind have, or might come to the knowledge of, merely by the strength of unassisted reason; as that, which reason sees to be right, and feels the force of, when it is known." This harmony between natural and revealed religion was asserted by the moderate (or Old Light) Calvinists and Arminians alike, because they felt that a divorce of the two would lead to either enthusiasm or deism.

Although they admitted that reason as well as revelation was the word of God, the supernatural rationalists had not placed unlimited confidence in man's reasoning powers, because they knew that they were often misused. They did not hesitate to prove, however, that the Bible was God's own word by resorting to an argument based on internal evidence; namely that there was nothing in the Bible contrary to reason. Faith in the eighteenth century, therefore, was preeminently an intellectual matter; it depended on testimony. Although the Christian rationalists constantly expressed a horror of infidelity, they had actually accepted the assumptions of the deists. They agreed that Christianity was something founded on argument, which had to be supported by external proof or testimony. Thus they had helped the deists to break down the distinction between the Bible and secular history and to apply the same critical standards to both.

When morality began to divest itself of its former theological sanctions, English thinkers had become preoccupied with ethics. As might be expected, rationalists like John Locke and Samuel Clarke were inclined to an intellectual ethic. God, they said, always acts in accordance with the eternal fitness of things; rational creatures should do likewise. Channing's favorites, Hutcheson and Shaftesbury, had claimed that men choose good not for rewards, but because it is naturally agreeable. Joseph Butler went a step further and insisted that conscience drives men to *do* good, not merely to *approve* it.

In New England Jonathan Mayhew had accepted both Clarke and Butler. Wherever they turned among the systems of the British moralists, the Arminians found an assertion of the natural capacities of all men for holiness, and a declaration that the content of morality was piety and benevolence. Piety had meant to Mayhew "love of God" but not "enthusiasm" and reason alone was quite sufficient to establish its obligations. As far as future rewards and punishments were concerned, New Englanders had seldom resorted to arguments drawn from inequalities in this life to prove that God's benevolence demanded a future balancing of the scales of justice. They were not always agreed that whatever is, is *good;* but they were fairly certain that it was right.

On the negative side, the theological position of the Arminians had been expressed in a denial of election and original sin; its positive side was contained in their doctrine of justification and regeneration. Christ's merits, they had declared, were sufficient to wash every man spotless without any action on his part. Where the covenant theology

and strict Calvinism, of which Hopkinsianism was representative, had
described justification as a divine operation by which man was saved
from guilt but not from sin, the Arminians had conceived of salvation
as freedom from both. Men were justified by faith—such a faith as
bears fruit in repentance and righteousness. Faith and works had no
merit in themselves, however. They secured man's salvation only because God had made them the terms of acceptance. Justification was
by the free grace of God, because men could never be perfect enough
to deserve it.

Over the subject of regeneration a triangular dispute had arisen
among the Congregational factions. The Old Calvinists had been
forced into siding first with the New Lights and then with the Arminians. All three parties agreed that man could do nothing of himself,
but grace meant something different to each of them. To the Arminians, it was nothing special, since they had already discarded the idea
of election. This was not true of the Old and New Lights, who still
held on to a covenant of grace. The latter group interpreted regeneration as an instantaneous act by which God came into a man's heart.
The Old Lights agreed with this interpretation, but they emphasized
the gradual development of the individual's moral powers following
regeneration. Only the gradual development, or conversion, was
stressed by the Arminians. Men like Mayhew denied that justification
was a sudden act. Like Channing, they looked upon it as a standard to
attain and stressed the fact that man's spiritual powers were capable of
development from birth onward. Man's happiness rather than God's
glory appeared to them to be the purpose of redemption.

The Arminian doctrine of justification and regeneration had been
completely developed and elaborated by the 1760's. It made a man's
salvation depend on his obedience to God's will, an obedience consisting of both faith and righteousness, and within the power of everyone.
The pattern of this thought was, in all essentials, the same as Channing's. But the Arminians still adhered to the orthodox Christian vocabulary. As Channing saw it, the difference between his own beliefs and
those of his predecessors was simply a problem of language or, as a
later age would call it, a question of semantics.

His own contemporaries were largely responsible for the new emphasis upon the dignity of human nature, Channing was convinced;
but it was equally true that the Arminians deserved a major share of
credit for their insight into the benevolence of the Deity. From the
time of the Puritans and even until the American Revolution, the
majority of men had pictured God as a king and father, and his govern-

ment as a constitutional monarchy ruled by laws. But the Calvinists' insistence that God acted only for His own glory had met with determined opposition from the Arminians, who were adamant in their stand that man's happiness was the end for which God worked. Once the idea of monarchy had fallen into disrepute in politics, it quickly lost its force in liberal theology as well, so that now belief in the pure concept of the fatherhood of God and His moral government was making rapid progress.

no longer God as king

Of course the change in attitude concerning the character of God had created some new problems for the Arminians. Could a truly benevolent Deity condemn any of His creatures to eternal destruction? Channing himself held no brief for the idea of an unending hell, but neither could he have much respect for the subterfuges employed by certain Arminian apologists. Some, using a variant of the "greatest-good" argument, had given the lame excuse that some men might be damned by God as a warning to others, but few who heard it took this response seriously. A more positive answer was that which Charles Chauncy published in *The Salvation of All Men: the Grand Thing Aimed at in the Scheme of God.* Universalism, as Chauncy's solution came to be known, had attracted great numbers of adherents; but this new belief still lacked an answer to the question of how one might reconcile the goodness of God with the existence of moral and physical evil.

Here the Arminians had been especially vulnerable because of their very insistence on benevolence. Accustomed to thinking in terms of the "Chain of Being," they naturally resorted to its principles to explain away evil. But such talk as "degrees of perfection" and "unrealized stages of development" offered only a negative, and hence unsatisfactory, solution. Arguing that God could not create perfect beings was no more convincing, since it involved a contradiction with His omnipotence. Moral evil, said some apologists, was a kind of medicinal unhappiness to make men appreciate good. Natural or physical evils, they added, were the result of established laws whose purpose and tendency are beneficial; and they cited hunger and thirst as examples. None of these proposed solutions answered the riddle. When all was said and re-said, the Arminians had to admit that God permitted evil. At no time, however, had they conceded that He was the author of evil, much less the father of sin.

The role of Christ in man's salvation had also been the subject of controversy in the eighteenth century. The Anselmic theory of atonement named after its originator, St. Anselm, carried the historical im-

primatur of the Catholic Church. Calvinism had adopted it, and Jonathan Edwards had reasserted it with his own peculiar emphasis. According to Anselm, God required satisfaction for every transgression
against Him. Any offense against God, however, was an infinite offense
and required an infinite atonement. The only possible infinite redeem-
er, therefore, was a God-man. This idea had originated in a cultural
period when sovereign lords treated their subjects as they pleased, and
prisoners were ransomed through the payment of a price. It was only
natural, therefore, for men to think of Christ's sacrifice as a ransom
which redeemed the world from the curse of God, its Sovereign Ruler.

The spirit of the eighteenth century, however, differed greatly from
that of the medieval world. The reason of the age saw the functions of
government to be the establishment of civic order through the administration of just laws. Justice was defined as the enforcement of these
laws instead of the punishment of transgressions, and perfect justice
became the mark of perfect government. This transformation in political theory was soon reflected in theology. The governmental theory
of atonement, derived from Hugh Grotius, the great international jurist of the Renaissance, soon came into vogue. Grotius had argued that
God was a Ruler who must maintain order and prevent crime. He
must insist on obedience to His laws, but He might remit penalties
when He saw fit. Christ's death was intended to serve as an example to
sinners, warning them of the horrible nature and consequences of sin.
His sacrifice therefore upheld the dignity of God's government, even
without the punishment of every individual transgressor.

This argument had enabled the Arminians to reject the imputation
of the righteousness of Christ and to emphasize the benevolence of
God. Christ no longer was considered the cause of God's benevolence,
and the traditional doctrine from Scripture that he was a king, who
judged man's transgressions; a priest, who served as an intercessor for
man before the throne of the Almighty; and a prophet, who was the
chief source of revelation of God's will, had been abandoned bit by bit.
By Channing's time Christ had become for liberals simply a source of
revelation from God, who taught chiefly by example. His duty was to
reconcile man to God, not God to man.

Between the Grotian or governmental theory of atonement and antitrinitarianism there was no inevitable connection. If adherents to the
theory did not stress the divinity of Christ, it was only because their
scheme had eliminated the necessity for a God-man. There was likewise
no necessary link between Arminianism and unsoundness on the Trinity, since there were a number of Arminians like the Reverend Pre-

served Smith who remained sound trinitarians. The Trinity had been neglected for a long time in New England, but in the 1750's the orthodox Calvinists had become disturbed enough to overhaul a number of Church covenants in an effort to avoid ambiguity. But the damage had been done. Doctrinal unsoundness was too far advanced for such patchwork. Jonathan Mayhew openly ridiculed the Athanasian Trinity in his *Seven Sermons,* and was doubtlessly instrumental in publishing that ancient document of English Arianism, Thomas Emlyn's *Inquiry.*

Controversy over the doctrine of the Trinity might have developed into a full-fledged revolution if matters of pressing political significance had not intervened. Mayhew became interested in the events that were leading up to the Revolution and withdrew from the theological arena. His successor Simeon Howard, who was regarded as unsound on the Trinity, was attacked by Samuel Hopkins in a strongly worded Trinitarian sermon. Hopkins had preached it in Boston, because he had a strong conviction that "the doctrine of the Divinity of Christ was much neglected, if not disbelieved by a number of the Ministers of Boston." If anything, Channing was certain, Hopkins had been guilty of understatement rather than hyperbole. But what a waste of time these endless arguments had been! Channing could not understand why so much energy had been used up in defending or attacking a position that was obviously unscriptural.

His own views were not much different from those of Samuel Clarke, whose *Scripture Doctrine of the Trinity* had been the chief fountainhead of Arianism in the Church of England and among dissenters. Clarke and Thomas Emlyn had been well known in New England before the Revolution, and most antitrinitarians owed something of their doctrinal divergence to them. There were few New Englanders, however, who had gone as far as William Bentley of Salem, who was outspoken in his Socinian, or purely humanitarian, ideas of Christ. For the most part, Channing's contemporaries in liberal theology were satisfied with the doctrine that Christ was divine and pre-existent, although subordinate to God the Father and not a part of the Godhead.

Their views were seldom challenged now, at least not openly, but the present state of affairs had been preceded by a series of hot skirmishes in numerous church bodies. Orthodox members of the Congregational family had begun to smoke out dissenters within their midst as early as the 1750's. Prizing doctrinal soundness more than Christian fellowship, they had revised Church covenants to establish a doctrinal standard for admission.

The Arminians denounced this "system of exclusion" and persistently fought the use of creeds and confessions of faith as tests of orthodoxy. Since they were by no means certain that all truth had been revealed to men, they preferred to leave the separation of sheep and goats to judgment day. Good evangelicals in the sense that they were wary of departing from the Bible, they stuck to the language of Scripture and accused the orthodox of departing from it. Since they took for granted differences of interpretation resulting from the study of Holy Writ, they did not believe in any society's imposition of creeds. All creeds, confessions, catechisms, they insisted, must be tested by the Word of God. Private judgment, in the light of these beliefs, became not only a right but a duty.

Channing's venture into history left him with no regrets. Since the founding of the theocracy, the New England mind had undergone many changes, but change in this instance was synonymous with progress. True, the path of progress had seldom been smooth or straight, but that was the price one always paid for improvement. The text of New England theology had been almost completely revised in the process, and many men and much effort had entered into the work of revision. No one place nor one group could take the credit. Harvard College was not the fountainhead of the new "latitudinarianism," nor could Boston ministers claim a monopoly on the growing liberalism. A congeries of forces and a mixture of diverse personalities and often unrelated ideas had gradually become fused and integrated. The result was a homocentric scheme of things in place of the old theocracy.

In Channing's mind there was no question that the new theology was better suited to the needs of a dynamic age than the old. Though he himself was much too modest to think it, he was, in many ways, a culmination of the main lines of religious development flowing from the previous age. New Light Calvinism and Arminianism were in strong disagreement, but both had opposed the Old Lights in the years following the Great Awakening. The New Light disciples of Jonathan Edwards had tended toward disinterested benevolence, and through Samuel Hopkins, this tendency had caught up with Channing and become an integral part of his liberal theology. Fully as important was the moral argument against Calvinism that Channing had inherited from Chauncy and the Arminians.

CHAPTER NINE

A HOUSE DIVIDED

WHEN CHANNING WAS ordained as minister of the Federal Street
Church, divergence of theological opinion had not yet become cause
for "the system of exclusion and denunciation in religion" to which
Channing vehemently protested in 1815. Trinitarians, Arminians,
Arians, and Socinians could still meet socially and converse amicably
together. But tension was increasing, and the state of relative calm existing from the time of the Revolution was about to end, and in no
uncertain terms.

When Channing preached John Codman's ordination sermon, he
could scarcely have foreseen how far Codman would travel down the
road to reaction. Only a short time after the latter had been installed,
he blew up a storm in his Dorchester Congregation by refusing to exchange with certain liberal ministers of the Boston Association. He
was backed up in this move by Morse and Samuel Miller of the Princeton Theological Seminary, who were eager to put the liberals in their
place. An extract of a letter which Miller wrote to Codman is typical
of the reasoning behind the policy of exclusion. He asks, "What has
led to that awful degeneracy of Boston with respect to evangelical
truth, which the friends of the faith once delivered to the saints have
so long endured?" And then answers himself with the statement: "I
have scarcely any remaining doubt, that the principal cause of the
effect in question, is to be sought in the subject of this letter, viz: indiscriminate exchanges with all classes of heterodox ministers."

Codman fought a bitter battle with the liberal faction of his own
congregation over the question of his right to exchange with whom he
wished. Two mutual councils were called, and Codman was exonerated
of charges of negligence, but the parish was still up in arms. Finally,
another minister was placed in Codman's pulpit, with a guard on the
pulpit-stairs, so that Codman was obliged to preach from the platform
below. The sight was so unedifying that he was overwhelmingly vindicated. The oppositionists in his parish were forced to leave, and Codman was free to do as he pleased in the matter of exchanges. The entire
incident proved that tempers were growing warm and that discretion

was rapidly being tossed to the wind; but the exclusionists only took heart from their victory in Dorchester, and looked for new ways to unify and increase their strength. According to William Bentley, "It seems Morse and Co. had contemplated a Union, a Consociation of Churches as I might call it." Morse's plans fell through, because even the orthodox cherished their congregational system. As Nathanael Emmons, the leading Hopkinsian of the day, put it: "Association leads to Consociation, Consociation to Presbyterianism, Presbyterianism to Episcopalianism, and Episcopalianism to Popery." After such a broadside, what was there left to say? Efforts to combine congregations were quickly discontinued, and for good.

In the same year that Codman was ordained, Andover Theological Seminary was established by a coalition of the Old Calvinists and Hopkinsians. Moderates like Morse and his friend Leonard Woods of Newbury had become extremely worried that their cause would shrivel and die unless they had a way to train young men in the Calvinistic faith. Harvard could no longer be entrusted with the task: they were certain of that. The Hopkinsians too were greatly concerned over the inroads of liberalism and were thinking of setting up a seminary in Woods's own town. Woods informed Morse of this development, and Morse wrote back, declaring that he feared a division of forces. Woods's reply is interesting:

> I am more and more convinced that we can't keep any terms with the Socinian crew. They are not honest. They hate the true gospel and the true God. We have suffered by treating them too well. I think heaven has placed you in the front of the battle against the powers of error and wickedness. The Lord support and guide you, and give you victory. If we can only get all Calvinists together, we need not fear. Hopkinsians must come down, and moderate men must come up, till they meet. Then the host will be mighty.

Morse thought Woods's idea excellent and set about immediately to woo the Hopkinsians, whom ordinarily he would have disdained. He convinced Gardiner Spring, the local Hopkinsian leader, but had to concede many points before the coalition was finally accomplished. On September 28, 1808, Andover opened its doors for the first time, and Jedidiah Morse wrote jubilantly: "A new institution, the offspring of Christian liberality, broad and scriptural in its foundation, richly endowed, consecrated to the interest of Evangelical truth, rises to bless our country." The editors of *The Monthly Anthology*, however, were not quite so happy about the event. William Bentley declared that the liberal elements among Boston ministers were alarmed because "they wish no religious establishment at present which is an enemy to religious moderation."

Such was the state of affairs when Channing emerged from the shadow cast first by his father's religion and later by the doctrine of Samuel Hopkins. Never a Trinitarian, he had still taken a decade in the ministry to throw off his early Calvinism. He had become a political and social liberal long before he was emancipated theologically, but such was the pattern of Boston liberalism. Channing placed such confidence in reason that he feared worse results from its repression or neglect than from its free exercise; and he distrusted theological precision because he thought it created sectarianism. Freedom of inquiry in religion was an absolute necessity, although he admitted "that the right of private judgment may be abused." Cloistered virtue was no virtue at all; Channing saw this just as clearly as had his hero, John Milton; and he insisted that "It was the wish and intention of the great Founder of our religion, that his religion should be examined, should be received on very different ground from false religions, should have no support but what is derived from its own excellence, and from the evidences of a Divine interposition by which it was accompanied."

His confidence that free inquiry was responsible for uniformity rather than diversity in religion lay behind his destestation of all forms of exclusiveness. He could endure almost anything as long as men were free to express their opinions and to search for new truth. Though opposed to infidelity (he had preached two sermons on the subject in 1813), because it resulted from ignorance, vice and pride, he nevertheless argued that the only way to combat it was by seeking the truth through free investigation. The same note of freedom rang from the Preface of the catechism which he and Samuel Thacher had prepared for the younger children of their respective societies in the same year that the battle over infidelity was being waged. And in a letter written late in December of 1812 to Eloise Payne, sister of the well-known dramatist, he had advised his correspondent to read Noah Worcester's *Bible News* "not so much with the hope that it may influence your judgment, as that it may teach you respect for those who differ from you."

Several months later he wrote Worcester, author of the book he had recommended, asking him to become the editor of a periodical that he and his liberal colleagues were contemplating. *The Monthly Anthology* had been discontinued in 1811 and *The General Repository and Review* of Andrews Norton had lasted only twenty-two months, because, as Norton himself said, "It was too bold for the proper prudence, or the worldly caution, or for the actual convictions, of a large portion of the liberal party." Since the failure of Norton's magazine had left the liberals without any medium of public expression at a time when the orthodox magazine, *The Panoplist,* was doing everything in its power to stir up criticism against them, Channing had been asked to make the overtures to Worcester, who was known in Boston only through his unusual publication.

In his letter to Worcester, Channing explained that he and his friends wished to have a periodical that would be adapted to the great mass of Christians and whose objective would be "to increase their zeal and seriousness, to direct their attention to the Scriptures, to furnish them with that degree of Biblical criticism which they are capable of receiving and applying, to illustrate obscure and perverted passages, and, though last not least, to teach them their Christian rights. . . ."

As to the peculiarities of Calvinism Channing remarked: "We are opposed to them, without censuring those who embrace those sentiments. We are opposed to that system particularly, inasmuch as it prostrates the independence of the mind, teaches men that they are naturally incapable of discerning religious truth, generates a timid, superstitious dependence on those who profess to have been brought from darkness into light, and so commonly infused into its professors a censorious and uncharitable spirit." He concluded by assuring Worcester that contention was the last thing in which the liberals wished to indulge. Worcester was convinced by his sincerity. Moving to Brighton in May, he took up his duties as editor of *The Christian Disciple,* the new magazine of the liberals.

After Worcester began his editorship, the man who seems to have had a veritable genius for provoking disputes—Jedidiah Morse—went so far in his one-man campaign of needling the liberals that he figuratively drew blood. If it had been his intention to force the liberals into the open with a yelp of pain, he succeeded admirably by jabbing their egos with a reprint of Thomas Belsham's chapter on American Unitarianism, which had appeared three years earlier in London as part of the English dissenter's *Memoirs of the Life of the Rev. Theophilus Lindsey.* The information contained in the chapter concerning the American Churches was innocent enough; but Morse prefaced the thirty-eight pages of Belsham's work with ten of his own which very adroitly insinuated an identification between the Boston liberals and the English Unitarian.

After Morse had seen his reprint through the press, he withdrew and let others carry the brunt of the attack against the liberals. Jeremiah

Evarts was prevailed upon to write a favorable review of Morse's pamphlet. It appeared in the June, 1815 issue of *The Panoplist*. Ably written and admirably slanted to produce discomfiture among the liberals, Evarts's review was like a lighted fuse dropped in a keg of powder. Its purpose was three-fold: to identify American liberals with English Unitarians; to convict the former of dishonesty in concealing their Unitarian opinions; and to demand the exclusion of all Unitarians from Christian courtesy and fellowship. On the last point it stated significantly, "Let the orthodox come out and be separate... in worship and communion from Unitarians; but let them meekly give a reason for their separation."

The explosion that resulted from the review was so great that it rocked Boston Congregationalism to its very foundations. Even Channing with his deep-seated opposition to controversy was strongly moved. The Boston liberals were thoroughly aroused. Samuel Thacher, the "Harry Percy" of the younger ministers, was about to reply to the *Panoplist* article, when discretion won the day, and he bowed out, leaving the task to Channing. Channing's masterly defense was *A Letter to the Rev. Samuel C. Thacher, on the Aspersions contained in a Late Number of The Panoplist, on the Ministers of Boston and the Vicinity*.

Channing's first concern in his *Letter* was to repudiate the identification of the Boston liberals with Belsham. "We both of us know," he said to Thacher, "that their Unitarianism is of a very different kind from that of Mr. Belsham." He admitted that there were, among the so-called Liberal Christians (Evarts's appellation for the liberals), differences of opinion regarding the nature and offices of Jesus Christ, ranging from high Arianism to simple humanitarianism (Socinianism); but he categorically denied that the Liberal Christians were in agreement with the materialistic, necessitarian, Socinian doctrine of Belsham.

"The fact is," Channing said, "that the great body of Liberal Christians would shrink from some of these opinions with as much aversion as from some of the gloomy doctrines of Calvin." As to himself, he added, "I have ever been inclined to cherish the most exalted views of Jesus Christ, which are consistent with the supremacy of the Father; and I have felt it my duty to depart from Mr. Belsham, in perhaps every sentiment which *is* peculiar to him on this subject." In pursuing this line of argument he was on firm ground.

Where the English Unitarians were materialistic philosophers, most of the Boston liberals were not; the necessitarianism in morals among

the former was simply anti-Calvinism in the latter. Belsham's Socinianism was in contrast to the high Arianism of most of the liberals,
and the radical political beliefs of the English dissenters (ardent
sympathizers with France and the Revolution) were anathema to
Boston Federalism.

The second part of Channing's rebuttal was of greater importance
than the first. His opponents had asserted that Liberal Christians "are
guilty of hypocritical concealment of their sentiments; behave in a
base, cowardly and hypocritical manner." This charge, he declared,
was infinitely more serious than the first; and he took great pains
to clarify the position of the liberals. Since he contended that the
charge was founded on the false premise of identification between
Belsham and the Boston ministers, he argued that the liberals could
certainly not express a sentiment which they did not believe. "Most
of us," he said, "have often contradicted Mr. Belsham's opinions; and
they who insist that these opinions are ours will be forced to maintain
that we practice deceit. They start with a falsehood, and their conclusion cannot therefore be true."

Morse and Evarts had placed the question of the Trinity in the
very center of their arguments against the liberals, but Channing
argued that it did not have "an immediate bearing on the temper
and the life" of the people. He went on to explain the liberal stand
on this matter: "We seldom or never introduce the Trinitarian controversy into our pulpits. We are accustomed to speak of the Father as
the only living and true God, and of Jesus Christ as his Son, as a distinct being from him, as dependent on him, subordinate to him, and
deriving all from him. . . . We have aimed at making no false impression. We have only followed a general system, which we are
persuaded to be best for our people and for the cause of Christianity;
the system of excluding controversy as much as possible from our
pulpits."

"Why is it," he then asked, "that our brethren are thus instigated to
cut us off, as far as they have power, from the body and church of
Christ?" Certainly it is not because "we refuse to acknowledge Jesus
Christ as our Lord and Master"; because we "neglect to study his
work"; or because "our lives are wanting in the spirit and virtues of his
gospel." No, indeed! "It is because, after serious investigation, we cannot find in the Scriptures, and cannot adopt as instructions of our
Master, certain doctrines which have divided the Church for ages,
which have perplexed the best and wisest men, and which are very differently conceived even by those who profess to receive them. It is, in

particular, because we cannot adopt the language of our brethren in relation to a doctrine which we cannot understand, and which is expressed in words not only unauthorized by the Scripture, but, as we believe, in words employed without meaning (unless they mean that there are three Gods) by those who insist upon them. This is our crime, that we cannot think and speak with our brethren on subjects the most difficult and perplexing on which the human mind was ever engaged. For this we are pursued with the cry of heresy, and are to have no rest until virtually excommunicated by our brethren."

Although Channing considered the doctrine of the Trinity abstruse and confusing, and not a suitable subject for controversy, he made no bones about his attitude towards the Trinitarian position. He steadfastly refused to acknowledge the concept of three persons in one God and left the orthodox with the choice of either monotheism or tritheism. He wanted peace and he wanted a reconciliation, but not at the expense of sincerely held beliefs. It was not at all unlikely, therefore, he told Thacher, that a storm might be gathering over them and their friends and he warned against bending before it.

"Let us never forget," Channing said, "that the most honored condition on earth is that of being sufferers for the sake of righteousness, for adherence to what we deem the cause of God and holiness; and let us welcome suffering, if it shall be appointed us, as bringing us nearer to our persecuted Lord and his injured apostles. . . . We profess to look up to a heavenly inheritance, and to hope that we shall one day mingle with angels and just men made perfect. And with these sublime hopes, shall we tremble before frail and fallible fellow-creatures, be depressed by difficulties, or shrink from the expression of what we deem important and useful truth? God forbid!"

Fearing that further controversy would perhaps be unavoidable, he concluded his argument by expressing the hope that sectarian heat and obstinacy might be avoided: "I cannot but look forward with pain," he said, "to the irritations, hatreds, bitter recriminations, censoriousness, spiritual pride, and schismatic spirit which will grow up under this system of denunciation and exclusion, and which may not only convulse many Churches at the present moment, but will probably end in most unhappy diversions among the very Christians who denounce us. . . . Error of opinion is an evil too trifling to be named in comparison with this proud, censorious, overbearing temper, which says to a large body of Christians, 'Stand off, we are holier than you.' "

All the passion of which Channing's nature was capable was exerted in these remarks to Thacher. His appeal was doubly effective. Not only did he mirror the faith of the new age and soothe the uneasiness of the people who were not entirely emancipated from the Calvinism that they had been gradually sloughing off, but he also stood forth as a champion of truth against the narrow and obstinate defenders of an exclusive religious spirit. He advocated friendship among Christians based upon benevolence and compliance with the ethical principles of Jesus. For this he was being persecuted and reviled. His message, therefore, was most satisfactory, because it not only reached the emotions but also satisfied reason as well.

The orthodox soon discovered that they had to deal with a brilliant orator who was "able to arouse the passions and inflame the prejudices of thousands." Dr. Samuel Worcester, younger brother of Noah, who had been terribly shocked by the defection of his brothers from "pure" Calvinism, took up the cudgels against Channing. By protesting against his free indulgence in "vague declamation, poignant invective, and fervid appeal to popular prejudices and passions," Worcester made it quite clear that he was aware of Channing's success in carrying the people before him. Consequently, he went to some trouble to show that Channing had put passages from the *Panoplist* article together in a way most favorable to his interpretation, and he made capital out of Channing's rather obvious excerpting out of context. But the real issue between his opponent and himself as Worcester saw it was the divinity of Christ.

He did not, however, offer a direct answer to Channing's charge of tritheism. He recognized that the doctrine of the Trinity was a necessary part of the orthodox scheme of salvation; but instead of making Channing's denial of it, which was actually undermining the whole Calvinistic edifice, the issue between them, he concentrated on the Trinity itself and the authority of Scriptures as the two major questions in dispute.

In his *Letter* to Thacher, Channing said that he would not feel bound to notice any replies which might be made to it; but Worcester's *Letter* had no sooner appeared than rumor had it that Channing would make a reply. His *Remarks on the Rev. Dr. Worcester's Letter to Mr. Channing, on the "Review of American Unitarianism," in a Late Panoplist* appeared on August 12. Although he asserted that Worcester was leagued with those who wished to drive the liberals from the Church as unworthy of the name of Christian and that "this is infinitely the most important part of Dr. Worcester's letter. All the rest is comparatively trifling," Channing knew better. Because he realized that Worcester was still unaware of the implications of his attack upon the central belief of Worcester's faith, he was now eager to discuss the Trinity.

Charging Worcester with ambiguity and failure to show the great significance which he attached to the doctrines deriving from the Trinitarian scheme, Channing had his opponent at a disadvantage, because Worcester had done nothing to repudiate the charge that the orthodox "mysteries" were anything but unintelligible metaphysical subtleties. Channing continued to repeat that the Calvinistic doctrines were insignificant and unnecessary for genuine piety. But he was careful nonetheless to give his opponent the benefit of being sincerely ignorant.

A similar tolerance induced him to minimize the differences between the orthodox and the liberals. "According to Trinitarians," he said, "Jesus, who suffered and died on the cross, is a derived being, *personally* united with the self-existent God. According to the Unitarians, he is a derived being, *intimately* united with the self-existent God. . . . The differences between Trinitarians are very often verbal. . . . Ought distinctions so subtle and perplexing to separate those who love the same Divine character and respect the same Divine will?"

Channing sincerely believed his over-simplification. His stress on love of neighbor and the golden rule made it almost impossible for him to comprehend fully the emotional rewards of the orthodox system, which involved a cosmic drama of unparalleled magnificence with such highlights as the Fall, damnation of mankind, ransom by the Son of God, and a new birth. For the orthodox, these were rooted deeply in the very soul of Calvinistic piety, and their eradication could not be accomplished by a simple act of nay-saying.

After replying to Worcester's first letter, Channing resolved not to continue the controversy; but Worcester's *Second Letter* was off the press by the end of August. Once more the charge against Channing was "misstatement." Worcester had advanced no new arguments: he simply repeated his conviction "that the errours of the Unitarians are subversive of the gospel, and most dangerous to the eternal interests of mankind."

Channing's second reply, therefore, continued the attack on Worcester's indefiniteness in stating his conception of the trinity. Again he wrote, "The differences between Unitarians and Trinitarians lie more in sounds than in ideas . . . would Trinitarians tell us what they mean, their system would generally be found little else than a mystical form of the Unitarian doctrine."

"What are the questions which divide us," he asked. "First, whether the One God be three distinct substances, or three persons, or three *'somewhats' called persons,* as Dr. Worcester says, for want of 'a better word'; and, secondly, whether one of these three substances, or improperly called persons, formed a personal union with a human soul, so that the Infinite Mind, and a human mind, each possessing its own distinct consciousness, became a *complex person."* Should phrases like these separate those who are united in great principles? he inquired; and there was a reassuring tone of negation in the very way he phrased the question.

Still not discouraged by the tenacity with which Channing defended his central thesis that the difference between them was really only semantic, Worcester tried once again to demonstrate the clarity and truth of the doctrine of the Trinity. But he was not nearly so clear in his own mind as he intimated in his remarks to Channing, for he came dangerously near to substantiating the latter's charge of tritheism. He reiterated the idea that "persons" as applied to the Trinity did not have the same meaning as it did when applied to human beings; but he soon forgot the distinction and began to use it as a biological analogy.

Fully as incapable as Channing of thinking of the word "person" in any but a biological and psychological sense, Worcester declared, "It will not be doubted even by Unitarians, that the Father knows the Son perfectly, as he knows all other beings; knows him intuitively; has an immediate, intimate complete perception of all that is in him. Even so then the Son knows the Father; has an intuitive perception, an intimate perfect knowledge of all his Father's infinite mind and will. . . . Such is their cooperation, their unity of will, and of action, that all that is done by the Father is in the same manner, and at the same time, done by the Son." To exchange his view of "the three adorable Persons" for the Unitarian concept of a solitary Deity and a philosophical heaven was unthinkable to Worcester, but his declamatory utterances did not convince Channing, who was both temperamentally and reasonably opposed to mere enthusiasm.

Worcester's emphasis upon a vicarious atonement was likewise doomed to rejection. Worcester's theory involved a God-man who suffered and shed his blood for man and thus became a propitiation to the Almighty Father. "Blood was poured, and sins were cancelled, the sins of those who believe in 'infinite atonement' by the blood of the son." Such an interpretation was abhorrent to the rationalism of which Channing was a spokesman. The new ethic of individualism regarded collective guilt as a relic of barbarism, and the new philosophy of right conduct considered self-sacrifice irrational. Unitarians, said Channing, can only "shudder when they hear that the ever-blessed God suffered and died on the cross."

In the debate between Channing and his opponent, the last word went to Dr. Worcester. According to John Quincy Adams, "Dr. Worcester had the right side in the discussion and altogether the advantage over Dr. Channing"; but Channing did not quit the race because of defeat. When he saw that the differences between him and Worcester were irreconcilable, he withdrew from the controversy and concentrated on a clear enunciation of the principles and doctrines of the liberal movement. His *System of Exclusion and Denunciation in Religion Considered* appeared in 1815. In it he contended that the honor of religion would never suffer by admitting men of irreproachable character. What good had the exclusive spirit done? "Could the thunders and lightenings of excommunication have corrected the atmosphere of the church," he said, "not one pestilential vapor would have loaded it for ages. The air of Paradise would not have been more pure, more refreshing." Branding characters out of dislike for the religious opinions of men, he declared, was certainly non-Christian and bespoke the ancient spirit of persecution. "Persecution has given up its halter and fagot, but it breathes venom from its lips, and secretly blasts what it cannot openly destroy."

Channing's resentment of the imputations levelled against the liberals was justified, but he did not permit himself to indulge in mere recrimination. His primary objection to the "exclusive" system was that it "entirely subverts free inquiry into the Scriptures." Why send men to the Scriptures, he asked, if they are told before they go "that they will be driven from the church on earth and in heaven, unless they find in the Scriptures the doctrines which are embodied in the popular creed." Such a system was also hostile to the great principles of Congregationalism, he added. "Since argument is insufficient to produce uniformity of opinion, recourse must be had to more powerful instruments of conviction . . . ECCLESIASTICAL COURTS . . . a vassalage, which reaches and palsies the mind, and imposes on it the dreams and fictions of men, for the everlasting truth of God!"

In concluding, Channing gave a more elaborate prophecy than he had in the second letter to Worcester of the evil effects that would result from the continuance of the exclusive and denunciatory policy. Picturing the spirit of discord entering into Church and family and separating friends and loved ones, as though by an impassable gulf, he begged his readers to "watch and pray" that the spirit of free inquiry might arise triumphant from its present hour of trial.

Measured by the number of sermons and articles that Channing contributed to the Unitarian Controversy, his part in it was conspicuously
small. Not to strike often but to strike hard was his policy. It was not
until some four years after his controversy with Worcester that he
spoke again, and then the occasion was to make him famous.

Meanwhile, other liberals joined in the controversy. One of these
was the Boston lawyer, John Lowell, uncle of the poet, and after Fisher
Ames's death in 1808 Boston's leading publicist and political authority.
At the same time that Worcester was correcting final proof on his *Second Letter,* Lowell published a pamphlet entitled *Are You A Christian
or a Calvinist?* Aggressive where Channing had been defensive, Lowell
attacked the orthodox very sharply. But his assault was not unprovoked, since his question was only an excellent rejoinder to another
that had been stealthily making the rounds in Boston, "Are you of the
Boston or the Christian Religion?"

To Lowell, the quarrel looked like a fight between Massachusetts
and Connecticut, between Harvard and Yale; and he attributed the
acrimony of the orthodox (Yale men mostly, with some from the College of New Jersey) to jealousy of the University of Cambridge which
"yields to no other seminary in our country." The main significance
of Lowell's pamphlet was not its arguments but rather its tone, which
was indicative of the spirit that animated so many of the controversialists in the years to follow.

CHAPTER TEN

BALTIMORE PENTECOST

CHANNING HAD BEEN drawn into controversy because he dared not be silent; but disputation was so distasteful he begrudged every moment it took him away from his parish and extra-curricular activities.

Pastoral visits, exchanges with other ministers, and ordination sermons (he was sought after because of his power to inspire young men just beginning their ministry) would have been sufficient to use up the entire energies of ministers in much better health; but he also had several important extra-parish activities to take care of.

He was a member of the executive committee of the Society of Seamen, which Joseph Tuckerman and he had organized in 1812, as well as chairman of the executive committee of the Bible Society of Massachusetts, for whom he prepared carefully detailed annual reports. As a member of the Harvard Corporation, he kept track of every aspect of the College's administrative and academic functions in order that he might propose reforms whenever they were needed. Certainly, if happiness consisted of activity, as he was accustomed to say, then he had no reason to be unhappy.

Oftentimes when a man is as busy as Channing was, he becomes so engrossed in his various activities that he loses sight of the larger philosophy of life that makes his participation in affairs worthwhile. The common touch of humanity forsakes him; he becomes insulated from his fellows. Such was not Channing's fate because the strain of otherworldliness in his make-up more than balanced his preoccupation with worldly matters.

Just two months prior to the publication of his *Letter to Samuel Thacher,* he drove to Salem to preach the ordination sermon for one of his former students, John Emery Abbot, who was about to be installed as pastor of the Second Church. Although Joseph Story was not there to greet his old classmate—for over three years now, it had been Mr. Supreme Court Justice Story—there was in Channing's audience, completely unbeknown to him, a young miss of nearly eleven years who thought him quite the most remarkable man she had even seen or heard. The name of the young lady was Elizabeth Palmer Peabody, the oldest of three daughters of a local dentist.

Elizabeth's infatuation was not born at the moment, although the speaker's appearance on this occasion brought to her youthful mind an impression received two years earlier, when her mother had brought her to this same Second Church to hear Channing speak. She had seen "a small man, with a rapid, nervous motion, dressed in a traveller's great-coat, go into the pulpit, and, without sitting down (for he was a little belated), take up the hymn book, turn its leaves quickly, and enter the desk; then slowly lifting up his large, remarkable eyes, with the expression of *seeing something*, begin to read a devotional hymn." It was this expression that had so impressed Elizabeth, because it gave her the feeling that the little man was "communing with God, face to face." Never before had she realized that "any man now, like a prophet of old, conversed with God as a friend to friend."

Upon her second view of the Reverend Mr. Channing, Dr. Peabody's precocious daughter was confirmed in her initial impression. She was probably too taken up by the speaker's appearance to pay much attention to his words; but had she listened carefully, she would have heard her idol discoursing on his favorite topic—perfection of the human character as the end towards which every minister must work.

"We should preach," he told his audience, "that we may make men perfect christians; perfect, not according to the standard of the world, but according to the law of Christ; perfect in heart and in life, in solitude and in society, in the great and in the common concerns of life."

Simply to preach the perfection of social duties was not enough for Channing: he had to be active in social enterprises. When he heard Noah Worcester lament the lack of any organization to oppose war, he quickly invited him to bring to his parsonage anyone interested in doing something militant about peace. The result was the organization of the Peace Society of Massachusetts on December 28, 1815, just three days after the celebration of the nativity of the Prince of Peace. It was the first society of its kind in America. The following May, when the Congregational ministers of Massachusetts gathered to hear Channing, instead of delivering a controversial sermon, he spoke on War in order to give the infant Society a good send-off. Later, he addressed a memorial to the Senate and House of Representatives in Washington, asking for a profession of pacific principles and urging an inquiry into methods whereby a pacific spirit might be infused into the laws of the land.

In addition to his work for peace, he advocated reform in penal institutions, and as early as 1816, he was preaching sermons in favor of Temperance. Missionary activity interested him greatly, but his physical infirmities made it impossible for him to participate personally in this kind of work. He was spreading himself so thin that there was danger of his being unable to do anything at all, yet he was so wrapped up in his vision of human perfection that he found it difficult to hearken to his own doctrine of gradualism. Fully believing that such a vision could be realized if only human minds could be made to give it credence and work toward its achievement, he felt morally obligated to provide encouragement and leadership to anyone moving in the direction of social progress. Soon his seminal influence would begin to make itself felt in far-reaching developments.

His confidence that everything in this world happens for the best sometimes needed bolstering. His sister Ann died in London on February 2, 1815, after a brief illness. Word of her death did not reach him until May 5. The following day, he recorded the sad event in his journal. The disjointed sentences reveal how sorely he had been stricken.

When Francis Dana had died five years before—like Ann, away from home and among strangers—he had found consolation in the thought of God's love and benevolence; but this second loss, coming, as it seemed to him, on the heels of the first, led him to write somewhat querulously in his journal, "Our family is falling to pieces. Is there no bond of union? Are we to be lost to each other?" Then, as if ashamed, he wrote down, "She is gone, not lost. Let me rejoice in her joy."

Several days later, he could even write to a friend, "I find that events of this kind disturb my mind much less than formerly. My increasing conviction of the *perfect* goodness of God, of his *paternal* character, of his minute and tender care, and of the riches of his *mercy* in Jesus Christ, the last truth in religion which men truly believe and feel, enables me more cheerfully to resign all things to his disposal."

His "conviction" was tested again sooner than he could have imagined. In October of the following year, the Channings' first-born child, a daughter, was taken from them almost before they were able to realize what had happened. In the journal the simple story of her life was recorded as follows:

> I remembered the love of Jesus to little children. I remembered the kindness of Him who has called himself our Father, and whose love must be infinitely purer than mine. Still my heart clung to her; and when I saw the last struggle on Wednesday afternoon, about twenty-four hours after her birth, I wept over her as if I had been deprived of a long-

possessed blessing. . . . Thursday afternoon I carried her to the tomb,
in the full and certain hope of a blessed resurrection. . . . I hope yet to
meet her and to see that my child is more excellent, more happy, than
I could have rendered her.

Sorrow, however, was not his only portion. Two years later, another
baby girl was born. Little Mary was a source of continuous wonder to
her father, who took the responsibilities of parenthood most seriously,
as only a man who considered birth "the entrance of an immortal soul
into existence" could. In his journal he struggled to set down his reactions as a father. Finally he managed to formulate a few statements
that were half wish, half self-admonition:

> May this child never have cause to reproach us for evil example, neglect,
> ruinous indulgence. Through its whole everlasting being, may it remember
> us, as, under God, its earliest, best friends, by whose kind care it learned
> to form itself upon the principles which are the foundation of eternal
> peace. Here is a mind to labor for, which is to live forever. Our influence
> on it is to be perpetual. What a claim this little being brings with it!
> What latent capacities!—yet not one developed. Here is a being whom I
> may taint or raise to immortal glory.

On the following Sunday he preached on the subject of parental responsibility and brought a smile to the lips of many of his parishioners,
when he reminded them that "no man should live for himself." All the
world loves a new father, and the patriarchs in the Federal Street Congregation could afford to indulge their pastor in his new-found happiness.

One of his first gestures upon becoming pastor at the Federal Street
Church had been to organize the women of his parish for religious instruction. For many years he had held these discussions at the home of
Mrs. Catherine Codman, a parishioner. According to Mrs. George Lee,
one of the participants in these conversation meetings, there were usually fifty or more present, largely members of the Federal Street Society,
though others often requested the privilege of attending. Years afterwards, when the theories of Frederick Froebel were being praised to
the heavens in New England, it was not at all unusual to hear these
same women, now grandmothers, exclaim: "But this is nothing new;
more than fifty years ago Dr. Channing taught us to *live with* our
children."

While he was still luxuriating in the pride of parenthood, he realized his goal of having a vestry-hall in which the catechetical and in-
structional work of the parish might be conducted. He had spoken the
previous year to his committee about a permanent building near the

Church, where the parish schools could be taught under proper supervision, and where he would have a more satisfactory meeting-place for the women's discussions. Now the hall was completed and in dedicating it, he threw out the hint that nothing would gratify him more than to meet occasionally the young men of the parish for free conversation or more regular instruction in religion. Nearly four years would pass, however, before his constant urging and goading would result in the organization of the Wednesday Evening Association for men only.

"I wish I could make you feel that no power is more noble than the power of swaying the mind, and impressing the heart," Channing had written to his schoolmistress friend, Eloise Payne, a few years before his marriage. Certainly in the years immediately following his controversy with Worcester, he did all in his power to effect social improvement through moral suasion. Because education was foremost in his plans for the reconstruction of society, he felt that the minister should be a prime mover in this cause.

In 1816, for example, he delivered a discourse on the subject of increasing the means of theological education at Harvard in which he argued that preparation for the ministry ought to be more extensive than that of any other profession because the Christian minister is intrusted with the most valuable interests of the human race. When his health permitted, he gave gladly of himself to any cause that promised to work good in society. The favored classes of Boston held no higher place in his affections than the poor and underprivileged. "The poor bring with them into being the same faculties with the opulent," he declared. "Nature knows none of our arbitrary distinctions."

Believing that all men should be educated, he was constantly pressing for better education for indigent boys, for tradesmen and mechanics, for those interested in business—for all those who had neither the means nor the academic ability to benefit from the scholarly curriculum at Harvard. But he was also very much interested in higher education and asked his brother Edward to write George Ticknor, then a student at the University of Göttingen, about the kind of metaphysics taught in the schools in Germany. Ticknor was only too glad to oblige. He wrote Edward of the revolution in philosophy by the great triumvirate of Kant, Fichte, and Schelling and the rebellion of common sense that had dispossessed all three.

"You may observe," said Ticknor, "an extreme unwillingness to receive any new system. The whole generation, in this respect, seem like men who have just come out from a long campaign, and are pleased with nothing less than the thought of beginning a new one."

Channing took this to heart when he read it, and it is quite probable that he had it in mind when he later remonstrated against the attempts of his fellow Unitarians to set up a new orthodoxy in place of the old system from which they had only recently managed to free themselves.

When Ticknor arrived home from England in June, 1819, Channing was among the first to benefit from the rich stores of knowledge accumulated in four years abroad. Ticknor became a member of Channing's congregation soon after his return. He, Channing, and Edward Tyrrell, who was now Boylston professor of rhetoric and oratory at Harvard, together with John Kirkland, President of Harvard, and Edward Everett, who had received the degree of Doctor of Philosophy from the University of Göttingen in 1817 ("the first American," he informed Stephen Higginson, "and as far as I know, Englishman, on whom it has ever been conferred"), spent many worthwhile hours exchanging ideas and projecting plans for the future.

Channing and Kirkland, who were older than the others, acted as a steadying influence; and their maturity of experience blended in well with the "higher learning" of the bright young men. Channing was saddened by the thought that Buckminster was not with them to add sparkle to their discussions, and he missed the friendly face and lively spirits of Sam Thacher, who had succumbed to tuberculosis the previous year, but he was pleased to think that he might carry on in their stead.

Channing was now nearing the age of forty, that magic year during which man is supposed to step forth from the outworn husk of his early life into a richer and more expansive existence. He was a recognized force for social and intellectual progress in the Boston community, even though he was always the first to deprecate his importance. After the Worcester controversy fellow Unitarians had come to rely upon him for religious leadership, and his manifold educational and philanthropic activities had brought him into intimate contact with people of every class in the city. Residing on Beacon hill, preaching in Federal Street near the marts of trade, and serving on the Harvard Corporation, he exerted an influence in practically every field of endeavor that the community could boast. His domestic life was all that he could have wished: he told a friend that "his condition was as prosperous as he could well bear," and the suffering brought on by his physical debility gave him "the discipline of pain which every being needs to purify away his self-love."

It was at this halcyon period that he was called upon once more to speak for his liberal friends. The controversy initiated by Morse in 1815 and developed through the debate with Dr. Worcester had been going merrily on all this time, with laymen taking their turn at pamphlet warfare, and the ministers having their say in the annual Convention Sermons.

The liberals, who up to this time had perhaps deserved their title of "Ministers of the Boston Religion," were now branching out, and Unitarianism was spreading wherever converts could be found. Joseph Priestley had established two congregations in Philadelphia in 1797, but they were formed on the English principle and had almost no ties with the Massachusetts groups, so that Unitarianism was almost an unknown quantity outside New England. The seed had been sown in Baltimore in 1816, and by 1819, it had developed enough to warrant a full-time minister to nourish it to full strength. Jared Sparks was chosen for the job, but Channing was selected to go before him and make straight the path.

There were numerous reasons for Channing's being chosen to preach the Baltimore ordination sermon. In addition to being the spokesman of the liberals and a fine ordination speaker, he had also been the strongest influence in making Sparks a minister. As a Freshman at Harvard, Jared had listened to Channing's sermons; and in 1812 he had met Channing and Josiah Quincy in Havre de Grace. Far away from home and feeling low in spirits at the time, he had been so encouraged by Channing's account of his own early despondency and homesickness in Richmond that he never forgot his visit with the older man.

After his graduation from Harvard in 1815 Sparks had served as a tutor in the College and editor of the *North American Review*. All this time he was attending the Federal Street Church regularly. Once he had even spent a week at the Channing home. Shortly afterwards he decided to enter the ministry. After a number of assignments in and around Boston he preached to the congregation of the First Independent Church in Baltimore for four successive Sundays, and the people gave him a call to settle permanently with them. He accepted and invited Channing to preach his ordination sermon.

Since the trip from Boston to Baltimore was neither easy nor pleasant, Channing decided to make it by easy stages. Accompanied by Ruth's sister he and his wife went first to New York, where he preached Sunday services in a private drawing room before a small group of people interested in "liberal" religion. The occasion was historically

significant, because it was the first Unitarian sermon ever preached in
New York. The date was Sunday, April 25.

After a brief visit the three Bostonians journeyed on to Baltimore,
arriving in plenty of time to enable Channing to rest and revise the
sermon that he had prepared for the occasion. It was an unusually long
sermon, but he had worked hard to polish it. He knew that he was
being counted on to make a complete and positive statement of Unitarian principles, and the other members of the ordaining party were
unanimously agreed that his remarks would receive wide publicity.
Although the final draft of his address reveals that he tempered earlier
versions of it by striking out such loaded phrases as "damned heretics"
and "incarnate fiends," he had resolved to be as explicit and firm as it
lay in his power to be.

That the Baltimore ordination ceremony was no ordinary event may
be gathered from the unusual circumstances surrounding it. First of
all, the cast of supporting ministers was an unusually brilliant one,
composed of carefully selected individuals from the liberal stronghold
in Boston as well as from the more remote congregations in New
Hampshire and Maine. Although he did not participate in the ceremony proper, Henry Ware, Sr., whose election to the Hollis chair had
been a big step forward in the liberal cause, was there to lend dignity
to the occasion. John Palfrey of Brattle Square Church gave the right
hand of fellowship; Dr. Eliphalet Porter of Roxbury delivered the
charge; Nathaniel Thayer of Lancaster addressed the Baltimore Society; and the Reverend Ichabod Nichols of Portland, Maine, said the
concluding prayer.

Secondly, on the evening preceding the ordination, Palfrey gave a
dinner for Sparks at which plans for publication of the sermon were
carefully mapped out and an unusually large number of copies (two
thousand to be exact) was decided upon. Ordinarily, no thought was
given to the printing of a sermon until there was a demand for its publication, which fact leads to the conclusion that there was a carefully
premeditated campaign to give Channing's message as wide distribution as possible.

"Unitarian Christianity," as Channing called his discourse, was the
strongest he ever preached on distinctly Unitarian lines. The plan of
the discourse was simple: first, to set forth the principles adopted by
Unitarians in interpreting the Scriptures and then some of the doctrines which the Scriptures seemed clearly to express; second, to demonstrate the unreasonableness of Trinitarian dogma, its perplexity for the
understanding and its "confusion for the pious heart"; and third, to

oppose the doctrine of Christ's double nature by emphasizing His unity.

As always, Channing's argument was directed to the reason of his listeners and leaned but slightly on the authority of Scriptural texts, although the following quotation might seem to indicate the converse:

> We regard the Scriptures as the record of God's successive revelations to mankind, and particularly of the last and most perfect revelation of his will by Jesus Christ. . . . Our religion, we believe lies chiefly in the New Testament. . . . Jesus Christ is the only master of Christians, and whatever he taught, either during his personal ministry or by his inspired Apostles, we regard as of divine authority, and profess to make the rule of our lives.

But this declaration of attitude prefaced a spirited defense of the use of reason in interpreting the Bible as a consistent unit from cover to cover. "The Bible," said Channing, "is a book written for men, in the language of men, and . . . its meaning is to be sought in the same manner as that of other books."

After stating this principle, he proceeded to set forth the views which he derived from it, particularly those which distinguished Unitarians from other Christians:

> In the first place, we believe in the doctrine of God's Unity or that there is one God, and one only. . . . We understand by it that there is one being, one mind, one person, one intelligent agent, and one only, to whom, underived and infinite perfection and dominion belong. . . . We object to the doctrine of the Trinity, that, whilst acknowledging in words, it subverts in effect, the unity of God. According to this doctrine, there are three infinite and equal persons, possessing supreme divinity, called the Father, Son and Holy Ghost. . . . The Son is mediator, and not the Father. The Father sends the Son, and is not himself sent; nor is He conscious, like the Son, of taking flesh.

He then went on to a discussion of the unity of Christ:

> We believe that Jesus is one mind, one being, as truly one as we are, and equally distinct from the one God. . . . That Christ is not the one God, not the same being with the Father, is a necessary inference from our former head, in which we saw that the doctrine of three persons in God is a fiction.

Because these remarks are telescoped, they may not illustrate the importance Channing attached to confuting the concept of two natures in Christ—a human and a divine—a concept which led Trinitarians to say that the redemptive Christ is God in his human nature atoning for the sins of human kind. There could be no compromise for him. He believed that "Christ's humiliation was real and entire, that the whole

Saviour, and not a part of him suffered, that his crucifixion was a scene of deep and unmixed agony."

The third point of Channing's discourse was the one upon which he placed the greatest stress:

We believe in the *moral perfection of God*. We consider no part of theology so important as that which treats of God's moral character. ...We believe that his almighty power is entirely submitted to his perception of rectitude; and this is the ground of our piety . . . it is not because his will is irresistible, but because his will is the perfection of virtue, that we pay him allegiance.... To give our views of God in one word, we believe in his Parental character.... We believe that he has a father's concern for his creatures, a father's desire for their improvement, a father's equity in proportioning his commands to their powers, a father's enjoyment of their progress, a father's readiness to receive the penitent, and a father's justice for the incorrigible.

This emphasis upon God's moral perfection led naturally to the denial of man's depravity and of the predestinarian doctrine of an elect. His mind filled "with a horror that wants words to express" when he considered these perversions of God's paternal relationship to His children.

Channing's views of the mediation of Christ and of the purpose of His mission differed somewhat, as he pointed out, from those held by many Unitarians. He felt that the influence of Christ's death on man's forgiveness was not purely a moral influence. But however he might waver on this point, he categorically denied that Christ's suffering was a price to God to buy His mercy to mankind: "We eminently maintain that Jesus, instead of calling forth, in any way or degree, the mercy of the Father, was sent by that mercy to be our Saviour; that he is nothing to the human race but what he is by God's appointment."

He also rejected the Anselmic doctrine that man, by sinning against an Infinite Being, had contracted infinite guilt. In its place he put the more "reasonable" argument that the guilt of a being must be proportioned to his nature and power. The former view, he declared, not only lacks New Testament confirmation but also dishonors God by making Him an ogre of injustice dealing out punishment disproportionate to man's offense. Moreover, he added, it fastens on Christ a dual nature and makes His mission a negative one of averting punishment rather than of communicating holiness.

He concluded his sermon by stating his view of Christian virtue: "We believe that all virtue has its foundation in the moral nature of man, that is, in conscience, or his sense of duty, and in the power of forming his temper and life according to conscience. We believe that these moral faculties are the grounds of responsibility, and the highest distinction of human nature, and that no act is praiseworthy, any farther than it springs from their exertion." Though this last statement might appear to place undue emphasis upon human efforts and to belittle the importance of God's aid, Channing was really objecting to the necessitarians who made man a completely passive receiver in moral actions and God an irresistible Agent. For him the love of God and the love of Christ were virtue's top and crown. Love of God was a moral sentiment consisting of a higher esteem and veneration of His moral perfections, and love of Christ was gratitude for His redemption and admiration of His perfection.

The Baltimore sermon shows how closely Channing's thought had become intertwined with the secular humanitarianism that had been growing in New England for over a half century. His clear and comprehensive statement of faith in human power and dignity and his brilliant defense of human reason and rectitude gave strength to the principles of a moral Christianity that was congenial to the interests and the ideals of a new age. Although one of his opponents was later to condemn his Unitarianism as "modified deism" and to declare that "infidels everywhere prefer this system to any other that bears the Christian name, and feel no reluctance in uniting in worship with its adherents," the condemnation was actually a kind of left-handed compliment, because Channing and his fellow liberals had been trying all along to plot a middle course between deism on one hand and orthodox Calvinism on the other.

A clue to this effort is to be found in a letter that Joseph Buckminster had written ten years before to Thomas Belsham in England: "It is the prevailing opinion all over the United States that the clergy of Boston are little better than Deists. Those very men who, in New York and Philadelphia, would probably be unbelievers because they could not be Calvinists are, among us in Boston, rational Christians,—the most constant supporters of public worship, the most intimate friends of the clergy, and not a few of them professors of religion." It was to attract this group who had turned to deism because they could not accept total depravity, election, etc. that Channing made such an effort. By establishing reason, experience, and conscience as a tribunal of truth before which revelation must stand and by declaring character to be the test and proof of true religion, he succeeded in reconciling faith with the cardinal theses of moderate deism.

If the orthodox were displeased with Channing's efforts, Jared Sparks was not. Two days after his ordination, he wrote to a friend:

"Mr. Channing has surpassed himself. His sermon was nearly an hour and a half long, giving a full exposition of *our* principles. He has never come out in so bold and decided terms, not even against Worcester."

The "bold coming out" had exerted a heavy toll upon Channing's strength, and the remaining events in the ordination schedule drained what little energy he had left. The following day he remained in his rooms, resting and conversing with friends who came in to chat about his sermon. On Friday his wife and sister-in-law went to Washington to see the sights, leaving him to relax and take care of his correspondence.

He wrote Sparks a note, asking to be excused from preaching the next day but telling him that he would make a strong effort to get the text of his sermon ready for early printing. His colleagues in the meantime were busy preaching morning, afternoon, and evening services in the Baltimore Church. Channing, however, left Baltimore without making another public appearance. On the return trip north he stopped off in New York, where he preached to a large audience in the Hall of the Medical College.

Back home again in Boston he picked up his labors where he had dropped them nearly a month before. He had promised Jared Sparks to prepare his address for publication as quickly as possible, and the work of checking proofs (they had to be sent to Baltimore for correction) kept him hard at work in the moments he could snatch from his regular duties. Despite all his care, however, the first copies came off the press without his having seen the final proofs. He wrote to Sparks with a reasonable amount of impatience of its being an "unauthorized and incorrect edition."

Meanwhile, as he had expected, he was beginning to come under fire from the orthodox. Professor Moses Stuart of Andover brought his *Letter to the Rev. Wm. E. Channing* before the public, and Andrews Norton, Channing's successor in the Dexter chair at Harvard, answered him with *A Statement of Reasons*. According to Stuart, the great question between him and Channing was, "What does the Bible teach on the subjects proposed?" Using this as his point of departure, he proceeded to set forth an erudite philosophy of Biblical authority. Norton, who was easily Stuart's equal at the business of picking over texts, retaliated with a defense of "rational" Christianity that rejected a literal acceptance of the Bible on the grounds of "the intrinsic ambiguity of language." The controversy dragged on: other disputants took up the contest, but neither side was able to gain a decided advantage.

Although Channing did not enter directly into the controversy himself, he defended Unitarianism against the charge of being "a half-way

house to infidelity" in an article published later in 1819 in *The Christian Disciple;* and in *The Moral Argument against Calvinism,* which
appeared in the same magazine the following year, he expressed his
views of the basic inconsistency between the tenets of Calvinism and
the perfections of God. "How is it possible," he asked with astonish-
ment, "that men can hold these doctrines and yet maintain God's
goodness and equity?" To the rejoinder that we cannot understand the
mysteries of God, he replied by justifying man's use of the moral reason God had given him. "The ultimate reliance of a human being," he
said, "is and must be on his own mind."

It is true, he admitted, that God is an infinite Being and that His
powers and perfections, being unlimited, are "incomprehensible," i.e.,
they cannot be "wholly taken in or embraced" by the human mind.
But—and here he made a distinction of great importance in his thinking—that does not mean that God is "unintelligible." Even though we
cannot pretend to know the whole nature and properties of God, we
can still form some "clear ideas" of Him from which we can reason as
justly as from any other ideas we may have. If the truth be told, we do
not "comprehend" anything, even the simplest plant or animal. Everything has hidden qualities. Still we do not question our capacity to
reason about people or things. Why then should we deny our ability
to know something of the true nature of God?

Here for the first time Channing had stated an idea that was to set
him apart both from the apologists of Roman Catholicism, his orthodox Calvinist opponents, and many of his own Unitarian brethren as
well. The time had not yet come for him to push the idea to its ultimate conclusions, but it was plain that he considered an error of the
first magnitude the view that man's mind is incapable of attaining any
definite knowledge of the divine nature, or of ascribing any qualities
to God in the same sense that these qualities are credited to man. The
key to his thought was to be found in two brief sentences: ". . . we
maintain that God's attributes are intelligible, and that we can conceive as truly of his goodness and justice as of these qualities in men.
In fact, these qualities are essentially the same in God and man, though
differing in degree, in purity, and in extent of operation."

"Essentially the same"—this phrase contains the basis of every word
and deed that fill his later life. Because he believed in man's essential
godliness, he was also confident of man's potential greatness. Others
might point to the sorry record of man's life past and present: he
countered with a vision of humanity perfected and brought nearer to
God. In point of emphasis at least, his viewpoint was unique. There

could no longer be any question of an open split between him and the
Calvinists when they held such divergent views of mankind.

Perhaps the best evidence of how far the liberals and orthodox had
travelled apart is offered by the "Dedham decision," which was handed
down by the Unitarian-dominated Massachusetts Supreme Court in
1820. When Channing had served as a member of the Reverend Alvan
Lamson's ordaining council at Dedham two years before, the church
and parish were united in their approval of their new pastor. This
harmony, however, did not last long, for a majority of the church members (the body of communicants) soon became dissatisfied with Mr.
Lamson's Unitarian views, which pleased a majority of the parish (the
secular organization). An appeal was made to Caesar, and the Supreme
Court ruled that "When the majority of the members of a Congregational church separate from the majority of the parish, the members
who remain, although a minority, constitute the church in such parish,
and retain the rights and property belonging thereto."

This decision left the members of the Dedham parish in possession
of the Church name, records and even the communion plate; but more
important, it set a precedent for all future disputes between church
and parish. By granting control over church property to the parish, it
reversed a long-established trend in the New England churches of sub-
ordinating the secular to the clerical powers.

Within a relatively short time, one hundred and twenty Congregational churches in New England, among them Plymouth Church,
founded just two centuries before, went over to Unitarianism. When
the parishes elected Unitarian ministers, the Trinitarian members of
the church seceded, leaving the church property to their opponents.
Although outnumbered three to one by the Trinitarians, the Unitarians held the upper hand, since they were technically intrenched as
non-seceders. Jedidiah Morse and his orthodox stalwarts inveighed
against this legalized plundering; but they were powerless to prevent
it. The "meek" had inherited the earth, and the powers of righteousness had been confounded.

CHAPTER ELEVEN

VOYAGES AND DISCOVERIES

GRANDFATHER ELLERY's death had long been expected—the old gentleman would have been ninety-three if he had lived through the year—but the news of his passing still came as a shock. The effect was all the more depressing, because Channing was not well and had to husband his strength carefully in order to carry out his pastoral duties. He needed a strong tonic, and his wife provided the ideal prescription. On Washington's birthday she presented him with his first son. They named the boy William after his father and Francis after his deceased uncle. Channing forgot his own troubles in the excitement of the moment and was soon well enough to expand his extracurricular affairs.

Shortly after his son's birth, he received a call from the recently organized Unitarian Society in New York to come and help them build up an "uncorrupted Christianity in this quarter of the Union." Much as he appreciated the honor, he was no polemicist; and he knew that the New York congregation really wanted a militant organizer. He wrote back, "Public, domestic, and private considerations leave me no liberty of forsaking the post which I now occupy . . . I regard the situation to which you invite me as honorable and important. But Providence has appointed me another lot."

On the evening of election day, a time when ministers of Massachusetts usually gathered to hold their anniversary meetings and to listen to the annual Election Sermon, Channing invited a group to the Federal Street vestry-hall. At this meeting he gave his reasons for bringing them together and urged closer ties than they then enjoyed.

"It was thought by some of us," he said, "that the ministers of this Commonwealth who are known to agree in what are called *Liberal and Catholic views of Christianity* needed a bond of union, a means of intercourse, and an opportunity of conference not as yet enjoyed. . . . For these ends it was proposed that an annual meeting should be held which should be spent in prayer, in hearing an address from one of our number, in offering reports as to the state of our churches, and in conference as to the best methods of advancing religion."

His colleagues welcomed the proposal and suggested that the new organization be called the Berry Street conference. Thus began an institution that was to endure throughout the nineteenth century and into the twentieth with its name, purpose, and spirit practically unchanged. Although Channing may have hoped it would gradually assume in an unsectarian manner the functions later assigned to the American Unitarian Association, whose founding he rather hesitantly approved five years later, every word of his address indicates that he had no desire to circumscribe the freedom of any individual minister.

The question he discussed at this first meeting was "How far is Reason to be used in explaining Revelation?" His answer was the one already given at Baltimore: "the great, essential principles of Christianity, such as God's unity and paternal character, and the equity and mercy of his administration, are there [in the Scriptures] revealed with noontide brightness, and . . . accord perfectly with the discoveries of nature, and the surest dictates of our moral faculties."

"The progressive influence of Christianity," he went on to say, "depends mainly on the fact that it is a rational religion . . . not that it is such a system as reason could discover without revelation, and still less that it is a cold and lifeless scheme of philosophical doctrines, but that it is a religion which agrees with itself, with our moral nature, with our experience and observation, with the order of the universe, and the manifest attributes of God." It was only because of this "practical influence," he concluded, that he considered the liberal views worth advocating. Controversy certainly was too great a price to pay for views of religion in no way superior to those of one's opponents.

At the Harvard Commencement in 1820 he was honored with the degree of Doctor of Divinity. Following his appearance at the college exercises, he went down to Oakland to rest. Since his marriage he had been accustomed to spend the summer months on the Gibbs estate, where the peace and quiet were a tonic to his weary spirit. Somehow these precious few weeks were sufficient to restore the energy the other months of the year had drained from his frail body. When autumn came, he was usually refreshed and eager to be back in Boston, ministering to the needs of his congregation and laboring in one or another philanthropic cause. This summer he needed even more rest than usual, because his health had been particularly bad. His vacation passed uneventfully, and in the fall he was back at work, ready for a new campaign and filled with a newly aroused interest in the spread of liberal principles.

He wrote to the Reverend Ichabod Nichols in Portland, after Maine had been admitted to the Union as a separate state, to ask what effect the new political organization would have on religion. Referring to "the more explicit avowal and defense of our peculiarities into which we have lately been driven," he asked whether "still more direct and exacting modes of holding forth the truth may not be our duty." In November he answered an inquiry from Jared Sparks regarding the feasibility of establishing a new periodical in Baltimore. "I highly approve," he said, "the plan of a periodical work, such as you propose, at the South, and I cannot but hope that a miscellany answering to its name, would do more good to numbers than our Disciple. We want a more various and entertaining work than we now have, and I wish that it may appear in a different part of the country from this."

Sparks was encouraged by Channing's remarks to begin such a periodical, and in January, 1821, he published the first issue of *The Unitarian Miscellany and Christian Monitor*. The new magazine was controversial in spirit and positively denominational, reporting all prominent Unitarian events, and those of a liberal tendency in all religious bodies. Five months after the first issue appeared, however, Channing wrote Sparks again to let him know that the Boston liberals were not completely pleased with the *Miscellany*: "Palfrey tells me he has expressed one view to you, which is very common among us. We think you identify yourself too much with the English Unitarians, men whose peculiar circumstances have given them more of a sectarian spirit, than we wish to cultivate."

He then went on to criticize Joseph Priestley and to warn Sparks against those who might wish "to blend with Unitarianism the doctrines of materialism and necessity, radicalism in politics, and a latitudinarian, half skeptical theology, which the learned shallowness of Germany would call naturalism." He closed the letter by asking Sparks to burn it "lest it rise up against him." Whether he was exercising his usual caution to prevent any harm that might result from a loose construction of his criticisms of the *Miscellany* and Priestley, or whether he was perhaps a little less than proud of the fact that his benevolence in this matter was not exactly "disinterested," he alone knew.

In November delegates from all over Massachusetts met in the Boston State House to consider revisions in the Constitution of 1780. Reverence for the Constitution rather than emancipation of the common man seems to have been the keynote of the convention. Federalist-dominated and well sprinkled with Unitarians, it stood for the *status quo* and voted down those who were for separation of church and state in the Commonwealth and who wished to abolish the test oaths for office holders.

At the same time that his colleagues were doing all in their power to keep the constitution of the Bay State sacrosanct, Channing was telling his congregation that "society is the school in which the heart is trained for the Creator." Men, he said, must become active in promoting both their own and others' present and future welfare. Though not exactly a voice crying in the wilderness, he was, at this point, some distance in front of the majority of the "liberal" Unitarians, who were still relying on hide-bound institutionalism to promote their own welfare.

Some two months after the Convention had tidied up its business and disbanded, Dr. Channing (he disliked to have people make a point of using his new title) travelled across the Charles to give the annual Dudleian Lecture to the students at the University. One of the Harvard boys in his audience was a senior named Waldo Emerson, son of his old friend, William Emerson, and soon to be his next-door neighbor in Federal Street.

1821

Waldo, whose birth had preceded Channing's ordination by a little more than three weeks, arrived at his final year in Harvard without any particular distinctions: he had joined none of the popular social clubs like Hasty Pudding, and his scholastic attainments had not entitled him to Phi Beta Kappa. As a matter of record, he stood number thirty in a class of fifty-nine. In the beginning he had felt no great attraction for his studies or teachers; but the scholarship of Edward Everett and George Ticknor had recently brought about a change in attitude toward the faculty, and he was now beginning to realize how much he had learned from the professor of rhetoric, Edward Channing.

The discourse on "The Evidences of Revealed Religion" that young Emerson heard on that wintry day in March, 1821, was greatly to his liking. And quite naturally so, for he was as much a friend of Christian revelation as Channing; and he had been brought up on the same philosophers and philosophies as the older man. Like his teachers Professors Frisbie and Hedge, who had dinned Scotch common sense into him, he had little or nothing to do with the new German thinkers and was as convinced as they that future advances in thought must be achieved under the guidance of men like Thomas Reid and Dugald Stewart. He was inclined to agree also that Price's *Morals* was a fine and true statement of man's moral sense.

Channing's Dudleian lecture proved him as thorough-going a supernaturalist as any of his orthodox opponents. Into the stock arguments of his time he breathed new life and made them seem vital and convincing to students like Emerson. He objected to those sceptics of the miraculous "who incline to rest their religion wholly on its internal evidence" and asserted that "Christianity is not only confirmed by miracles, but is in itself, in its very essence, a miraculous religion. It is not a system which the human mind might have gathered, in the ordinary exercise of its powers, from the ordinary course of nature." The shallowness of Channing's scriptural criticism would have been obvious to a scholar brought up on modern Biblical exegesis; but limited as he was by the times and by an essentially uncritical mind, he did the best he could to defend revelation. It was really his moral earnestness that carried the day.

The result, as far as Emerson was concerned, left little to be desired. In his journal he wrote, "the highest species of reasoning upon divine subjects is rather the fruit of a sort of moral imagination, than of the 'Reasoning Machines,' such as Locke and Clarke and David Hume. Dr. Channing's Dudleian Lecture is the model of what I mean, and the faculty which produced this is akin to the higher flights of the fancy." Channing never relinquished his supernaturalism, but after this lecture, he tended to move away from it toward a more strictly rational and moral point of view.

His health, which had been growing steadily worse since his Baltimore trip two years before, had become so poor by the summer of 1821 that he decided to forsake part of his usual visit to Rhode Island in favor of a trip to the mountains. He was in the New Hampshire ranges by the end of July, drinking in the pure air and glorying in the natural beauties of mountain peak and valley stream. By August he had reached Vermont and the Green Mountains, in whose gloomy recesses and cavernous depths he found much to wonder at.

Back in Oakland in September, he wrote of his journey as "a specimen of the life I have led for many years. One day undoes the work of many weeks." The trip had brought him much exhilaration and delight but little physical improvement. But he did not count his journey as lost. In words very likely inspired by his favorite poet Wordsworth, he wrote: "I should hardly dare to travel over the same ground again, lest the bright images which are treasured up in memory should be dimmed by a second sight."

During the winter and spring that followed he was too weak to perform his duties. Orville Dewey, his youthful protegé, substituted for him in the Federal Street pulpit, and Jonathan Phillips did what he could to take care of his administrative and philanthropic labors. Realizing that he was of no use to family or congregation in his present condition, he finally yielded to the suggestion that he take a year's

leave of absence and go abroad. His Society was agreeable, and Dewey
consented to supply his pulpit while he was gone.

He stood before his people on May 26, 1822, the Sunday before he
was due to sail, and told them that he was torn between his sense of
duty to them and his anticipation of the pleasure he would derive
from "traversing countries which have kindled my imagination almost
from infancy, whose literature has been the food of my mind, and
where nature and society present aspects hardly to be conceived amidst
the freshness of our own institutions." The next day he wrote his
mother a tender farewell, and on the morning of the twenty-seventh,
after bidding their children, relatives, and friends goodbye, he and
his wife sailed for England.

The voyage across the Atlantic was uneventful, though Channing
was confined to his cabin most of the time. When he did go on deck,
his wife wrapped him in four great coats and laid a fifth over his feet.
He wrote in his journal, "Nature breathes nothing unkind. It expands,
or calms, or softens us. . . . The soul and nature are attuned together.
Something within answers to all we witness without." This exquisite
correspondence between nature and the human soul had never before
been so manifest to him. Like Emerson later on, he was thoroughly
convinced that "the axioms of physics translate the laws of ethics."

Upon their arrival in Liverpool the Channings were warmly greeted
by friends who had come to know Channing through his writings and
by report from acquaintances who had visited in Boston. Social visits,
however, were out of the question, because the excitement of the long
sea voyage had left Channing weak and somewhat depressed in spirits.
He and Ruth bade their new friends a hasty farewell and set off for
the Lake Country.

Taking the post from Liverpool they travelled through Wigan,
Preston, and Garstand to Lancaster, where they stopped to inspect the
castle founded by Edward III as the seat of power for the House of
Lancaster. It was Channing's first glimpse of a monument of feudal
times. He was disappointed because he found it "crowded with felons,
debtors, lunatics, and . . . a workshop for convicts, an asylum for mad-
ness, and a court-house. . . ." Perhaps he felt that the castle had fallen
on evil days and that the justice dispensed in it was of an inferior
brand to that meted out by Edward in the good old days of chivalry.
Like Scott, whose novels he admired, he seemed subconsciously drawn
to the splendors of an age that had been sadly lacking in the humanitarianism he prized so highly. He was enough of a romantic also to

wish to unite into one social state the virtues, principles, and joys which had marked the different stages of human nature.

From Lancaster Castle he and his wife journeyed to Kirkby Lonsdale and then on to Lake Windermere, where the full realization of how much "beauty depends on connection and harmony" was brought to him. Next they visited Grasmere Water at the foot of Mount Loughrigg, and the spirit of this tranquil spot entered into Channing's inmost soul.

"It invites," he wrote, ". . . the mild enthusiast, who amidst the deformities of life still sees what is lovely in human nature, and at a distance from the tumults of society would resign himself to visions of moral beauty, of perfect loveliness, and of sublime virtue, unknown on earth,—who is conscious of the capacities of human nature for what is good and great, and desires, under the kindliest influences of the universe, to call forth into new life these high principles in his own soul." Unwittingly he had drawn a perfect self-portrait.

Mount Skiddaw impressed the travellers with its "tranquil majesty," and Channing was moved by it to expatiate upon the close relationship between moral greatness and love. Beauty, goodness, and truth had been identified in his mind since his college days; but the sublimities of nature always seemed to refresh his memory of the unity underlying spiritual concepts.

Much as he admired Grasmere and Skiddaw, however, his real reason for visiting the Lake Country was to meet the poet who lived nearby in the shadow of the mountain. Wordsworth had long been a favorite, although it was the spirit of the man and his philosophy rather than his skill as an author that attracted Channing. From his first acquaintance with the *Lyrical Ballads,* he had been won by the English poet's love of man and the air of genuine piety that pervaded his poems. Shortly after *The Excursion* was published, he had obtained a copy of it and "never read anything but Shakespeare more." Now he was to meet his idol face to face, and the prospect filled him with great excitement.

On Sunday, July 14, he set out for Rydal Mount in the only vehicle available—a rough cart, "dragged by a horse who had caught nothing of the grace of the surrounding scene." He found Wordsworth at home and received a cordial welcome. They chatted about poetry and religion—mostly about religion—and Channing warmed to his favorite argument that Christianity was divinely instituted because "it contained nothing which rendered it unadapted to a progressive state of society. . . ." Wordsworth, who was in complete agreement with him, read from a manuscript copy of *The Prelude* passages illustrating his own doctrine of communion with Nature as a part of human development.

When the interview was over, Channing started to walk back to the inn in the company of his host, who had accepted an invitation to go part of the way. At the end of a half mile Channing's strength began to fail. Finding his companion still earnestly talking, he invited him to get into the cart with him. Wordsworth did so, and the two made their way back to the village in the rough conveyance. As Channing wrote his sister: "Mr. Wordsworth's conversation was free, various, animated. We talked so eagerly as often to interrupt one another. And as I descended into Grassmere [*sic*] near sunset, with the placid lake before me, and Wordsworth talking and reciting poetry with a poet's spirit by my side, I felt that the combination of circumstances was such as my brightest hopes could never have anticipated." It was a rich experience —so rich that Channing felt fully repaid for the long pilgrimage he had made to the Grasmere shrine.

The following day he and his wife went to nearby Keswick, where they had an agreeable visit with another writer—this time it was the poet laureate, Robert Southey, to Channing as well as to posterity, a much lesser light than Wordsworth. Southey's Anglicanism was too much for Channing to stomach, because the Establishment had never held any attraction for him and Southey was a vehement defender of that institution. Channing's only account of his visit is contained in a brief remark addressed to his sister to the effect that he was somewhat disappointed to find "Southey had gone back so far into ecclesiasticism."

From Keswick the sightseers travelled back to London, which they used as a base of operations while visiting the "holy ground" in nearby Stratford and touring through Windsor Castle. There were a hundred and one places they had marked out for inspection, but time was passing so rapidly that they decided to cut short their English tour and cross the channel. Leaving London in the middle of August, they went first to Calais and then hurried on to Paris. After passing several weeks there, they travelled leisurely through the French countryside toward the Swiss border.

Channing's health gave little sign of improving, but his physical debility was no longer a clog to his spirit. From Geneva in late September he wrote to his sister-in-law Susan, "All that nature can do to lift us above the sordid and selfish is done in Switzerland; and who can doubt that where there is a deep purpose in the soul to elevate itself, much aid may be derived from the sublimity of the external world?" Only a few weeks before, he and Wordsworth had discussed this very matter; now he was actually experiencing the power of Nature not only "to inform the mind that is within us" but also to heal the body. Switzerland inspired him, and although he could not scale her towering peaks, he grew better almost as soon as he entered her borders. Grasmere had filled him with "a tender, grateful, melancholy feeling"; but "delicious" as this had been emotionally, it had done him no good physically. Now the ruggedness and wildness of the Alps were providing the stimulant that he needed.

Much as he preferred not to leave the inspiring sights of the Grimsel and Jungfrau, Channing knew he and his wife must go on. Winter found them in Italy. In November they came to Florence, where it rained almost daily. The wonders of European art exceeded all Channing's anticipations, but nothing seemed to strike him more than "the apparent insensibility of the mass of the people to the masterpieces; and the fact, that in the churches, side by side with these masterpieces, were the most miserable modern daubs and images of the Virgin adorned with tinsel. Yet it was before these, rather than before the masterpieces, that the people would be seen kneeling!"

Catholic Italy was truly an enigma to him. The omnipresent churches, crosses, and kneeling figures which he saw in Florence, Rome, and Naples, seemed part of an empty ritualism. To his way of thinking, institutional religion (Catholic or Protestant) was not the answer to man's problems, because it came between the individual and his Creator. Christianity firmly believed was not a dogma, but a spirit; the great foe of the Church of Rome was not the theologian—"It is human nature waking up to a consciousness of its powers, catching a glimpse of the perfection for which it was made, beginning to respect itself, thirsting for free action and development, learning through a deep consciousness that there is something diviner than forms, or churches or creeds. . . ."

One thing about Catholicism did impress him, however. In this respect he came closest to putting his finger on the pulse of a Church whose rich emotional life was not even remotely approached by his own Unitarianism. He recognized "its most skillful adaptation of itself to the different tastes, passions, wants of men." He was beginning to catch a glimmer of what Catholics mean when they talk of "Mother Church."

The "composition of forces in the Romish Church seems to me a wonderful monument of skill," he said. "When, in Rome, the traveller sees by the side of the purple, lackeyed cardinal, the begging friar; when, under the arches of St. Peter, he sees a coarsely dressed monk holding forth to a ragged crowd; or when, beneath a Franciscan Church, adorned with the most precious works of art, he meets a charnel house, where the bones of the dear brethren are built into walls, between which the living walk to read their mortality; he is amazed, if he gives himself time for reflection, at the infinite variety of machinery which Catholicism has brought to bear on the human mind; at the sagacity with which it has adapted itself to the various tastes and propensities of human nature."

Despite this insight he remained blind to most of the aspects of Catholicism, believing, among other things, that the members of that faith "worshipped" images and "adored" the Virgin. "The worship of the Churches of Italy," he wrote, "is directed chiefly to the Virgin. She is worshipped as *the Virgin*. The great idea of this Catholic deity is purity, chastity; and yet, unless all travellers deceive us, the country where she is worshipped is disfigured by licentiousness, beyond all countries of the civilized world."

While he was still in Circe's court, he took time to jot down some of the general impressions inspired by his new experiences among a society which had been class-conscious for centuries. He had viewed scenes of wealth and poverty in America; but nothing there could match the regal munificence of European palaces or the penury of the lowest classes in the great cities he was visiting. Before he started out on this extended journey, he had decided that the principal object in travelling was "to discover by comparison what is primary and universal in our nature, to separate the adventitious, secondary, temporary, to learn the deep principles on which all permanent improvements are to rest. . . ." Believing, like Thoreau after him, that a change of scenery was valuable only in so far as it helped "to enlarge our views of human nature, to learn what it can do, to what it is equal, under what influences its powers are most developed, by what most crushed," he seized upon every opportunity to scrutinize human nature in the different environments with which he came in contact.

Everywhere in Europe he found the "ruinous" idea that respectability and lofty rank go together. This concept, he knew, was not unknown in America, but here it flourished like a rank weed. As long as it existed, there would always be "a large class, cut off from the rest of the community, trained up in ignorance and vice, gross in manners, in no degree acted upon by other classes, and repressed only by brute force." This was all wrong. "The true organization of society," he de-

clared, "is that in which all improvements of the higher are communicated in the lower classes, and in which intellect and virtue descend and are diffused."

Absolute equality among men was impossible; even in his most sanguine moods he realized this, but he was not interested in a complete
levelling of mankind. There should be, he believed, a group of scholars
to maintain "an improving intercourse" among all orders of men; and
knowing that "there will be rich men," he insisted that they "ought to
regard property as a trust for the good of those who are in want." But,
he warned, "Let there be no literary *class*, no *class* of rich." These
views were idealistic, and he knew it; but it would always be his way
to measure the actual by the ideal. Most men, he was aware, preferred
the reverse of this procedure; but then they were not as certain of the
efficacy of Christianity and man's moral sense as he was.

When the Channings reached Rome in the middle of December,
they received the shocking news of twin deaths in their immediate
family. Although they were deeply grieved to learn of the decease of
Barbara Channing, Walter's wife, the news of the death of their youngest child left them broken-hearted. Less than a year old when they had
left him the preceding May, baby George had been in perfect health.
It seemed almost inconceivable that he could have been taken from
them.

Channing was particularly distraught, because poor health had prevented him from lavishing the same affection upon his younger son
that he had given William Francis; and now he was gone forever. But
his "Christian principle" provided the strength that he needed to bear
his loss, and once again he resigned himself to God's will, although he
now became impatient to return to Boston. "In a world so transient
and uncertain," he wrote his mother, "a year seems too much time to
be spent at a distance from one's home."

On his forty-third birthday, he and his wife were back in Florence
on the return leg of their journey to England. A fortnight later they
were at Fontainebleau, admiring the historically famous sites and listening to their guide's tales of the ill-fated Napoleon. By May they
were once again in Paris, but not even the allure of a Parisian spring
could break their determination to get back to England as quickly as
transportation and Channing's health would allow. They were in London by early June, seeking out Washington Allston's friend Coleridge.
They found him in excellent spirits at the Highgate residence of his
physician, James Gillman, where he had been living as a member of
the family for several years.

Channing presented Coleridge with some letters from Allston, and the two spent some time discussing him. Channing told his host that Allston was busily at work on his masterpiece, "Belshazzar's Feast," and that, as far as he knew, it was coming along fine. Coleridge expressed his admiration for Allston and remembered to tell Channing what a fine woman he had thought Ann Channing. Then they discussed the Channings' visit to Rydal Mount and spoke for a while about the current state of English literature.

Channing had long been an admiring reader of Coleridge, the latter's *Biographia Literaria* and *The Friend* having particularly impressed him by the spirituality of the philosophy contained in them. He would always have some reservations about the "abstractions of the philosopher," but the "exactness of the poet" never ceased to amaze him. Now, conversing with the poet-philosopher face to face, he was struck by the fact that Coleridge never used a word that was empty or even careless.

The Coleridge whom Channing visited was a very different man from the young revolutionary of the days when the Wordsworths and he had shouted their elation over the successes of the French revolution. Not only had he ceased to worry about the great political movements of the time, but he had also explicitly rejected his old religious heresies. The Unitarianism of his youth had long since evaporated, and his devotion to the materialism and necessitarianism of David Hartley and Joseph Priestley had given way to an evangelical type of piety. The Sage of Highgate now believed there could be no morality without religion and no religion without revelation. Christianity was for him, as it was for Channing, "the only Revelation of permanent and universal validity." A loyal member of the Church of England, and believing "That the Christian Faith . . . is the Perfection of Human Intelligence," he was hoping to prove the identity of true religion and true philosophy and thereby raise religion to its proper place in the sun.

Channing and Coleridge talked freely about religion and particularly about the doctrine of the Trinity. Coleridge was only too eager to discuss the Trinity, which he believed "to be the perfection of Reason, which can only be developed in us by our grasping the idea of the relation of infinite Love and infinite Wisdom in one Spirit, communicable to those who are filial by a free obedience." Channing found nothing except the phraseology to object to in his host's formula: "the relation perceived between the creating spirit and the created spirit in its purity, by which man finds intelligent and moral life in the Holy

Spirit"; and he also concurred with Coleridge's statement that such a formula should not be imposed on the mind arbitrarily, "because no abstract statement can really be believed that is not produced by the mind's own action on facts."

But the Trinity was only one of the subjects upon which Coleridge held forth. "He was so delighted," Channing said later, "to get a patient ear for his cherished thoughts, that he poured them out in a flood on all subjects,—the transcendental philosophy, Trinitarianism and Unitarianism, and especially on his idea of the Church of England, which was wholly new to me, and not at all acceptable in England to any party, for he included in the National Church not merely the pulpits and curacies in the Establishment, but all the spiritual forces at work in the land—the great schools and universities, and even the sectarian schools and pulpits!" Channing's part in the conversation —the part that he liked best to play—was that of Socratic interlocutor; and he never had a more willing or cooperative partner than the author of *Table Talk*.

Coleridge commented on the visit in a letter that he wrote shortly afterwards to Allston:

> My Friend: It was more than gratification, it was great comfort, to all of us, to see, sit, walk and converse with two such dear and dearly respected friends of yours, as Mr. and Mrs. Channing.
> Mr. Channing I could not be said not to have known in part before. . . . His affection for the good as the good, and his earnestness for the true as the true, with that harmonious subordination of the latter to the former, without encroachment on the absolute present him in a character which in my heart's heart I believe to be the very rarest in earth. . . . He has the love of wisdom and the wisdom of love. . . . I feel convinced that the few differences in opinion between Mr. Channing and myself not only are, but would by him be found, to be apparent, not real,—the same truth seen in different relation. Perhaps I have been more absorbed in the depth of the mystery of the spiritual life, he more engrossed by the loveliness of its manifestations.

For Channing the Highgate experience was rich and satisfying. He discovered that Coleridge's repudiation of Priestley's philosophy and the core of ideas designated as English Unitarianism did not mean that he condemned Unitarians personally, and though he gloried in being a member of the Anglican Church, he had not become nearly so much of a reactionary as Southey, or even Wordsworth. He discovered something else also—something which his friend Margaret Fuller was later to comment shrewdly upon: the infinite suggestiveness of the English poet's mind. "To the unprepared," Margaret wrote, "he is nothing, to the prepared everything." Channing's idealistic cast of mind and his theory of interior cultivation had prepared him admirably for Coleridge's idea of striving always to attain to higher truths. Both men looked for better things in theology, even though, as Coleridge remarked to Allston, they were inclined to see "the same truth . . . in different relation."

In comparison with Coleridge, most of the English people whom Channing afterwards met seemed rather lackadaisical. This was not true, however, of an acquaintance he made in Stoke Newington. He and his wife had been invited to the home of Mrs. Anna Letitia Barbauld, English moralist and critic (of whom Charles Lamb once remarked, "the cursed Barbauld crew, those Blights and Blasts of all that is Human in man and child"), and there they met Mrs. Barbauld's niece Lucy Aikin. Her *Memoirs of the Court of Queen Elizabeth,* published five years earlier, had won her a reputation that was about to be further enhanced by her *Memoirs of the Court of King James I,* then selling in the London bookstalls.

Although their meeting was somewhat by chance, Channing and Miss Aikin immediately recognized kindred spirits in each other and soon fell to discussing, as she later put it, "the neglect into which metaphysical science had fallen among us." When they parted company, it was with a promise to discuss the subject at greater length. As it happened, their discussion was to be carried on fairly regularly by letter over a period of more than sixteen years. Lucy Aikin became a lifelong friend and confidante and, in one sense, a kind of safety valve for Channing. Through her he was able to keep abreast of developments in England and on the Continent during the rest of his life.

There were no more such weighty discussions as those Channing indulged in with Coleridge and Miss Aikin, but he did have some interesting conversations with leading Unitarians in Bristol, Southampton, and London. He even managed to become acquainted among the nobility. Everywhere he went, he was especially impressed by the freedom with which the English conversed on politics; and in an interview he had with Thomas, Lord Erskine, one of England's leading advocates, he was very much surprised to hear that nobleman say, "Monarchy must go down!" He was not particularly eager to preach, but he could not deny the request of his London friends to address local Unitarian groups; and he was extremely gratified to see how much they enjoyed his sermons.

However, time was growing short for the travellers. In the middle of June they sailed to the Isle of Wight in a royal yacht and dined

nobly at Ryde. A week later they stood on the banks of the Wye, looking at Tintern Abbey and remembering the poet who made the scene
before them seem part of their former experiences. In July they were
again aboard ship on the long journey home. As each day brought
them closer to Boston and their family, they grew more and more
restive. On the last day as the shores of New England were coming
into view, William wrote in his journal thanks for a safe return and
then humbly resolved to strive to do God's will "more perseveringly,
to be more useful, watchful, temperate, kind, devout, than ever before."

When they landed, there were happy tears and broad smiles of welcome to greet them and a host of questions to be answered. They had
seen glorious natural beauties, viewed the wonders of European art,
talked with great men, and observed the lowly of the earth; but all
these experiences faded into the background when they stood in the
presence of those whom they loved. It was wonderful to be home.

Channing's European travels were highly significant both for his
own soul-expansion and for the cultural liberation of those whom he
was to influence through word and personal contact. Several years
earlier he had written to a Mrs. Catherine Cappe, widow of a Unitarian minister in York, England, telling her how pleased he was to see
that certain writers of Wordsworth's school had made the discovery
"that Unitarianism and imagination and poetry are not irreconcilable
foes."

Reiterating his view that "Unitarianism has suffered from a heart-
withering philosophy," he added, "it has suffered also from a too exclusive application of its advocates to Biblical criticism and theological
controversy, in other words, from a too partial culture of the mind. I
fear that we must look to other schools for the thoughts which thrill
us, which touch the most inward springs, and disclose to us the depths
of our own souls."

A year later he had considered the same problem, but from a different perspective: "I smile when I hear poetry called *light* reading. The
true poet has far-reaching thoughts, a perception of the harmonious
and exquisite relations of the universe, an eye that pierces the depths
and the miseries of the soul, placing him amidst the most gifted and
exalted intelligences."

His cultural horizon had begun to open up, therefore, even before
his trip abroad. Unlike many of the liberals, he was not content merely to consolidate the material gains resulting from the victory over
the orthodox. He knew that the theological break had come but that

the cultural was still to be realized. He knew, also, that the Calvinism of the early "Saints" and the "New Light" doctrines of Jonathan Edwards had possessed a power to arouse the emotions and kindle the imagination that was woefully lacking in current Unitarianism.

Temperamentally opposed to the "pale negations" of the liberal system and firmly convinced of the dynamic possibilities of human nature, he never ceased to warn against the danger of the new liberalism's degenerating into another orthodoxy. Thus he turned to the English romantics for the development of imagination and poetical enthusiasm which he deemed so necessary to supplement the "partial culture of the mind" afforded by the empirical philosophy and sensational psychology of his day. His visits in England with Wordsworth, Southey, and Coleridge and his first-hand contacts with the natural surroundings and cultural environment of the Old World confirmed the opinions that he had previously formed through reading. As a result of these new experiences, a warmer current of life had been breathed into his cold New England theology. Henceforth, it would be tightly woven into the fabric of his philosophy, poetry, and social reforms.

While he was scarcely "the first ambassador plenipotentiary of the English Romantic Movement who was accredited to the American people," as one modern scholar has remarked, he was certainly better equipped after his trip to Europe to carry out what he considered to be the chief work of his life—"to act upon other minds, and to act through sympathy as well as instruction."

No better proof of this could be found than the statement he made soon after his return: "The poetry of the age has a deeper and more impressive tone than come to us from what has been called the Augustan Age of English Literature. . . . Men want and demand a more thrilling note, a poetry which pierces beneath the exterior of life to the depths of the soul, and which lays open its mysterious working, borrowing from the whole outward creation fresh images and correspondence, with which to illuminate the secrets of the world without us."

Laying open the inner life of man now became Channing's primary endeavor. His critics might blame him for withholding sympathy and support from movements they considered important, but he would be quietly working in the background, effecting changes whose far-reaching consequences not even he could have anticipated.

CHAPTER TWELVE

BETWEEN THE BLACK AND THE WHITE

IN THE PRESENCE OF his congregation once again, Channing gave thanks for his safe return and dedicated himself anew to the service of God. Asking his listeners to pray that he might be given grace and strength to carry out his obligations, he reassured them of his convictions concerning the great role Christianity was to play in the future of the world.

"I return," he said, "with views of society which make me rejoice as I never did before in the promise held out by revealed religion of *a moral renovation* of the world. I expect less and less from revolutions, political changes, violent struggles,—from public men or public measures,—in a word, from any outward modification of society. Corrupt institutions will be succeeded by others equally, if not more, corrupt whilst the root or principle lives in the heart of individuals and nations; and the only remedy is to be found in a moral change, to which Christianity, and the Divine power that accompanies it, are alone adequate."

Although this statement revealed his distrust of political reform—of institutional reform in general—it did not signify any indifference to external social change. Neither did it imply any attempt to sabotage the efforts of those who were opposed to his theory of internal reform. An intensive survey of his "undercover" activities in promoting social amelioration would show that while he always put moral suasion first, he never stopped working for practical reform. It was simply a question of emphasis. Unlike the economic determinists of a later age, Channing believed internal reform must precede external change. And so he urged critics of humanity to forget the time-worn but hardly axiomatic statement that "human nature never changes" and to begin investigating the possibilities of moral renovation. The idea was not novel, but its application would have been.

Some in his audience undoubtedly could not share his enthusiasm in full measure, but none could gainsay his sincerity. Want of faith in improvement, which Channing always considered the "darkest

154

symptom" of the age, was certainly not one of his faults; and his job, as he saw it, was to stimulate the faith of others. All he asked was God's grace and the trust of his people.

Although his European travels had inspired him spiritually, they had done little for him physically. One sermon alone was enough to convince him that he was not up to performing the duties of a large and growing congregation. To add to his problem, Orville Dewey had accepted a call to New Bedford and could no longer assist him. From his Oakland summer home he wrote to the officers of his Society asking for help. Though he did not say so, he wished for a colleague; and the officers were quick to divine his purpose. By the end of September arrangements had been made to provide for a permanent assistant under terms that were acceptable to both parish and pastor. Channing agreed to relinquish one-quarter of his annual salary of two thousand dollars, and the Society commissioned him to select a young man who would be agreeable as a colleague.

While this matter was under consideration, Channing was faced with the unpleasant duty of bidding goodbye to a very dear and very special friend. This was John Cheverus, Bishop of the Boston diocese and the leading member of the Catholic hierarchy in New England. Cheverus had come to Boston nearly thirty years before, a simple priest driven into exile by the forces of revolution and anti-clericalism in France. Here among the descendants of the Puritans, who were still suspicious of "popery," Cheverus had labored with apostolic zeal to minister to his small flock. So successful were his efforts to breed tolerance and to diffuse charity throughout his adopted city that by the time of his consecration to the episcopacy in 1810, the forty-two-year-old priest was beloved by Protestants and Catholic alike.

Channing had become acquainted with Cheverus through his interest in social reform. Both men entertained pretty much the same ideas about philanthropy, and they often found themselves working together in the same charitable enterprises. Respect for each other as Christians soon deepened into personal friendship. When Channing sailed for Europe, he received a warm personal letter from his friend, wishing him godspeed and a safe return, as well as letters of introduction to leaders of the Catholic faith in Europe.

Channing knew that he would never see Bishop Cheverus again because the Catholic prelate had been called by the Vatican to assume charge of the See of Montauban in France. For Cheverus it was an important rise in the hierarchy of the Roman Church; but Channing could only regret that the Bishop's superiors had seen fit to take him away, because toleration was still a mighty rare thing in Massachusetts, and Cheverus had been a bulwark against bigotry and dissension. He bade his friend a simple goodbye and wished him success in his labors. The memory of their friendship grew dimmer with the passing years, but Channing never forgot the example of what one good man might accomplish by a "pure and apostolic life."

If there was peace between the Catholics and the Unitarians in Boston in the fall of 1823, a state of open conflict still existed between the liberals and orthodox. The former now had another periodical besides *The Christian Disciple* to spread their views. *The Christian Register* was a general religious newspaper, but it defended and interpreted the liberal cause whenever necessary; and its columns were always open to Unitarians. On the occasion of the Dedham decision and the recriminations that followed, it had spoken out vehemently for the liberals, exonerating them from the charge of stealing churches from the orthodox. Otherwise it was mild and placid enough, striving to be tolerant in its attitude toward all kinds of doctrines and reforms.

During Channing's absence abroad one phase of the argument precipitated by his Baltimore sermon was concluded. The celebrated Wood'n Ware controversy, as it was popularly called, had begun in the spring of 1820, when Dr. Leonard Woods of Andover, a good friend of Jedidiah Morse, had written his *Letters to Unitarians*. This was soon followed by *Letters to Trinitarians and Calvinists*, from the pen of Henry Ware, Sr.

In September, 1821, Dr. Woods published his *Reply to Dr. Ware's Letters;* and in May, 1822, Dr. Ware published his *Answer to the Reply*. This was followed in September by a pamphlet entitled *Remarks on Dr. Ware's Answer* from Dr. Woods. *A Postscript to the Second Series of Letters* by Dr. Ware ended the debate in the spring of 1823.

Since both men had conducted themselves calmly and decorously, their discussions had never degenerated into name-calling. Instead of the doctrine of the Trinity, which played so prominent a part in the earlier phases of the controversy, the ideas of total depravity, vicarious atonement, election, and reprobation had received primary consideration. Woods believed that Unitarians overlooked "the ruined state of man," while Ware insisted that Woods should drop even the metaphorical meanings of the old Calvinistic doctrines.

The whole debate sounds unappetizing to the modern ear but to Elizabeth Peabody, Channing's youthful admirer—then grown to the ripe age of nineteen—"Stewart and Norton's Controversy" and "Wood and Ware's Controversy" were stimulating, and she recommended them as ideal reading matter for her fourteen-year-old sister, Sophia.

Controversy might have been stimulating to Elizabeth, but Channing had other things on his mind. The question of the moment was to find a suitable assistant who could help him in his ministry. He didn't have long to wait.

On a Saturday morning in early October, Ezra Stiles Gannett called with a friend to pay his respects. He had just completed his theological studies at Cambridge and was eager to begin preaching. Frank and open of countenance, and with a volatile temperament, Gannett was his own best advertisement; but he had an added attraction for Channing because he was the grandson of Ezra Stiles.

Despite the tie between Stiles, Gannett, and Channing, the visit was somewhat stiff and formal. The fault was all Channing's, because his young visitor could hardly have been expected to break the conversational ice. One of Channing's great faults, and he realized it only too well ("I am strong," he said, "before the multitude, but weak before the individual") , was that he talked too often for his own sake, forgetting visitors and self in his preoccupation with ideas.

Just a week or so before Gannett's visit, Edward Everett had been in to talk over Channing's European jaunt and had departed shaking his head and saying, "I have never met anyone to whom it was so interesting to listen and so hard to talk when my turn came." It wasn't rudeness that led Channing to neglect his responsibilities in conversation, for he was the soul of courtesy. It was more a failure to bend to the frailty of human nature and to recognize that few people are capable of always addressing their thoughts and words to high themes.

Although Gannett felt that he had failed to pierce his host's reserve, he had made such a good impression that Channing soon asked him to preach part-time at Federal Street. Even then Channing exercised his habitual caution, because Gannett recalled that "he was very particular in impressing upon me that I was not to preach as a candidate but merely to relieve him." The opportunity to assist Dr. Channing was one that no young man in his right mind could afford to pass up, and Gannett agreed to the proposal immediately. Channing told him they would alternate the morning and evening services.

At first the neophyte found himself in a trying position. Gannett seldom knew whether he would preach in the morning or evening or at both times. He could be bursting with a message for the congregation; but he had to go to church on Sunday morning prepared either to unburden his soul or sit quietly by while Channing addressed the congregation. Plain living and high thinking were all very fine, but for an enthusiast like Gannett, it was sometimes difficult to measure up to the lofty ideal of self-denial which his senior colleague was always talking about.

He stuck the situation out, however, and after preaching fifteen sermons, was invited to become Channing's permanent colleague. He had been put through a very severe inspection, but had won Channing's complete confidence and affection. Looking back at the experience, he could find little to criticize in the older man's behavior.

Another young man was also becoming better acquainted with the Federal Street Church. Although he was no longer a close neighbor of Channing (Ruth Emerson and her sons had migrated from Federal Street to Roxbury the previous spring), Waldo Emerson walked into Boston almost every Sunday to hear Channing preach. He had become a member of the First Church of Christ a few months earlier, but he was irresistibly drawn to the frail little man who stood in his pulpit Sunday after Sunday and preached that religion was a spirit and not bound up in creeds or dogmas. Granting even that Channing held on to certain core beliefs—the historicity of Scriptures, Christ's pre-existence, and the miracles of Jesus—doctrines no longer fully believed in by Emerson, still young Waldo found him closer to his own way of thinking than any other minister around.

When the Emerson family was faced with a weighty problem in the fall of '23, they very naturally turned to Channing for advice. William Emerson, who was twenty-two now and eager to begin his preparation for the ministry, was debating whether to go to Göttingen to study divinity or to stay at Harvard. Channing protested against Germany, arguing that, while it was better for literature, one who intended to preach in New England had better study his divinity there. His logic failed to carry the day. William sailed for Europe in December, carrying in his trunk letters from his Harvard professors Edward Everett and George Ticknor.

In a way, young Emerson's decision was a portent of things to come in New England theology. German literature and German philosophy could not be separated, as Channing seemed to believe, for the impulses underlying the one were also at work on the other. The "higher criticism" could not be kept out of New England any more than the writings of Goethe or Schiller.

As Channing approached his forty-fourth birthday, he began to take stock of himself as he had done annually for many years. For the first time he realized that he occupied a somewhat peculiar position among his liberal comrades in Boston and the neighboring communities. He could see clearly two fairly distinct divisions in the liberal ranks. There were the white-haired men and the dark-haired men. But just where did he stand? The older liberals like Henry Ware, Sr., Noah Worcester, and John Kirkland probably counted him as a member of their group, but actually he belonged mid-way between them and such "dark-haired youngsters" as James Walker, John Palfrey, John Pierpont, Henry Ware, Jr., and Orville Dewey, who had begun their careers less than a decade before.

Thinking back, Channing was reminded of the dead Thacher and Buckminster. For a moment he considered somewhat wistfully what might have happened had they been spared to work with him. He thought then of his near-contemporary, Andrews Norton, but he concluded somewhat humorously that Norton, who was six years his junior, actually belonged among the white-haired men. There was really no one else whom he could place by his side. The thought was saddening, but he brightened quickly when he considered that his position actually allowed him to keep a foot in both liberal camps.

From pondering on the people about him, Channing turned to a consideration of the local scene. Since he had first visited it some thirty years ago, Boston had grown up. Then it had been a country town of perhaps twenty thousand inhabitants. Now it was a city—had been legally for two years—and it was bulging with a population of more than fifty thousand.

Physically, Boston was terribly cramped, being confined almost entirely between Beacon Hill, Dover Street, and the water front. Wealth, immigration, and growth were rapidly upsetting the order that Channing had known when he first came up from Newport; and he could see how increasing industrialization and urbanization would create even greater problems than those now facing the city fathers. Pauperism and crime were extremely distasteful for a conservative well-to-do community like Boston to face; but he was heartened by the results of private and public philanthropy. One of the most encouraging signs of the trend toward scientific and practical reform, was the report of the state committee on poor relief, which had been submitted three years before by the chairman of the committee, his good friend and parishioner Josiah Quincy.

But Channing also knew that the steps already taken to cope with the growing evils of the young city were only a beginning. Great divergence of opinion still existed among those responsible for formulating future policies, and no systematic method had yet been applied either to the care or the prevention of pauperism, crime, and intemperance. Many of the city's vices demanded prompt treatment if they were to be prevented from becoming chronic and malignant. He was eager to find new avenues by which he could prove his oft-repeated statement that religion was a social principle. His own role in the battle to improve Boston culturally and socially could hardly be in the front lines, because his health would not permit such active participation; but if he could find willing and hardy disciples, he might still accomplish his purpose. He resolved to redouble his efforts to encourage "any useful design which the benevolence of the age and the wants of the community . . . [might] suggest."

For many years now, Channing had been gathering materials which he hoped to embody in systematic form and publish as his share in the work of elevating human nature. By reading, observation, and patient thought, he had formulated certain principles about man and his place in the universe, and he was looking forward to the day when both health and physical opportunity would enable him to write his treatise.

In the spring of 1824, Channing wrote to Lant Carpenter, one of his English Unitarian friends, "I hope that I shall be spared to execute a work of some extent, for which I have made some preparation; but time flies away, and nothing is done but the accumulation of more materials, and my plan continues to grow, whilst the space for accomplishing it is contracted."

The plaintive tone of this letter was to become familiar in the years to follow. Perhaps he half suspected that he might never accomplish his purpose, because in the same letter to Carpenter he remarked, "it is certainly well for the world that so many schemes of authorship prove abortive." But he never ceased to look for materials for his work on Man, and much of his inquisitorial manner during the last twenty years of his life was due to his eagerness to squeeze dry all possible sources of information.

A few months before his departure for Europe he had played host to a group known afterwards as the "Wednesday Evening Association." Samuel J. May, later a renowned anti-slavery leader, but in 1822 a young man of twenty-five acting as a part-time assistant for Channing, attended these meetings, and remembered that they "often called from the Doctor his happiest and most precious utterances." May also seemed to think that this Association was partly responsible for providing the impetus that "led to the institution of courses in public lectures—the Lyceum and the Lowell Institute."

Whether he exaggerated or not, the "Beneficent Association" had continued to flourish during Channing's absence; and now that he was back home, he began to urge its members to renewed activity. To keep things moving in its own congregation, he established the "Association of the Members of the Federal Street Society for Benevolent Purposes," an organization designed to facilitate contributions to various charitable enterprises in the city and to discuss such projects as Sunday Schools, missions, the ministry at large, and the support of needy students of divinity.

Although he was kept busy "acting upon minds" at home, Channing still managed to keep up with the ever-increasing number of his acquaintances abroad. Actually, he had made very few personal contacts during his brief visit to England, but the impression that he left upon those whom he did meet was so deep and lasting that they extolled his virtues to their friends. They in turn read some of his sermons, liked them, and asked for more, so that his reputation was made almost overnight.

An example of the esteem in which he was held is to be found in an article on "American Writers" which appeared in *Blackwood's* the year after his return to America. The writer of the article refers to him as a Boston clergyman who, "without any question, may rank among the first sermonizers that ever lived. Such of his writings as have been published are remarkable for simplicity, clearness, and power. The diction is of the heart not of the schools. It is, as it were, a language of his own—a visible thought."

On the same page and in the same piece William Cullen Bryant is called a minor poet: "He wants fire—he wants the very rashness of a poet—the prodigality and fervour of those who are overflowing with inspiration." Such criticism makes it plain that the Scottish School of criticism had changed very little from the days when Wordsworth's *Excursion* and *The White Doe of Rylstone* were under fire.

By the mid-twenties, then, Channing had a number of steady correspondents—from literary as well as religious circles—who were eager to keep him informed of developments in the British Isles. One such informant was Felicia Hemans, the English poetess, whose reputation as a lyricist was just beginning in England and America. Another, and a more regular correspondent, was Joanna Baillie, the Scotch dramatist and poet, who was an acquaintance of Mrs. Hemans and a close friend of Sir Walter Scott. Mrs. Baillie had long been a resident of Hempstead, the scene of Lucy Aikin's labors, and the two of them were intimate friends and mutual admirers of Channing. Through Mrs.

Baillie he was able to keep up with literary happenings in Britain and to find out what effect his writings were having on her country-men. It was she, for example, who informed him of Lord Byron's death and who quizzed him about that "rake" Tom Moore.

Both Byron and Moore were choice targets in America. Byron's private life generally colored the judgment of critics who were con-cerned that literature might make vice attractive, and Moore's "coldly voluptuous" verse often came in for censure. Unlike most critics, Channing was primarily concerned with the positive principle of moral idealism. He might deprecate the "impiety" of certain authors, but he never questioned "Does this man make vice attractive?" Like Emerson, he preferred to become excited about the good. All literature, he argued, must be based on sound religious principles. It was in these terms that he answered Mrs. Baillie's question about Lord Byron:

> I can hardly express the feeling the news of Lord Byron's death has given me. That a mind so gifted should have been left to devote its energies to the cause of impiety and vice, and should be so soon and sud-denly taken without making reparation to insulted truth and virtue . . . in all this we see the mysterious character of God's providence. I always hoped, that after the fever of youthful passions, this unhappy man would reflect, repent, and prove that in genius there is something congenial with religion.

The rest of his letter indicates that he had been taken in as com-pletely as any of his fellow-countrymen by the "Byronic pose." Still, there was no evidence whatsoever to indicate that he denied Byron's claim to genius. As he saw it, Byron's tragedy lay in his failure to affirm man's potential for moral greatness.

Similarly, he wrote Mrs. Baillie that he disagreed completely with Thomas Moore's contention that men of genius are naturally unsuited to friendship or domestic life. He did not doubt that genius was often joined with vice—"but not naturally or necessarily." Generally, he said, genius is characterized by self-mastery; and the highest genius is a self-guiding comprehensive power. "It creates in the spirit of the Author of the Universe, in the spirit of order. It worships truth and beauty." As to Moore's notion that genius, because it delights in the ideal, is soon wearied and disgusted with the real, he claimed exactly the opposite. "He who conceives and loves beauty in its highest forms is most alive to it in its humblest manifestation. He loves it not by comparison, or for its degree, but for its own sake; and the same is true of beauty."

The Wordsworthian quality of these remarks is evident, but the

basis for Channing's statements goes back much farther than Wordsworth—at least as far back as his reading of Price and Hutcheson. His
study of Plato had also done much to substantiate it. Universal harmony, or the unity and parity of beauty, goodness and truth, was an
integral part of his philosophy, and he was bound to reject any doctrine which taught that God "has sown discord between the noblest
attributes of the soul."

Harmony rather than discord characterized the gala affair that took
place in Boston on the final day of June, 1824. The occasion was the
ordination of Channing's colleague, Ezra Gannett. All the clergy of
the city with the exception of the Methodists (even Harmony needs
occasional protection) were invited and the Secretary of the Russian
Legation, Baron DeWallenstein, was present. Channing delivered the
ordination sermon, and according to young Henry Ware, outdid himself. "It is not possible," Ware wrote his sister-in-law, "for you to
conceive the excitement produced by Dr. Channing. I have never seen
the enthusiasm equalled. To hear such a sermon, is one of the memorable things in a man's life. It forms an epoch in his existence."

The subject of the sermon was "The Demands of the Age on the
Ministry"; and if Henry Ware did wax exceedingly enthusiastic about
its merits, he had good reason, because Channing spoke with great
fervor about ideas that were closest to his heart. Mind, he declared,
has become the sovereign of the world, and kings and heroes are becoming impotent by the side of men of deep and fervent thought. An
enlightened age demands an enlightened ministry, and the moral
teachers of the present must cloak their message of truth in the garb
of imagination and reason. Too often religion has been made a separate business, "and a dull, unsocial, melancholy business, too, instead
of being manifested as a truth which bears on and touches every
human, as a universal spirit, which ought to breathe through and
modify all our desires and pursuits, all our trains of thought and
emotion." But a new spirit of improvement is abroad, and "multitudes, unwilling to wait the slow pace of the great innovator, time, are
taking the work of reform into their own hands."

"Who," he asked, "that can compare the present with the past, is
not struck with the bold and earnest spirit of the literature of our
times?" Fiction no longer merely amuses but has become part of the
moral steam enginery of the age, and poetry is equally useful in un-
folding new theories of education and morals. Men will no longer be
trifled with; they want a religion that will lay hold upon them and
grip them by its power to awaken a real and deep interest in their

souls. The minister today must be prepared, therefore, to impart a message that is both truthful and thrilling. He must know the external proofs of his religion—its history and the record of its miracles—but even more important, he must be thoroughly familiar with its inward proofs—"its adaptation to the spiritual wants, to the weakness and the greatness of human nature . . . its unbounded benevolence, corresponding with the spirit of the universe . . . its views of God's parental character and purposes, of human duty and perfection, and of a future state."

As if anticipating future criticism of his policy of moral revolution, he took exception, before he concluded his address, to the charge that "romantic expectations of great changes in society will do more harm than good." It isn't true, he insisted. "If there be one striking feature in human nature, it is the susceptibleness of improvement." If science and art, intellect and imagination are extending their domains, "who is authorized to say . . . the moral and religious principles of our nature, are incapable of increased power and elevation?" Channing's reasoning might have left something to be desired, but many like Henry Ware were lifted beyond the plane of logic by his eloquence and were convinced by the magic of his sincerity that perfectibility was as natural to man as eating and sleeping.

Channing's conviction that moral reform was impossible except under the true awakening of conscience and the quickening of religious inspiration was the primary feature which now distinguished his hopes for the world from his student dreams of Rousseau, Godwin, Coleridge, and Southey: dreams of a golden age of justice, equality, and fraternity secured either by revolutionizing the world or by quitting its corrupting influences. Then his schemes had depended on social construction or reconstruction by men as they are. Now after reading the long record of man's imperfections, he was relying upon the prior perfecting of the individual for the regeneration of the world. He could hope to bring heaven down to earth, because there was no need for any new machinery or unheard-of forces to bring about such a result. The power was ready and waiting in the soul of every man. It needed only the sympathetic call of a faithful witness to evoke it and put it to work. This much did the Age demand of the ministry.

Channing's remarks were probably the inspiration for a project undertaken the following spring by the Wednesday Evening Association. At a February meeting of the group, a committee was appointed to study the state of morals among the young men of the city, and the means of improving it. Channing was named chairman. He lost no time getting the survey under way, and several months later reported to the larger group a series of recommendations that his committee had drawn up.

In working out their "means of improvement" the committee had discovered three fairly distinct classes among the young men of Boston: the first, who were "the sons of opulent families," were profiting from their superior opportunities for education by exhibiting a higher standard of character than formerly; the second, consisting of apprentices in stores and shops, manifested a less favorable condition. Country-bred usually and ignorant of city ways, they received little attention from their masters; and as a result, were neglecting public worship in favor of "riding, or reading novels, if not in less innocent employments"; the state of morals among the third class, the apprentices of mechanics and the sons of laborers, was becoming steadily worse. The basic cause was cited as "the free use of ardent spirits among their masters and fellow-laborers," and the subsequent indulgence into which they, themselves, were soon led.

The committee's solution to these problems was education. It recommended that another group be appointed to inspect the Apprentices' Library "for the purpose of ascertaining whether it contains the best moral and religious books for readers of their age and condition, and of supplying what deficiencies may exist." It also proposed that single seats be reserved in churches for young men who could not afford an entire pew. Sunday evening lectures were also prescribed for these same young men to deal with subjects "which shall be spiritually adapted to their condition, dangers, wants, etc." Finally, an investigation was urged "into the nature and operation of the institutions lately formed in Great Britain and particularly Scotland, for giving lectures to young mechanics on the scientific principles of their various arts."

Education and internal reform were on the march, but workers themselves were going at reformation in a different way. In Boston the House Carpenters were calling a strike to secure shorter working hours—the first great strike in which the ten-hour working day had ever arisen as a major issue.

Quite a different problem confronted Channing at about the same time that he and his committee were completing their study. The time had come, or so thought the "dark-haired" members of the liberal group, to organize into a distinctive religious body. They had been trained in the independent spirit of the Harvard Divinity School by Andrews Norton. Though conservative in theology and opposed to sectarian measures, Norton was nevertheless a radical and stimulating teacher, and often led his students to go far beyond his own limits. Having grown up under the freer life of the liberal churches, they had no fears about becoming another sect, but were persistent in their efforts to secure an organization that would represent distinctively Unitarian thoughts and sentiments.

The first step toward forming a separate body was taken in the autumn of 1824 by the members of the Anonymous Association, a group of leading Bostonians who were in the habit of meeting at one another's homes to discuss religion, morals, and politics. At a gathering in the home of Josiah Quincy, the discussion came round to certain articles in *The Christian Register* and the importance of promoting liberal principles through the printed word. Unity seemed of paramount importance to the group, and they appointed a committee to report on the expediency of forming an association.

Late in December the committee sent out a circular to all who were interested in such an organization to confer some time in the near future. In response to this call, a meeting was held in the vestry-hall of the Federal Street Church on January 27, 1825. Channing opened the meeting with prayer; and after a few preliminaries, the discussion began. Aaron Bancroft, father of the future historian, voiced the sentiments of the older ministers when he pointed out the inexpediency of rushing from the dangers of one sect into the possible perils of another. Andrews Norton defended the proposed organization but declared that its purpose should not be to make proselytes. At this point, Channing arose and cautiously approved the suggestion that provision "be made for future meetings of Unitarians and liberal Christians generally." He thought the object of the convention, as he wished to call it, should be to "spread our views of religion, not our mere opinions, for our religion is essentially practical."

For Channing to speak, even thus guardedly, indicated that he felt such an organization could skirt the shoals of sectarianism. His firm stand against every phase of religious organization that put bonds upon men was well known to everyone present. Time and again he had condemned "the guilt of a sectarian spirit" and had said that "to bestow our affections on those who are ranged under the same human leader, or who belong to the same church with ourselves, and to withhold it from others who possess equal if not superior virtue, because they bear a different name, is to prefer a party to the Church of Christ." In future years his distrust of sectarian influence would increase; but the time had not yet come when he could say, "I am little of a Unitarian . . . and stand aloof from all but those who strive and pray for clearer light, and look for purer and more effectual manifestation of Christian truth." For the time being, he would urge moderation and hope that the group would proceed soberly and cautiously.

His friendly attitude, however, did not dissuade several prominent laymen, as well as three or four of the older ministers, from arguing against labelling the group Unitarians or Liberals. John Pierce, Channing's old Latin teacher, thought the measure of the committee "very dangerous" and got up three times during the course of the meeting to remonstrate. The debating grew warmer and warmer, until it became apparent that no final decision could be reached at that particular time. Before adjourning, the group appointed the inevitable committee (Channing was a member) and empowered it to call another and larger meeting. The committee never acted, however.

The zeal of those who had proposed organization in the first place did not slacken. During the late months of the winter they continued to gain new adherents. Finally, when they felt they had enough support to win the battle, they called another meeting. On May 25 the Berry Street Conference met in an afternoon session and voted to form "a new association to be called the American Unitarian Society." A few days later, a nominating committee selected Channing for president of the new organization and Ezra Gannett for secretary.

One of Gannett's first jobs was to notify his senior colleague. He wrote to Channing, who was then at Oakland, of the honor that had been conferred upon him. Channing wrote back quickly, declining the office. "I was a little disappointed," he said, "at learning that the Unitarian Association is to commence operations immediately. I conversed with Mr. Norton on the subject before leaving Boston, and found him so indisposed to engage in it that I imagined it would be let alone for the present. The office which in your kindness you have assigned to me I must beg to decline."

His refusal to assume the direction of the new organization was certainly not due to any quarrel with its aims. On the contrary, its statement of purpose—to promote pure and undefiled religion—was one that he himself might easily have formulated. Poor health and the urgency of other duties were his reasons for declining, and his friends knew only too well how valid these excuses were. It was not the Association that filled the sleepless hours of his nights with fears of "a Unitarian orthodoxy," because he was never a foe of group effort as such.

"The value of associations," he said, "is to be measured by the energy, the freedom, the activity, the moral power, which they encourage and diffuse." It was by this standard that he would judge the Unitarian Association. In so far as it was "fitted to call forth energy, active talent, religious inquiry, a free and manly virtue," it would justify its existence and would deserve the confidence and support of every member of the community. If it proved, however, to be only another means for usurping the rights of the individual, then he would condemn it with all his strength. Until the evidence was in, he would reserve judgment. Meanwhile the thing to remember was that "there is no moral worth in being swept away by a crowd, even towards the best objects."

After the stirring events of the winter and spring he was content to relax at Oakland. By the end of summer he was ready for another assault upon Boston, and September found him back at his home in Mount Vernon Street. Shortly after his return, he paid a visit to Susan Channing's were he found that enthusiastic admirer of his, Elizabeth Peabody. More than four years had passed since they had last met, and Elizabeth was thrilled to see her "great little man" once again. She had corresponded with him about her religious questionings and doubts, and he had been able to dispel the fog of Calvinism that had beclouded her youthful vision; but letters were a poor substitute for seeing him in the flesh, and she resolved not to let him get so far away from her again.

The truth of the matter was that she was now developing a romantic passion for the good Doctor. That fall, while she was sharing the duties of schoolmistress with her younger sister Mary at their suburban retreat in Brookline, Channing's sermons became the great events of her life. Her enthusiasm carried her on foot to the Federal Street Church through the winter drifts when the omnibus refused to run, and it was a rare occasion indeed when she missed a church service or a meeting connected with the parsonage. She was eternally grateful to her new pastor for opening up the vistas of hope upon which his religion was based, and she took strongly to heart his doctrine of service. She heard him preach on self denial and afterwards wrote in her diary that the passions ought to be "brought into strict and entire subordination to our moral and intellectual powers." "Power over ourselves . . . is the beginning and end of virtue," Dr. Channing had declared, and she felt the weight of his authority as she never had that of the Scriptures.

On Saturday mornings after her classes were over, she would walk in from Brookline to the Mount Vernon address to join Channing for their weekly discussion. When the weather permitted, they adjourned

to the nearby Common and became peripatetic philosophers, saunter-
ing like the Greeks of old beneath the shady trees or strolling along the
winding paths of the Green. Oftentimes Plato or Socrates would be the
subject of their conversation, for Channing was especially fond of the
dialogues; and he never tired of discussing the relative merits of the
Apology and the *Phaedo*. He thought the former contained a pro-
founder argument for immortality than the latter and delineated a life
in the world that was close to Jesus' own spirit of devotion to the will
of God. Socrates, he maintained, was inferior to Jesus as a revelation
to man, because he was only intellectual, while Jesus was spiritual and
humane as well.

In the role of Socratic questioner, he would often quiz Elizabeth
about theological matters, and he was delighted to discover what an
apt pupil she was. She in turn was gratified at Sunday services to hear
him expatiating upon the subject of their Saturday's talk. Both were
good for each other; Channing seldom had such an eager and inquisitive listener, and Elizabeth could not have found a more inspiring
teacher.

On one occasion, when they were discussing the ethics of Thomas
Brown, a philosopher of the Scotch School, Channing told her that he
thought Brown's system very interesting but unsupported by his metaphysics. "He *felt* more truths," he said, "than he *saw* and stated." She
was bothered by this judgment, because she was a conscientious teacher
and Brown was one of the authorities upon whom she relied. She told
Channing her problem, and he received it very sympathetically.

"No education of children," he told her, "can be adequate, unless
their nature is carefully studied and reverently dealt with. I am glad
that you are impressed with this great truth, for unfortunately there is
prevalent the practical error—and often it is theoretical also—that children are mere blank paper to be written upon, or plastic material to
be moulded at the will of the teacher."

Channing went on to explain his objections to Brown and Locke
and the school of philosophers who failed, in his estimation, to give
adequate expression to the moral powers and intuitions of man. No
being whose consciousness includes only images of outward nature and
mere emotions could feel the sense of responsibility that God had im-
planted in all human beings, he asserted. The laws of physical inquiry
certainly were inadequate to explain some of the great insights that
had helped to revolutionize human thought.

Men like Brown and Locke often expressed ideas for which they
could give no logical justification, but this was to be expected. Incon-

sistency was as much a part of human nature as consistency. The important consideration was not to judge of a man's philosophy by the occasional insights that transcended his metaphysical theory but to remember that, nine times out of ten, his thinking would rise only to the level permitted by his system of thought. He agreed with her that the Scotch School had improved upon Locke, because it did affirm the reality of intuition and the authority of conscience, but he warned her against accepting all of its ideas. Brown's error was that he defined cause as mere antecedence. Believing this, he could not say anything about moral responsibility that would give it any real meaning.

Lessons like this were invaluable to Elizabeth, who put them into practice as soon as she was able. She felt obliged to Channing for his help and sought ways to do something for him personally. Her opportunity came when she heard several of his parishioners bemoan the fact that his sermons were never available, either in print or manuscript. She went immediately to him and proposed that she copy out his sermons so that they could be passed around. She could never decipher his handwriting, he argued. Besides the task would steal valuable time from her reading. He was interested in her education, and there were books that he would like to read to her. She replied that she could copy while he read.

"I will test that at once," he exclaimed, and going to his bookcase, he picked out a copy of Plato's *Timaeus* in a French translation by Cousin. Then he gave her one of his sermons and some copy paper and told her to begin while he read. It was a severe test, but she passed it with flying colors. Channing agreed to continue the arrangement as long as it was of mutual benefit. In this way some fifty of the sermons were put into shape for printing.

More than likely Elizabeth's faithful copies were indirectly responsible for the request that he received shortly afterwards to publish them. An indication of the esteem in which his work was held can be gathered from the list of names attached to the request. Isaac Parker, presiding Justice of the Massachusetts Supreme Court; Nathaniel Bowditch; William Prescott, father of the historian; Daniel Webster; and Joseph Story, Associate Justice of the United States Supreme Court, were among those who urged authorship upon him.

Mary Channing, the Doctor's eight-year-old daughter, became a pupil in Elizabeth's school, as did the daughters of many of Channing's parishioners. This new bond of interest between the minister and his protegé strengthened their relationship and resulted in many interesting discussions on the subject of education. Channing preferred oral instruction to any other method of training and never neglected to press home his point. "Could we use books less and talking more," he often said, "one of the chief objects in early teaching would be attained more certainly,—I mean *distinctness of conception.*"

On the score of religious instruction, a subject about which he was continually talking, he had definite ideas. He didn't believe very young children should be sent to Sunday School, and he dreaded everything parrot-like in devotion. "True worship is spontaneous," he said; "nothing should ever be done to force children to worship." On the other hand, "It is vain to say that children should be left to choose a form of religion for themselves. They cannot escape the influence of family, of country." Thus he baptized his own children when they were still babes in arms, but did not send them to Sunday School until they were eight or nine.

One of the highlights of Elizabeth's early acquaintance with Channing was the week-long visit he spent in the fall of '25 at the home of Mr. Guild, the father of one of her pupils. He was in an expansive mood and talked quite freely about world problems. Great changes were due, he assured his listeners, and he hoped they were not far off. He was conscious of the change within himself since his trip to Europe, and he attributed it to the new perspective that a comparison between the decaying institutions of the old world and the growing ones of the new had given him.

"Progress is not everything," he warned; "It is a mere change indeed, and a snare, when it is divorced from the art of *keeping* that which we are competent to gain." Change, he knew, was a law of all finite things, and man could not hinder it, but it was up to him to give it the right direction. One of the growing trends of the times was a tendency for the social classes to grow apart from each other. He wished more of the old equality of New England society could be preserved. "I love the motto, 'God preserve the *Commonwealth* of Massachusetts,'" he said. "I would have it make progress in refinement and beauty, as well as in wealth, continually putting *more and more in Common.* We too much ape the customs of the Old World. . . . There would be more artists, if there was more demand for them."

He was probably thinking of Allston when he spoke of the problems confronting the artist. Allston had returned from Europe eight years ago with great visions in mind and the desire to complete his colossal composition, "Belshazzar's Feast." But money difficulties had forced him to lay aside his masterpiece and to keep body and soul together by painting small canvasses for immediate sale. Finally, in a moment of

weakness or perhaps desperation he allowed a group of Boston gentlemen to buy the "Belshazzar" in advance for ten thousand dollars. It
was a bad bargain and he was stuck with it. He no longer felt the way
he did when the painting was originally conceived, and now he was
forced to paint something for which he had no heart. The result was
that he was beginning to talk about art instead of creating it. His
schoolboy dreams were still little more than dreams—and all because
art went begging in the marketplace.

Some short time later, Elizabeth sat in Federal Street Church and
heard Channing discourse on "Christianity free as Nature." Church,
home, place of business—all were equally sacred, he said. God does not
shut Himself up in tabernacles, and He does not appoint a special
time for His worship. Religion is for all the days in the week; the only
shrine that must be kept sacred and unprofaned is the soul of man.

At another time, however, Elizabeth heard him warn against too restricted cultivation of the soul. He was speaking of the Quakers and
their doctrine of the inner light. Though they called their "light" the
"light of Christ," he claimed they had divested it of the personality of
Christ. Thus it tended to vanish into an abstraction. "The Quaker is
wrong," he said, "in neglecting the revelation made through Nature to
the human reason. He worships God with his heart and might, but not
with his *mind* and banns [*sic*] the spontaneity of the intellect in *art*
as ruthlessly as the carnal appetites." His explanation for the Quakers'
limited vision was that "they suffer from the old dogma of the depravity of human nature; they do not reverence the spontaneity of the
intellect and imagination as immediate gifts of God no less than conscience."

Early in the new year Channing was busily at work in the moments
he could steal from his regular duties preparing an essay for the *Christian Examiner* (the old *Disciple* under a new name and a new editor).
He told his congregation that teachers of religion should be exempt
from temporal matters, and he explained why. They no longer have a
ready-made creed that they can dole out week after week, he reminded
them. Instead, they must be prepared to set forth a dynamic system
that will urge the people on to greater endeavor. "Once they had time
for secular business," he said; "now nobler conceptions and higher
views of religion obtain, and seclusion, quiet, leisure, a great never-
ceasing culture of mind is necessary to find in Revelation something
new, to meet the new questions continually asked by the spirit of the
times."

Still he did not believe that the minister should be set apart. He once chided Elizabeth for her "awe of the preacher," and when Jonathan Phillips remonstrated about Channing's being a clergyman during a discussion they were having, he replied, "Yes, I know it; and always remember the disadvantage." When Josiah Quincy's mother told him of her son's joining a militia company, he replied, "Your son, madam, is to be greatly congratulated, for he will now have the satisfaction of seeing men as they really are; and this is an inestimable privilege which has always been denied me. The moment I enter any society, everyone remembers that I am a clergyman, puts off his natural self and begins to act a part. My profession requires me to deal with such men as actually exist, yet I can never see them except in disguise. I am shut out from knowledge which is essential to my work." The "sanctity of persons" was a favorite thesis with him, and he never tired of hammering away at the idea that the individual was always more important than the office he filled.

The first issue of the *Examiner* of 1826 contained Channing's essay on Milton. A number of his fellow citizens were somewhat surprised to see "Parson" Channing in the guise of author, but Elizabeth Peabody was not one of them. Her conversations with Channing had taught her to respect his literary judgment just as much as his religious pronouncements.

Channing himself remained undisturbed about the minor furor caused by his essay and went on with other work. He might talk about being exempt from temporal duties, but he couldn't resist any opportunity to improve Boston or its citizens. Life, he found, was a gift constantly increasing in value. He wrote in his journal: "I have not found it a cup foaming and sparkling at the top, and growing vapid as I have drunk. In truth, I dislike altogether this old-fashioned simile. Life is not a little cup dipped from the stream of time. It is itself a stream; and though at birth it may dance and send forth cheerful murmurs as it does not afterwards, still it is intended to flow as it advances, through more beautiful regions, and to adorn its shores with richer verdure and more abundant harvests." His conviction on this point was due primarily to the continually broadening sphere of activity in which he found himself able to participate.

Sometimes, of course, he had to deny requests upon his time. Matters of lesser import often had to be neglected. Thus he had to refuse Andrews Norton, when Norton asked him to review the works of Mrs. Barbauld, who had recently died. Instead of turning reviewer, he prepared an address for the Wednesday Evening Society, urging its members to consider the practicability of a ministry to the poor. Joseph

Tuckerman, who was still at Chelsea but whose health was growing increasingly worse, heard him and thought that he might be able to engage in such a work. During the summer he talked the matter over with Channing and received his blessing. In November, after his resignation from his pastorate in Chelsea was accepted, Tuckerman came to Boston and began his missionary work under the auspices of the Unitarian Association. Henceforth, Tuckerman the social worker and Channing the sociologist would work together as a team.

Channing resigned as a member of the Harvard Corporation in the spring of '26, but his relations with the College remained cordial. In the fall at the dedication of the new Divinity Hall he delivered a discourse on *The Christian Ministry* in which he reemphasized his belief in free inquiry. Truth, he exclaimed, endures, while error carries with it the seeds of decay. The minister, like the good knight, should be without fear. "Let him make no compromise with evil because followed by a multitude, but, for this very cause, lift up against it a more earnest voice."

Whether he appreciated it or not, he was limning the course of his own future actions. Not long before he had scandalized a casual visitor at Federal Street by his strictures on slavery, and one of his critics already thought him "half mad on the subject." The time was still some years distant when former friends would pass him by on the street without speaking; but when that time came, he would not flinch, because "virtue which flies to the shade when God gives a work to be done in the world . . . is not the virtue of Christianity."

When his protegé Waldo Emerson was approbated to preach on the tenth of October, he was highly pleased. Two years before Waldo had taken "a hebdomadal walk" to him "for the sake of saying I am studying divinity," and he had provided the young "seeker" with some books and a reading list that he might exhaust at his leisure. It was a meager list by comparison with some that Channing usually gave out. Perhaps he thought that Waldo was not up to more serious study.

Following a somewhat irregular preparation, Emerson had entered the infant theological school in Cambridge, where he desultorily began a systematic course of study. Eyestrain had led him to ask for permission to be excused from Andrews Norton's lectures, and he had finally left to teach school. Now he was licensed to preach, even if he was not ordained, and no one but himself really knew how ignorant he was of divinity. Ignorance he could overcome easily, but the doubts in his mind were something again. Only time could tell how he would resolve them.

When Channing dedicated the new Divinity school in the fall of 1826, he had in his audience an attentive listener. Charles Follen, a refugee from European persecution, had arrived in Cambridge only a few months earlier to accept an appointment as a teacher of the German language at Harvard. He had made few friends up to that time, because he knew little English and was kept busy at the University. Channing's sermon helped to relieve much of his disappointment over the paucity of literary men and literary institutions in America. He recognized in the speaker a man who loved liberty as he did and who understood the destiny of free spirits; and he resolved to make his acquaintance at the earliest opportunity. When he came home to the Cabots, where he was boarding, he told Eliza, one of the Cabot daughters, of his wonderful experience; and she promised to introduce him to her pastor at the next meeting of her Sunday School group. She did so, and the two men became fast friends. The triumvirate of Channing, Phillips, and Tuckerman now became a foursome.

Originally, the teachers who assisted Channing in the catechetical work at Federal Street had organized to discuss methods of instruction for the Sunday School. Religious teaching soon yielded to the larger question of general educational methods, and as the group enlarged its purpose, its membership increased. George Ticknor, Jonathan Phillips, Eliza and Susan Cabot were charter members; and Elizabeth Peabody, William Russell, the editor and founder of the *American Journal of Education,* and Follen became regular participants at the end of the organization's first year of existence. When Joseph Tuckerman joined them the following year, the subject of children's training was superseded by the problems of adult education; and the scope of "The Society for Education," as the group was now called, became as broad as the visions of its total membership. Walter and Edward Channing came into the fold; and the range of discussion topics was widened to include the wealth of their practical experience.

The importance of such an organization to Boston and its citizenry can scarcely be overestimated. Ticknor, whose training at Göttingen had left him with an eager interest in renovating the Harvard curriculum; Jonathan Phillips, philanthropist and ardent exponent of self-education and Baconian empiricism; Russell, with his training in Scotch universities and his desire to spread educational ideas through the medium of the printed word; Follen, patriot and teacher, whose training and teaching in German and Swiss universities and contacts with the new philosophers of France and Germany made him an invaluable addition to Harvard and the entire Cambridge community;

Walter Channing, with his clinical training and medical experience among the sick and poor of Boston; Joseph Tuckerman, just beginning to find out what the underside of Boston looked like; Edward Tyrrell, Harvard professor and mentor of the most brilliant scholars of tomorrow; and finally, William Ellery himself, nudger and goader—what a wealth of talent and experience was here represented!

In a few years Boston and the neighboring village of Concord would produce a crop of writers, reformers, and educators destined for greater fame; but what proportion of their success would be owing to the efforts of this group and others derived from it, whose inspiration and stimulation had come originally from the master in Federal Street? Waldo Emerson's answer was as good as any, and he concluded that "we could not then spare a single word he uttered in public, not so much as the reading a lesson in Scripture, or a hymn . . . there was no great public interest, political, literary, or even economical . . . on which he did not leave some printed record of his brave and thoughtful opinion."

CHAPTER THIRTEEN

THE TEST OF TENDENCY

EARLY IN 1827 THE host of books, pamphlets, and articles which had appeared in the wake of the controversy inaugurated in 1815 was supplemented by an anonymous review of a sermon delivered by Channing the previous December at the dedication of the Second Unitarian Church of New York City.

The reviewer, a staunch Calvinist, prefaced his criticisms of Channing's "Unitarian Christianity Most Favorable to Piety" by an illuminating survey of the conflict between the orthodox and the Unitarians. In his opinion it had already moved through two phases and was now entering a third: in the first of these "the weapons of attack and defense . . . were chiefly derived from *Biblical literature*"; in the second "the trial of orthodoxy was transferred to another tribunal, that of philosophy"; finally, the opposing creeds were "brought to another test, that of *tendency*," the main question being "which of the two systems, the Unitarian or the orthodox, is of superior tendency to form an elevated religious character."

This was an important question. In the next decade it would become the focal point of the many discussions resulting from the desertion of such leading figures as Waldo Emerson and Theodore Parker from the ranks of Unitarianism. True, most of the participants in the controversy never seemed to worry whether Unitarians exhibited more actual Christianity in their lives than their Calvinist neighbors, or vice versa. They were so engrossed in the theoretical aspects of their particular system of piety that piety itself was shunted into the background or relegated to the limbo of things unimportant.

Channing's reasons for coming forth to do battle again were neither to indict nor praise individuals but, as he had done in 1815 and again in 1819, to make an explicit statement of what Unitarians believed and then relate those beliefs to practical piety. His New York Sermon was by no means the first to argue the superiority of Unitarianism for man's spiritual welfare. At Sparks's ordination he had unequivocally stated that Calvinism "tends strongly to pervert the moral faculty"; and in his "objections" article printed in the *Christian Disciple* a few months later, he had defended the liberal system against the charge of being "a half-way house to infidelity." He had also emphasized the moral and rational qualities of Unitarianism and its consistency with the great principles of human nature in his sermon at Gannett's ordination.

In his introduction to the New York Address, he stressed the fact that he would "speak only of systems, not of those who embrace them," and then went on to explain why men's opinions do not always determine their characters. "Nothing is more common than to see a doctrine believed without swaying the will," he declared. "Its efficacy depends, not on the assent of the intellect, but on the place which it occupies in the thoughts, on the distinctness and vividness with which it is conceived, on its association with our common ideas, on its frequency of recurrence, and on its command of the attention, without which it has no life. . . . A creed is one thing as written in a book, and another as it exists in the minds of its advocates. In the book, all the doctrines appear in equally strong and legible lines. In the mind, many are faintly traced and seldom recurred to, whilst others are inscribed as with sunbeams, and are the chosen, constant lights of the soul."

Once he had disclaimed any intentions of measuring individual character by opinion, he proceeded with his reasons for contending that Unitarian Christianity was more favorable to piety: it presents to the mind One, and only one, Infinite person, to whom supreme homage is to be paid; it holds forth and preserves inviolate the spirituality of God; it presents a distinct and intelligible object of worship, a being simple and suited to human apprehension; it asserts the absolute and unbounded perfection of God's character; it accords with nature, with the world around and the world within us; it opens the mind to new and ever-enlarging views of God; it assigns to Christ his proper place as the first of the sons of God and teaches that his highest office is to call forth and strengthen piety in the human breast; it meets the wants of sinful man by assuring him of his Creator's mercy; and finally it is a rational religion.

Each of these reasons or arguments was taken up in a separate section of his discourse, and under each heading the Unitarian position was contrasted with that of the Calvinists—always to the latter's disadvantage. The eighth section, which was the most elaborate part of the whole sermon, brought down upon him the most severe criticism. Essentially an attack upon the Anselmic theory of atonement, it charged the orthodox with teaching that "the Creator in order to pardon his own children, had erected a gallows in the centre of the universe and had publicly executed upon it, in room of the offenders, an Infinite Being, the partaker of his own Supreme Divinity." He had warned his hearers beforehand that he might wound the feelings of some, but he could scarcely have anticipated the fierce attack that followed. A critic from his native state voiced the typical orthodox reaction to the "central gallows" image when he exclaimed, "It forces upon our recollection the foul account of the incarnation contained in the celebrated "Age of Reason." Another, the anonymous author already mentioned, saw Channing as a moderate deist and by substituting the word *deists* wherever the word *Unitarians* appeared in Channing's address attempted to prove that there was absolutely no difference between the two.

The Unitarians were of course pleased because Channing had summed up their most cogent arguments in his usual clear and forceful manner. Henry Ware, Jr., who never had anything but superlatives for Channing's eloquence, wrote his customary encomium: "It was altogether and beyond all comparison the greatest oral communication I ever listened to. The man was full of fire, and his body seemed, under some of his tremendous sentiments to expand out into a giant. He rose on his feet, thrust up both arms, and screamed, as one may say, at the top of his voice, and his face, say those who saw it, was, if anything, more meaningful than his words."

The latter part of Ware's description seems more applicable to a revivalist like John Davenport; but Ware evidently was trying to impress his correspondent with the fervor of Channing's address and was probably carried away by his own natural excitability. Certainly Channing himself would have been amazed had he been able to view himself in such a ranting pose; for had he not told the young men at the Divinity School but a short time before that "we would not train here, if we could, agents of terror, to shake weak nerves"?

Andrews Norton reviewed the sermon for the *Examiner* and found its claims virtually unassailable. "There will be, we think, no attempt to answer it, except, perhaps, by some one incapable of estimating, either his own powers, or the *force* of argument." But there were a number of the orthodox who either did not see this warning or else did not heed the advice, because the years following Channing's summation of the Unitarian position were filled with the clamor of rival voices.

Lyman Beecher, father of Harriet Beecher Stowe and a renowned laborer in the orthodox cause, had been called to the pastorate of the Hanover Street Church in 1826; and he made his presence quickly felt.

LYMAN
BEECHER

By setting up evening meetings and similar inducements to the religious-minded, he began to attract sheep from the Unitarian fold and to disprove at least in Boston Channing's contention that the orthodox system was not conducive to piety. Sermon after sermon was preached and pamphlet after pamphlet written to emphasize the "negative" qualities of Unitarianism and its fatal "tendency" toward infidelity.

Jeremiah Evarts, former editor of the *Panoplist* and Jedidiah Morse's right-hand man in the first stages of the Unitarian controversy, carried on the spirit of his now-departed friend by starting a new magazine, *Spirit of the Pilgrims.* In a very short time, he proved that his spirit was more like that of a John Cotton than a Roger Williams.

Following his appearance in New York, Channing returned to his duties in Boston and was carrying on as usual, when his strength suddenly gave way. It was still early spring; but his brother Walter told him that he must give up his work. Despite Channing's remonstrances Walter was adamant and bundled him off to Oakland. When summer came he was nearly restored to health. Dr. Follen, who had decided to prepare for the Unitarian ministry, joined Channing in Newport, and they spent most of the summer going over the texts that Follen should know and discussing the immortality of man's moral nature. Late in the summer, Channing left Oakland on a trip to Niagara Falls. He had never been there, and he was anxious to corroborate by personal observation the glowing reports he had received from friends and visitors from abroad.

Travelling through the small communities of central New York, he passed in the wake of the great Charles G. Finney, one of the leading revivalists of the day, and everywhere it seemed to him "as if a hurricane had passed." The moral effect of such preaching he thought very enervating, and it took the wonders of the Falls to restore his usual equanimity. Before he reached his objective, however, he was persuaded by Myron Holley, a free-thinker of the town of Lyons, New York, to stay over Sunday and preach for him in a public hall. He spoke on Self-Denial, and the calmness of his manner and his lesson of moderation were obviously intended to show how little he appreciated the "storming" of men's souls by emotional outbursts.

Niagara proved far more beautiful and exciting than Channing had ever dreamed. He agreed with Catherine Sedgwick that "justice has never been done to its beauty," and he wrote that "a visit to this spot is an era in one's life." It took him back in memory to Terni and Velino, which he had visited when he was in Italy; and he was reminded of Byron's description of the "hell of waters." The phrase, he decided, was no more appropriate for Niagara than it had been for the beautiful Italian waterfalls.

Back at Oakland in August, he corresponded with Andrews Norton about tackling the job of reviewing Walter Scott's *Napoleon*. He was willing to undertake the task but only on condition that he would find in the book "sufficient materials to form a fair judgment." He believed a just estimate of Napoleon was needed and he feared Scott would not do the job faithfully. By September he had part of the job completed, and the remainder was finished in November. The *Examiner* carried one of his articles in the fall issue, and the second appeared early the following spring. This time Bostonians took his authorship in stride, for they had learned to expect almost anything from Dr. Channing.

Although the burden of "half-health" was particularly oppressive during the winter, spring found him in a cheerful mood. He was human, and there were times when he desired to be released from his infirmity; but it wasn't often that he indulged in self-pity. As he wrote Follen, "true courage fights the enemy *within* as well as abroad."

No better example of his expansive mood could be found than the ordination sermon which he preached that spring for the Reverend Mellish Motte. His topic was "The Great Purpose of Christianity," a favorite subject with him; and he gave it his characteristically idealistic treatment.

The glory of Christianity, he explained, was "the pure and lofty action which it communicates to the human mind. . . . The highest existence in the universe is Mind; for God is mind; and the development of that principle which assimilates us to God, must be our supreme good."

He went on to urge his listeners to cultivate a true freedom of mind and gave them his own philosophy of man thinking. "I desire," he said, "to escape the narrow walls of a particular church, and to live under the open sky, in the broad light, looking far and wide, seeing with my own eyes, hearing with my own ears, and following truth meekly but resolutely, however arduous or solitary be the path in which she leads." He had many other things to say about man and his role in the universe, but they could all be summed up in this doctrine of self-reliance. The kingdom of Christ, he said, was in the human soul, and man must look for his blessings within himself and not from abroad. He could not make man's inheritance any clearer.

Such emphasis on human agency was not likely to earn the approval of the more orthodox members of the Boston community. Evarts belittled the whole performance, asserting that Channing made Christ a mere reformer and concluding that his sermon was not "calculated to produce any great effect, one way or the other." But the response to the Motte Sermon was as an idle whisper compared to the strident chorus that greeted Channing's discourse in the fall at the ordination of Frederick Farley.

His health was so bad when Farley extended the invitation to come to Providence that he agreed to accept only if Farley were prepared with a substitute. His strength held up, however; and he obliged his Rhode Island friends with one of his most noble utterances. He had a theory that physical illness brought him "a singular clearness and brightness of mind"; and his sermon on man's "Likeness to God" would seem to be proof of it, for he never gave a more lofty or transcendental address.

"The idea of God, sublime and awful as it is," he declared, "is the idea of our own spiritual nature, purified and enlarged to infinity. . . . God is another name for human intelligence raised above all error and imperfection, and extended to all possible truth. . . . We see God around us, because he dwells within us."

These were exalted views of humanity, he knew, and he had never before stated them so explicitly; but he rested his case on the intuitions that he derived from his own soul: "I do and I must reverence human nature. Neither the sneers of a worldly skepticism, nor the groans of a gloomy theology, disturb my faith in its god-like powers and tendencies. I know how it is despised, how it has been oppressed, how civil and religious establishments have for ages conspired to crush it. . . . But, injured, trampled on and scorned as our nature is, I still turn to it with intense sympathy and strong hope. The signature of its origin and its end are impressed too deeply to be ever wholly effaced."

If the originality of Channing's view of man's likeness to God is to be fully appreciated, it must be contrasted with the position taken by orthodox Christianity down through the ages. For centuries, theologians had maintained that the human intellect was incapable of knowing the essence of an infinite God. That human reason could arrive at proof of God's existence was an entirely different matter: it was readily conceded in Christian circles that man could know that God *is*. But that he could determine *what* God is was denied by Protestant and Roman Catholic theologians alike.

Despite such denial many attempts had been made to chart the divine nature, and one of the most frequently used methods was that of analogy. But analogical reasoning of any sort implies that the subjects under comparison have differences as well as something in com-

mon: that there is dissimilarity as well as similarity between the
analogues. Hence, analogical argument had always resulted in the conclusion that man is essentially different from God.

But Channing had already rejected the analogical method of determining the God-man equation. In *The Moral Argument against
Calvinism* eight years previously he had declared his belief in the doctrine of "essential sameness." Now he was concerned to make absolutely clear that he had not been indulging in a mere figure of speech.
"God does not sustain a figurative resemblance to man," he declared.
"It is the resemblance of a parent to a child, the likeness of a kindred
nature." Gone completely from his theology was the idea of God's
sovereignty. The fatherhood of God and the sonship of man now constituted for him a divine relationship.

To some of the orthodox such preaching was blasphemy. A reviewer
for Evarts's *Pilgrim* would not say that Channing was an out-and-out
pantheist; but he did declare that his language, if it were not poetry,
was close to that of pantheism and universalism, too, for that matter.
If this was a true sample of Unitarian thinking, then the orthodox had
complete proof that their "liberal" brethren had become so emancipated from right views of religion that there was no longer any reason
to consider them Christians. When the revelation of God was become
secondary to the revelation of man, then there were no further depths
into which Unitarianism could sink. The end had come, and the orthodox would say, in all sincerity and with a spirit of Charity, "I told
you so."

However, Channing had said that he was not disturbed by "the
groans of a gloomy theology," and he wasn't. As long as Unitarianism
could enlist men like Charles Follen in its cause (Follen had been admitted to the Suffolk Association of ministers on July 28), he was not
fearful of its power to do good. His opponents might exclaim about
"the uncertainty and skepticism exhaled from the fogs and mists of
Germany"; but as far as he was concerned, he wanted to know more
about the German mind. Follen had shown him recently a review of
German philosophy in the *Edinburgh Review,* which had so impressed
him that he resolved to study German.

Channing was also reading George Combe's *The Constitution of
Man* but was finding the phrenological aspects of that volume little to
his liking, because, as he said, "I have a strong aversion to theories
which subject the mind to the body." The scientific theories of the volume, however, intrigued him. Physical science was high in his scale of
value, and he lamented the fact that he could not keep pace with the

discoveries of the age. "The universe," he wrote, "is a divine volume, and I wish that I could look on it with a more intelligent eye."

Channing recognized that there were avenues for knowledge denied to the minister but open to the layman; and he wondered "What would be the result of a superior man, not of the clergy, giving a course of lectures on the *teaching of Jesus*, just as he would give one on the philosophy of Socrates or Plato?" Christianity, he felt, was too often considered the exclusive property of religious teachers; perhaps that was why the majority of people were so callous towards evils like slavery. He was watching the efforts of the English to relieve themselves of this evil; and he wrote Jane Roscoe, daughter of the noted English historian and reformer, that the great wrong of slavery was not the physical harm it caused but the destruction it wreaked upon the intellectual and moral being of its victims.

In March, 1829, his *Remarks on the Character and Writings of Fenelon* appeared in the *Examiner*. Its immediate inspiration was a volume of selections from the writings of the French author which had recently been published in Boston, but Channing's thoughts about the saintly Archbishop of Cambrai went back at least as far as his college years at Harvard, and he wrote about him as though he were an old and intimate friend. Although he could not agree completely with the quietism of the French writer, he admired him as an exponent of the transcendent qualities of the human mind and paid tribute to his tolerance.

Shortly after his article had appeared, he wrote Joanna Baillie, thanking her for her interest in his writings but explaining his own lack of regard for them. "Whilst I have the deepest conviction of the truth and greatness of my leading views," he told her, "and look to them as powerful means of quickening and elevating the human mind, I am so dissatisfied with my expression of them, that I sometimes hesitate about sending my writings to my friends, after they have gone through the press." His comment was characteristic; for while he was intrepid in speaking his mind, he never felt that he had quite done justice to the great themes that filled it.

Always on the lookout for "moral genius," he was aroused by Joseph Tuckerman's praises of the benevolence of a newcomer to Boston and by Elizabeth Peabody's glowing reports of the stranger's prowess as a preacher. With Elizabeth as guide he went one Sunday morning, when the church was not crowded and the air was better, to hear Father Taylor, that nonpareil of sailor-divines. Taylor had come to Boston with instructions from his superiors in the Methodist Episcopal Church to set up a seamen's bethel, and his success in transforming the "whiskered, shaggy, untrim tarpaulins" of the Harbor into "sons of light and hope" had been immediate.

After listening to the sermon, Channing went up to the altar to receive communion. The husky preacher, who knew of him through his sermons and from the accounts of Tuckerman, Elizabeth Peabody, and others, addressed him as "father." Later he visited Channing's home with the Peabody sisters and after his visit remarked to them, "What a beautiful being Dr. Channing is! If he only had an education!"

When Channing received the comment afterwards from his never-failing informant Elizabeth, he replied seriously, "Yes, he is right. What I have needed is an education for my work. . . . He has had infinitely the advantage of me in his nearer approach to all classes of men and free range of Nature. . . . And this is the reason he is so effective a power, reaching from the zenith to the nadir of society; for *all* seem to open their hearts to him."

If there was a note of wistfulness in his voice, it was only because he was remembering his own early dreams of living *among* the people as one of them. The foolishness of his youthful disregard for his physical welfare came back to him, as it always did when he was reminded of the limitations of poor health, but there was no undoing it now. He could simply continue to hope that he was doing good in the only way that was left to him—by acting on the minds of others.

On Election Day the following May while Waldo Emerson, chaplain of the State Senate, sat comfortably in the pulpit, Channing spoke on the subject of Spiritual Freedom. Emerson thought it a truly noble discourse. Along with the preface to his first volume of sermons and articles, it was Channing's last great affront to New England orthodoxy. He began by asserting that spiritual liberty is the supreme good of men, and he followed up this remark by gainsaying those who argued that "practical truth . . . consists in knowing that we have an animal nature, and in making this our chief care. . . ." By spiritual freedom he meant "moral energy or force of holy purpose put forth against the senses, against the passions, against the world . . . thus liberating the intellect, conscience, and will" to act with greatest force and efficiency.

Not content with this general definition, he proceeded to expand it by a series of more specific explanations each beginning, "I call that mind free." It was a splendid enumeration that he gave his listeners, and the chaplain was impressed by the note of self-reliance that rang from every word. How could he fail to be? For he heard the speaker declare, "I call that mind free, which jealously guards its intellectual rights and powers, which calls no man master, which does not content itself with a passive or hereditary faith, which opens itself to light whencesoever it may come, which receives new truth as an angel from heaven, which, whilst consulting others, inquires still more of the oracle within itself, and uses instruction from abroad, not to supersede but to exalt and quicken its own energies."

Channing's method of developing his subject was to show that civil or political liberty is dependent upon and springs from spiritual freedom. Civil liberty, he declared, consists in the removal of all restraint except that demanded by the public welfare. The highest end of government is the freedom or moral strength of the individual mind: the individual is not made for the state, but the state for the individual.

"A man is not created for political relations as his highest end, but for indefinite spiritual progress, and is placed in political relations as the means of his progress. The human soul is greater, more sacred, than the state, and must never be sacrificed to it."

Religion and government, therefore, become the proper means by which the mind of man is to be freed and elevated. Of the two, religion is by far the more important, because it alone is equal to the task of freeing man from the domination of matter, to recall him from the outward to the inward world. In a civilization that is becoming increasingly materialistic in outlook, and in which the mind is more and more confined by the petty operation of a mechanized, industrial system, there is great danger that there will be "improved fabrics but deteriorated men." Religion must work to prevent such an eventuality.

On the other hand, the sense of justice in a community depends upon government more than on any other institution. But people must be careful not to put an idolatrous trust in free institutions. They need to learn that "the forms of liberty are not its essence; that, whilst the letter of a free constitution is preserved, its spirit may be lost; that even its wisest provisions and most guarded powers may be made weapons of tyranny. In a country called free, a majority may become a faction and a proscribed minority may be insulted, robbed, oppressed. Under elective governments, a dominant party may become as truly a usurper, and as treasonably conspire against the state as an individual who forces his way by arms to the throne."

If Channing had ever believed in an ideal form of government, as he claimed during the days that he was dreaming of world revolution in Richmond, he was by this time completely cured: "Free institutions secure rights, only when secured by and when invigorated by that spir-

itual freedom, that moral power and elevation, which . . . [is] the supreme good of our nature." Like De Tocqueville after him, he saw
that even in a democracy "the power of opinion grows into a despotism which more than all things represses original and free thoughts,
subverts individuality of character, reduces the community to be a
spiritless monotony and chills the love of perfection."

And this despotic power of opinion was most evident in religious
sects whose purpose was not to free man from custom and tradition
but to usurp his God-given prerogatives and refer him to some man-
made tribunal. In the past men had suffered from the outward evils of
religious persecution. That was bad enough. Today a far more griev-
ous harm is wrought by sects that attempt to enslave the mind and
destroy its powers for self-improvement.

"We say we have no Inquisition," he declared. "But a sect skillfully
organized, trained to utter one cry, combined to cover with reproach
whoever may differ from themselves, to drown the free expression of
opinion by denunciations of heresy, and to strike terror into the community by joint and perpetual menace,—such a sect is as perilous and
palsying to the intellect as the Inquisition. It serves its ministers as
effectually as the sword."

This application to the state of religion in and about Boston together with certain remarks contained in the preface to his *Discourses,
Reviews, and Miscellanies,* which had just been published, quickly
brought counter-charges. Moses Stuart, who had engaged in combat
with Andrews Norton after the Baltimore Sermon, brought forth a
pamphlet of fifty-two pages in which he categorically denied Channing's accusations. Professing to be deeply hurt by the injustice of
Channing's allegations, Stuart claimed that the only crime of his orthodox brethren had been to propagate their sincere views, to defend
them when attacked, and to expose the errors of those by whom they
were assailed. He did not approve of everything that every member of
the orthodox persuasion had said, but he knew of nothing that could
compare with the reiterated charges of bigotry and superstition that
the Unitarians were constantly levelling against them.

Stuart's letter was written in an earnest and sincere tone and
breathed an air of outraged innocence. Channing did not reply. In his
preface to the *Discourses* he had given a clear account of his reasons
for first entering into controversy together with an explanation of the
spirit in which he had always tried to conduct himself. If his opponents wanted to know where he stood, they could easily find an answer
there.

But while he was silent, the Reverend Bernard Whitman spoke out in his place with a series of letters indicting the orthodox for establishing ecclesiastical tribunals and working hardships on individual congregations. The *Spirit of the Pilgrims* retaliated, noting Whitman's "ignorance," "misrepresentations," and "inconsistencies." The Reverend George Cheever of the Harvard Street Church in Salem joined his voice to the orthodox chorus and reiterated the old charge of infidelity. "The fire of unbelief has been the ruling spirit in your system," he wrote in an article addressed to the editors of the *Christian Examiner* through the columns of the *Spirit of the Pilgrims*. "It is a system, as shifting as the sands, having no stability, no permanent creed, no grounds of certainty, nothing fixed but a mortal aversion to the evangelical scheme." He went on to enumerate the doctrines that the Unitarians had already abandoned: human depravity, the atonement, the existence of Satan, the eternal punishment; and concluded that there was not much more that they could throw aside.

Cheever's article was the last of any note before the controversy virtually ceased; and with its publication, the *Spirit of the Pilgrims* ended its short but stormy career. When church and state were disestablished the following year, the main reason for the orthodox charge of persecution was removed; and they directed their attention to other problems. "We are a community by ourselves," declared Henry Ware in 1835; and things would have remained that way, had not Waldo Emerson and Theodore Parker embarrassed Ware and his party by advocating doctrines that the Calvinists had all along predicted.

There would be further talk of infidelity, but the charge against its "latest form" would come from a Unitarian, and not an orthodox leader.

CHAPTER FOURTEEN

MAN OF LETTERS

ACCORDING TO ORVILLE DEWEY, who had abundant opportunity for observation during the last twenty years of Channing's career, preaching was "the *great* action" of his life and conversation, "the ordinary action." As far as the man of letters is concerned, Dewey does not give even an "honorable mention."

Certainly Channing never considered himself to be primarily a writer, for he wrote candidly to Joanna Baillie, "I have been an author by accident, not by profession or of set purpose"; and he was continually deprecating the efforts of friends and correspondents to play up his literary accomplishments. To be sure, the truths in his writings were "infinitely important," but he was ever conscious "of having done no justice to them."

Regardless of what he might think of his own value as a writer, he had definite opinions about other writers and about literature in general. Beginning with his years at Harvard and the months of strenuous study at Richmond, he had cultivated a taste for literature that was more catholic than scholarly, ethical rather than intellectual. Books regarded merely as gratification he considered "worth more than all the luxuries on earth"; but their primary usefulness was not, as he viewed it, for pleasure, but to help and interpret what he saw and experienced. "The grand volumes, of which all our books are transcripts . . . nature, revelation, the human soul, and human life, are," he said, "freely unfolded to every eye. . . . To open and fix our eyes upon what passes without and within us, is the most fruitful study."

Shakespeare and Milton were the first giants to appear on his literary horizon; and when he reached maturity, their lengthening shadows were blended in with the clearer silhouettes of more contemporary writers like Wordsworth, Coleridge, and Carlyle. In his serious reading he concentrated upon authors who exalted man's moral and intellectual powers and relegated to positions of secondary importance those who seemed content to deal with man as he was and with the actual conditions in which he lived. Thus among the older English writers, he ranked Milton in the order of "seraphs," while Dr. Johnson was, by comparison, an earth-bound spirit.

Among his contemporaries, he gave the place of poetic eminence to Wordsworth, who taught reverence for man's universal nature by breaking down "the factitious barriers between human hearts." Coleridge was Wordsworth's compeer by virtue of his philosophic insights. Byron, however, had given up all claim to greatness by reaching low for fame and had given clearer demonstration of his scope of intellect in his letters than in his poems. Shelley was "a seraph gone astray, who needed friends that he never found in this world."

Like his idol Milton, Channing believed that "he who would not be frustrate of his hope to write well hereafter in laudable things, ought himself to be a true poem." He filled his library, therefore, with only the best authors (*morally* best), so that he might build up a reverence for virtue that would strengthen him in his battle against the forces holding back human perfection. And like Milton again, he wanted to write a work that would "justify the ways of God to man" or—to put it more properly—demonstrate to man his potentialities.

Apparently the idea for such a work had come to Channing early in his career as a minister, but no mention of it occurred until after his return from England. From then on, scattered references to it, increasing in the frequency of their appearance as his life drew to a close, cropped up in his private papers and in his correspondence to friends at home and abroad. Apparently, it was to have borne the title of *The Principles of Moral, Religious, and Political Science;* and its purpose, as outlined in a rough draft, was to examine man's nature "so as to determine its central law, and the end for which all religious and political institutions should be established."

"All our inquiries in morals, religion, and politics must begin with human nature," he wrote. "It is the want of a true science of our nature, that has vitiated all past systems of government, morals, and religion. . . . Just views of human nature are, then, all-important. In comprehending man, we comprehend God, Duty, Life, Death, Providence; we have the key to the Divine administration of the world."

To accomplish his lofty purpose, Channing had planned a work consisting of three parts: the first to deal with man; the second with God; and the third with the duties resulting from man's relationship to God. Eight chapters only of the first part were composed—a rather pitiful fragment of accomplishment to represent the plans and aspirations of nearly an entire lifetime. Even at that, they are only outlines, first sketches: and they lack the clarity and careful ordering

so characteristic of Channing. Various threads of influence, some of
them inconsistent with others, are discernible; and there is evidence
that no pattern had ever been established to explain all of the material collected.

The general background of the fragment is eighteenth-century. It
begins in true Lockean fashion with a discussion of sensation; but it
does not follow the Lockean lead very far, nor that of the Scotch
School, which came after Locke. Sensations are described as "occasions" rather than "causes" of intellectual activity, and the mind is
cited as furnishing the universe from its own store instead of deriving
its riches from it.

The idealism of the piece is incontestable, but Channing's eclectic
method makes identification of the specific sources of the ideas in it
virtually impossible. He had drawn from Plato and Price, Wordsworth
and Coleridge, Cousin and Jouffroy, Kant and Carlyle; but a fundamental lack of critical acumen had prevented the welding of his materials into a coherent system. Not having been gifted with the mind
of an Edwards or a Hume, he was just as incapable of erecting a logical
edifice like the *Freedom of the Will* or the *Treatise of Human Nature*
as he was of arguing in behalf of human depravity and a blood atonement. A man of a few great ideas, it was his talent, not to devise systems of logic, but to drive home these ideas—through the dense barriers of stale custom and habit, and in spite of human inertia—by the
force of his example and by constant reiteration in conversation, sermon, and pamphlet.

Naturally, Channing was disappointed not to be able to do more
with his *magnum opus;* but he was accustomed to temporizing with
circumstances and comforted himself with the thought that he was
fortunate to have accomplished anything at all. He counted the time
devoted to the work well spent, because he could remember how this
sermon had been enriched and that discourse benefited by his study.
Besides, he had done a great deal more writing on account of it than
he would otherwise have done. Writing, he believed, was one of the
great means of giving precision, clearness, consistency and energy to
thought; and he had for a long time attempted to sharpen his powers
of concentration by increasing his efforts in composition.

"One of the great laws of our nature, and a law singularly important
to social beings," Channing said, "is, that the intellect enlarges and
strengthens itself by expressing worthily its best views. . . . Superior
minds are formed, not merely by solitary thought, but almost as much

by communication." Great thoughts, therefore, could never fully be possessed until they had been uttered.

In his emphasis upon clarity and precision in particular and upon the power of written communication in general to improve the mind, Channing was simply following in the steps of those eighteenth-century arbiters of taste, Lord Kames and Hugh Blair, both of whom he had carefully studied at Harvard and whom his brother, Edward Tyrell, was then teaching to Harvard undergraduates, along with Archibald Alison and Thomas Brown of the Scotch School. Moreover, when he declared that "the laborious distribution of a great subject, so as to assign to each part or topic its just position and due proportion, is singularly fitted to give compass and persevering force of thought," he was not only following the pattern of discourse established in New England by the early Puritan ministers, but also proving himself a good disciple of Addison by using the standard idiom of neo-classic decorum. Aesthetically, he looked both backward and forward, acknowledging as late as 1837 his humility before "the spontaneous graces" of Addison and Goldsmith, yet writing almost simultaneously in his projected treatise that beauty was in the mind and not in the objects perceived by the mind.

Up to the very close of his writing career, therefore, he was a typical exponent of eighteenth-century methods of writing as well as of the more mechanical and technical aspects of that century's rules on style. Perspicuity, force, and precision are spelled out in his many sermons and in his several critical articles, and his purism in language is demonstrated by the avidity with which he seized upon neologisms in the letters of his correspondents.

To the larger and less cut-and-dried features of style he devoted much attention; and he seldom neglected, especially in his ordination sermons, to emphasize the importance of developing a personal style in both written and spoken communication. It was, he believed, the primary factor in determining the creative power of a writer; and it depended very little upon the structure of sentences and size of vocabulary, but chiefly upon the mind of the person writing.

Thus he was asserting the power of the mind (or soul) to invigorate art and, by so doing, was putting aside the cold and mechanical standards of Kames and Blair for the warm and organic principles of the romantics. He was still a "judicious" critic of literature; but his moralism was rather the dynamic doctrine of Wordsworth and Coleridge than the negative didacticism of Addison and Steele. Insofar as he emphasized the spiritual relationship between man and nature, he was giving expression to the idealism of his age in much the same way as the English romantics were doing.

It was this dualism in attitude that accounted for the varying estimates of his work both at home and abroad. Philosophically akin to Wordsworth, Coleridge, and Carlyle, he was also accepted by the English quarterly reviewers as one of themselves. During the period between his return from England and the seven or eight eulogistic years following his death, he occupied in the estimation of his English critics a position only below that of Washington Irving and James Fenimore Cooper. This opinion aroused some criticism in America, not because of Channing's eminence, but because writers like William Cullen Bryant and Fitz-Greene Halleck had not been included among those worthy of English notice.

In general, his reputation at home ranged from the somewhat conservative judgments of Emerson to the enthusiastic encomiums of some of his parishioners. Even during the years when his name was an abomination in the ears of Southern slaveholders, the same lips that excoriated him for meddling in affairs that were none of his business paid tribute to his skill as an author.

There were several good reasons for his recognition by English as well as American critics, nor were they owing, in any great measure, to his reputation as a leading Unitarian apologist. His critical essays on Milton and Napoleon were the first specimens in America of the kind of judicial criticism that had made the *Edinburgh Review* famous, and his remarks on *The Importance and Means of a National Literature* anticipated by seven years the independence of mind proclaimed by Emerson in *The American Scholar*.

Far from being restricted to the exposition of controversial religious dogma, Channing's writing, as Emerson realized, was "almost a history of the times." And his religious idealism, which may seem outmoded to a generation of Americans emancipated from the tradition of moral strenuousness that he had inherited, was just what the more enlightened people of his age wanted to hear. Vice, poverty, and crime, he told them, were strange habiliments for the sons of God, and the words sounded very convincing when he uttered them. Self-culture seemed a natural program to men who had grown up in the expansive years following the revolutionary successes in America and France, and there was no more forceful or convincing expositor of the doctrine than he in the America of the twenties and thirties.

For his English readers and his American audience as well, he provided a link between Coleridge on the one hand, and Carlyle and

Ruskin on the other. The spirituality of the former found frequent echo in his journal and public utterances, while the doctrine of heroism that Carlyle later elaborated was illustrated in his articles on Milton, Napoleon, and Fénelon. Finally, the conception of the dignity of manual labor, which was to be strongly emphasized in the lectures of Carlyle, Ruskin, and William Morris, found full and adequate expression, a generation earlier, in his lecture on *Self-Culture, The Elevation of the Laboring Classes,* and *The Present Age.*

Up to the time of his visits to London, Bristol, Southampton, and other metropolitan centers of England in 1823, his reputation as a Unitarian leader had not penetrated very far into the British Isles. At home he was known only by his several articles on the Unitarian controversy and by a few sermons, the most important of which was the address at Sparks's ordination. After his return to America, however, his tracts and sermons were reprinted with great regularity in Liverpool, Manchester, Bristol, Glasgow, and London, and received frequent notice in the religious journals.

When his *Remarks on the Character and Writings of John Milton* was published in London in 1826, not much notice was taken of it until it ran into a second edition in the year of the pamphlet republication of his *Analysis of the Life and Character of Napoleon Bonaparte* (1828). By the time his article on Fénelon appeared the following year, his literary reputation was ready to keep pace in both America and London with his theological; and the reprinting in England of *The Importance and Means of a National Literature* was a matter of course. From 1830 until his death, his works were issued practically simultaneously on both sides of the Atlantic.

The London *Monthly Magazine* was the first to acknowledge the worth of the critical essays on Milton and Napoleon and found little to criticize in them except the strictures on Dr. Johnson in the *Milton.* *The Westminster Review* thought the Bonaparte article excellent, exclaiming that "Dr. Channing was the first man, whose bold and mighty breathings dissipated the delusive mist of fame which hung round the brow of Napoleon."

One man, however, disagreed sharply with this opinion. This was William Hazlitt—testy and bitter—for whom Waterloo had been a tragedy. The first two volumes of his *Life of Napoleon Bonaparte* appeared in the year of the *Westminster* article, and there were still two volumes to come. Scott's *Life of Napoleon* had anticipated his by a year, which fact was not calculated to improve his good nature, and now there was Channing's essay, which unsparingly attacked one of

Hazlitt's idols. Add to all this the fact that Channing had several times gone on record as being opposed to the English brand of Unitarianism of which Hazlitt's father had been one of the leaders, and it is easy to see why Hazlitt's usually tart pen was dipped in gall when he criticized the American writer.

After Channing's first essay on Napoleon had been reprinted in London at least four times and his second at least twice, Hazlitt wrote a "Review of *Sermons and Tracts,* by W. E. Channing" for the *Edinburgh Review,* in which he prefaced his criticism of Channing by some general remarks on American literature. "Of the later American writers, who besides Dr. Channing have acquired some reputation in English," says Hazlitt, "we can only recollect Mr. Washington Irving, Mr. Brown and Mr. Cooper." After giving grudging praise to Irving, he proceeded with increasing severity of criticism down the scale of writers, until he reached Channing and his *Napoleon:*

> Dr. Channing is a great tactitian in reasoning; and reasoning has nothing to do with tactics. We do not like to see a writer constantly trying to steal a march upon opinion without having his retreat cut off—full of pretensions, and void of offense. . . . He keeps an eye on both worlds; kisses hands to the reading public all round; and does his best to stand well with different sects and parties. . . . We like Dr. Channing's Sermons best; his Criticism less; his politics least of all. We think several of his discourses do great honour to himself and his profession. . . . His notice of Milton is elaborate and stately, but neither new nor discriminating. . . . This is the general feature of our author's writings; they cannot be called mere commonplace. . . . Dr. Channing's Essays on Milton and Bonaparte are both done upon the same false principle, of making out a case *for* or *against.* The one is full of commonplace eulogy, the other commonplace invective. They are pulpit criticisms.

Regardless of how involved emotionally he might become in the subject he was discussing, Hazlitt always managed to sow some wheat among the cockle of his criticisms. Thus, while he was grossly unfair in challenging Channing's intellectual morality—more to vent his spleen than for any other purpose, one imagines—he was more than three-quarters right in calling Channing's essays, "pulpit utterances," and in singling out the ethical obsession that led Channing to exalt Milton and belittle Napoleon.

The criticism that Channing never left the pulpit was just. Although he was sometimes painfully conscious of the degree to which he had immersed himself in his profession, he was seldom able to relieve the seriousness of his manner. In his letters and conversation he slid easily into the sermon tone, and so it was with his articles for the *Examiner.*

The best part of his essay on Fénelon reproduced his sermon on self-denial, the theme in both being that man should respect his reason and subordinate his passions to its rule. The second article on Napoleon read like a sermon on the temptations to the abuse of power, while the first swelled with passages that sounded as if they had been written for a Sunday audience in Federal Street. Without question, he was most at home in the sermon; and his writing took its form, because, in the author's mind, it was heard rather than read from the printed page.

However sincere Hazlitt might have been in regarding the Milton article as neither "new nor discriminating," he did scant justice to the new philosophical and religious concepts underlying Channing's criticism; for in addition to avowing the essential ideality of poetry, the latter had set forth, in his description of the "serious poet," a definition of abstract greatness (in terms of intellectual and moral superiority) that accorded with the most progressive tendencies of the age.

"Milton's fame," he said, "rests chiefly on his poetry. . . . Of all God's gifts of intellect, he esteemed poetical genius the most transcendent. He esteemed it in himself as a kind of inspiration, and wrote his great works with something of the conscious dignity of a prophet. We agree with Milton in his estimate of poetry. It seems to us the divinest of all arts." Thus, when he came to the end of his essay he used Milton as an example of the ideal "hero," although that word did not appear in his text:

> We believe that the sublime intelligence of Milton was imparted, not for his own sake only, but to awaken kindred virtue and greatness in other souls. Far from regarding him as standing alone and unapproachable, we believe that he is an illustration of what all, who are true to their nature, will become in the progress of their being; and we have held him forth, not to exile an ineffectual admiration but to stir up our own and others' breasts to an exhilarating pursuit of high and ever-growing attainments in intellect and virtues.

Using the same moral yardstick that he had used to judge Milton, he scrutinized Napoleon's character and the means by which he had risen to power and found him lacking in the moral stamina that means true greatness. "But some will say," he declared, "he was . . . a great man. This we mean not to deny. But we would have it understood, that there are various kinds of orders of greatness, and that the highest did not belong to Bonaparte." Then followed a classification which was to echo through the social criticism of the century. First came *moral* greatness, or magnanimity; second, *intellectual* greatness, or genius; and third, the greatness of *action,* or the power of "conceiving bold and expansive plans." To this final order belonged the greatness of Napoleon.

It was really Channing's "egotism" rather than his classification of greatness that bothered Hazlitt. "Dr. Channing," he said, "very gravely divides greatness into different sorts, and places himself at the top among those who *talk* about things—commanders at the bottom among those who only *do* them." It was the inevitable rejoinder addressed to those who would *teach* mankind, and it betrayed the usual ignorance of the behind-the-scenes action involved in the didactic function.

After this baptism of fire, Channing's position among American writers worthy of recognition in England was undisputed. The *Westminster* continued to be his loyal friend, reviewing in 1830 his essays on Fénelon and *Associations,* together with the *Sermons and Tracts,* which Hazlitt scorned. "We consider Dr. Channing as an incarnation of the intellectual spirit of Christianity," its reviewer wrote. "He is the tenth Avatar of the principle of reformation; and come to complete the work. . . . America has a right to be proud of Channing; and shame would it be for the criticism of England were he to be dismissed with affected contempt."

"You do not tell me what the French say about the American Channing," commented "The Lounger" in the *New Monthly Magazine.* "I am anxious to know. His works are reviewed in the proper spirit of reviewing in the last *Westminster.* It is high time that we English are willing to be the first to echo an American's praise. The fact is that when the Americans read our periodicals they suppose us hostile to them—no such thing." The writer was apparently unaware that Hazlitt had written the hypercritical article in the *Edinburgh,* for he went on to say, "The Scotch write our periodicals and it is the Scotch (the last nation in the world to do justice to a new people) who abuse them."

With the essay on *National Literature* in 1830, Channing's literary reputation in England reached its culmination. The *Athenaeum,* which had lumped him in with Irving and Cooper as an imitator of his English betters a short time before, now described him as "decidedly a man of high literary attainments, of a refined taste, a discriminating judgment, with an acute, vigorous, and comprehensive mind," but objected to his style as "frequently diffuse and elaborately redundant."

Five years later, in an article entitled "Literature of the Nineteenth Century, America," which was seemingly an answer to Sydney Smith's question (reworded slightly to "Who reads an American book in America?"), an American writer for this same periodical gave credit to the English for introducing Channing to the republic of letters. "Even the great Channing," he said, "though always revered for his piety and eloquence by the immediate circle of his sect, was never generally known and admired in America, as the most powerful writer of his time, until the echo came back from England."

Later this critic continued, "The *lay* productions, on which the literary reputation of this great divine is founded, are very few; a small volume of essays comprise them all. Yet in these small limits, the hand of the master are [sic] so visible—the thoughts are of such broad sculpture—the language is so severely beautiful—and the truth and loftiness of the author's mind are so stamped upon every line, that, if he were not the leader of a powerful sect, and should he never write more, his fame would have pedestal enough."

At home in America, Alexander H. Everett, reviewing Channing's discourse on the "Ministry for the Poor," was saying equally laudable things. Believing Channing even a better writer than Irving, he wrote, "as respects the mere form of language, we rather give the preference to the style of Dr. Channing. It is equally elegant, and a little more pure, correct and pointed than that of Mr. Irving."

Actually, however, he decided there was no competition: the latter was a poet, while the former was a philosopher. "Dr. Channing . . . deals in general truths:—he looks through the external forms of things in search of the secret and mysterious principles of thoughts, action and being. He takes little notice of the varieties of manner and character, that form the favorite topics of the novelist and poet. Mind in the abstract, its nature, properties and destiny, are his constant theme."

When a second collected edition of Channing's work appeared in Glasgow in 1837, it was greeted with praise as a matter of course. Although a reviewer for *Fraser's Magazine* could not "acquiesce in the meagre and unhappy creed" of its author or have "any sympathy with his republican preferences," he nevertheless proclaimed him "unquestionably, the finest writer of the age." The bestower of the compliment, an Anglican, labelled Channing "a low Socinian" in this article but declared in another that his "reviews of character, be it intellectual or physical, are models."

Not long after this enthusiastic judgment appeared, Channing had his second experience with an able and scornful English critic. This time it was "the learned friend," Henry Peter Brougham, Baron Brougham and Vaux, one of the original founders of the *Edinburgh,* who took exception to his writing. In their stylistic creed, these two writers had much in common, but Channing possessed one article of faith which Brougham could not admit: he preferred fitness to lucidity. In the *Milton,* he had said that "energy and richness" were much more important qualities of style than "simplicity and perspicuity" and had argued that a noble thought or emotion ought not to be reduced to a commonplace for the sole purpose of making it clear to inferior intelligences:

> The best style is not that which puts the reader most easily and in the shortest time in possession of a writer's naked thoughts; but that which is the truest image of a great intellect, which conveys fully and carries farthest into other souls the conceptions and feelings of a profound and lofty spirit. To be universally intelligible is not the highest merit. A great mind cannot, without injurious constraint, shrink itself to the grasp of common passive readers.

These were sentiments to which Brougham could not assent. In words that would very easily have fitted upon the pages of a twentieth-century periodical conducting its annual campaign against the omnipresent and irresponsible "incommunicables" of literature, Brougham berated Channing for what he designated his "false theory" of taste. "His favorite," he declared, "is the enigmatic style, not the lucid, not the perspicuous: his cry is 'riddle my riddle;' he stops you after a period with 'Ha! do you follow me? I'll warrant you can't tell what *that* means?'" Following this somewhat playful sally, he phrased a more serious complaint against Channing's taste:

> In every page we trace its evil influence in most careless thinking and faulty diction—a constant mistaking of strange things for strong ones—a perpetual striving after some half brought out notion, of which the mind had never formed to itself any distinct picture—a substitution of the glare of words for harmonious ideas. . . . Though he is among the most distinguished, he is yet but one of a pretty large class of writers, who, chiefly in affectedly written words of exaggerated sentiment, dictated by a Narcissus-like love of their own fancied charms—in many departments of the periodical press, and still more recently in the annuals written by ladies and gentlemen amateurs, are filling the republic of letters with productions all the more hurtful to the public taste, that these great faults of one class cannot be committed, any more than Dr. Channing's without some talents, though of a showy and shining rather than a sterling kind; while the emptiness of the other is balanced and set off by the art of the engraver.

The tenor of Brougham's other remarks was similar. In summary, Channing was found guilty of contaminating the taste of his age by laying down false rules of criticism and by forming his own writings on a false model of excellence.

If Brougham's criticism of Channing's style bore little relation to fact, Channing himself was partly to blame, because he had not chosen the most felicitous phrasing to explain his view of the relationship between force and clarity, and in selecting the "left-handed" prose of Milton as an example of "power" writing, had not been on the safest ground. Certainly he was farthest from a true description of his own style when he wrote, "We delight in long sentences, in which a great truth, instead of being broken up into numerous periods is spread out in its full proportions, is irradiated with variety of illustration and imagery, is set forth in a splendid affluence of language and flows, like a full stream, with a majestic harmony which fills at once the air and the soul." In attempting to elevate Milton's prose to a position "hardly inferior to his best poetry," he had done himself an injustice. Brougham was in a more tenable position when he declared, "Milton wrote Prose upon a False system and Poetry on a True."

News of Brougham's article travelled quickly across the Atlantic, so that Bostonians and New Yorkers were discussing the pro's and con's of its merits within a few weeks of its appearance in London. By and large, Channing's admirers were inclined to exculpate him completely from the charge of false taste; but there were some in whom the "green-eyed monster" lurked, as the following quotation from a letter addressed to Mrs. William Prescott, wife of a distinguished Boston judge, by a former Bostonian then living in New York, demonstrates:

> What do they say in Boston to the attack in the Edinburgh on the seraphic doctor—& what will the Dr. say himself to being classed with the Narcissus school—I am not sorry to see him combed down a little, for I do think he was mounted on rather high stilts. Since I heard of his purpose of writing a manual for the human race, I have thought it might be well for him to know, that he is not either an universal idol or an universal oracle—I am glad too that the attack is in the Edinburgh & not in the Quarterly & that it is in literary & not in religious opinions & still more that it is on the most recent of all the Dr.'s productions "The Character & Writings of Milton" & on the very point, for which his admirers have most commended him the beauty of his composition.

There were doubtless others in America who considered "Parson" Channing too big for his boots, but usually the charge was based not on literary grounds but rather on the score of "meddling" in politics or in some other arena deemed unsuitable for the appearance of a man of the cloth. After his entrance into the slavery controversy, reviews of his works became so colored by the personal bias of his critics toward that embattled subject that there was no way of telling most of the time whether friendly criticism was ironic, or unfriendly attacks pure malice aforethought.

There were other reviews of Channing's work in England after the second *Edinburgh* attack—some for and some against, few altogether complimentary, but all plainly indicating that Channing was a writer who could not be ignored.

Such a position would never have been granted him, had he not written acceptably according to the standards of the time and written in a mode familiar to his English reviewers. Both they and he had been brought up in the same schools of thought; they had read the same textbooks; their standards for judging were pretty much the same. Granting that they might not see eye to eye on all details, they possessed too much in common to be long at odds with each other. As a social and literary critic, according to the canons of the day, Channing had the necessary cultural background, breadth of humanitarian perspective, mastery of medium, and vigor of expression to earn a reputation and hold it.

By his own critical standards also he was worthy of a position among the better writers of his age. His *Remarks on A National Literature,* like Emerson's *American Scholar,* was the statement of a creed which its author believed by living. When he wrote his essays and sermons, he was simply trying to practice what he was always preaching. If he fell far short of the ideals that he had established for a great literature, it was only because he lacked ability—not the will—to realize them.

When his friends read the *Remarks* in the *Examiner,* they must have found it very familiar. Although the word *national* in the title may have thrown them off momentarily, for they knew there was nothing narrow or chauvinistic about his literary aspirations, they must have found themselves at home as soon as they got into the essay, because the core of the address was the familiar old doctrine of self-trust and self-idealization.

The essay began with a broad and all-inclusive definition of literature that was the stock-in-trade of the day's reviewers. It was described as the expression of a nation's mind in writing, which meant that no group of gifted men should be neglected "whether devoted to the exact sciences, to mental and ethical philosophy, to history and legislation, or to fiction and poetry."

After this and further definition of terms, Channing then proceeded, with the characteristic method of rhetorical exposition, to map out the different aspects of his subject and to go on to a topical development of each. A dynamic literature is needed in America, he said, because it is "among the most powerful methods of exalting the character of a nation, of forming a better race of men." America's greatness depends upon her contribution to mankind. As yet she has produced no national literature, because, however she may surpass other nations in providing for elementary instruction, she has fallen behind many in providing "for the liberal training of the intellect, for forming great scholars, for communicating that profound knowledge, and that thirst for higher truths, which can alone originate a commanding literature." The result is a paucity of original thinkers and a tendency to rely for intellectual stimulation upon Europe, whose social and political conceptions are alien to a truly democratic country.

The causes obstructing the advancement of an American literature were, as he saw them, a reverence for utilitarian knowledge which ministers only to "the animal man" and not to "the intellectual, moral and religious man"; and a passive acceptance of foreign culture.

There were other reasons, hardly less important than those already mentioned for wishing a national literature. It would aid not only in expressing but in forming the national mind. It would improve style through exercise. It would stimulate new investigations among the country's leading thinkers. Finally, it would be an admirable medium for diffusing the doctrine of democracy throughout the world. The time was ripe for the history of the human race to be re-written, and only men free from the prejudice of the old aristocracies could hope to participate in such a work.

The means of producing this national literature were thought to be a general fostering of it wherever and whenever it might appear; the enlargement of literary institutions and the staffing of them with competent personnel; the improvement of universities and other educational institutions; and a new development of the religious principle. Channing was quick to assert, however, that these were only means and not causes, for "literature depends on individual genius, and this, though fostered, cannot be created by outward helps."

Finally, he suggested that Americans turn their attention to the continent and curtail their interest in things English lest they become imbued with the utilitarianism of that country.

Few American critics of the nineteenth century managed to escape the pitfall of cultural nationalism, and Channing's essay could very well have contributed to their downfall. But the respect that he himself held for man *per se* kept him from falling into the error of exalting his own national group above man in general. As he put it, "We love our country much, but mankind more." True independence of mind knows no national boundaries, and he was fully aware that America could not progress in a literary vacuum any more than she could remain politically free while the rest of the world was in chains.

This essay marked his final appearance in the *Examiner* as a literary critic. He had kept his promise to the editors to help them get the magazine off to a good start, and it had become, largely because of his efforts, the most important periodical of the day. His article on Milton had been the first significant piece of criticism to appear in its pages, and its campaign for an American literature had been inaugurated by his essay. Up to 1829 it had an appeal that was primarily theological; but after Channing's challenge, it took to literary criticism with a vigor and freshness that enabled it to assume a commanding position among literary journals in the years 1830 to 1835. The moral idealism of its spiritual godfather permeated the criticism of its editors and contributors and left its impress upon nearly every article that appeared in it during the thirties.

Although he never again resorted to a periodical to express his views on literature, he had by no means said his last word on the subject. In 1838 while introducing the Franklin Lectures to the Boston working classes, he took the opportunity to summarize the basic creed of Self-Culture that underlay all his hopes for an improved literature, and hence for an improved race. Of all the discoveries men need to make, he told the apprentices sitting before him, the most important at this moment is the self-forming power treasured up in ourselves. Once this is done, he went on to say, men can begin to appreciate properly the idea that "the beauty of the outward creation is intimately related to the lovely, grand, interesting attributes of the soul." Literature, he concluded, is one of the most valuable means for making that relationship clear.

Three years later, he echoed the same sentiments in his oration before the Mercantile Library Company of Philadelphia. Speaking upon "The Present Age," the same topic which had been assigned to him more than forty years before at the Harvard Commencement, he dwelt upon those developments of the age which seemed to him worthiest of being encouraged. Literature was, of course, high on his list. Signalling out those writers whose works seemed to express the most universal sympathy for human nature—Wordsworth, Scott, and Dickens—he paid particular attention to Wordsworth. "The great truth which pervades his poetry," he said, "is that the beautiful is not confined to the rare, the new, the distant, to scenery and modes of life open only to the few; but that it is poured forth profusely on the common earth and sky."

This remark and many others like it reveal his general optimism. A true disciple of Rousseau, at least to the extent that he believed "Human nature is not a tiger which needs a constant chain," he looked with unclouded eye to the future, willing "to see some outbreak of enthusiasm, whether transcendental, philanthropic, or religious," as long as it indicated that the human spirit was not wholly engulfed in material considerations.

When the first collected edition of his writings appeared in 1841, he wrote a lengthy introduction for it, which constituted a kind of apologia *properibus suis.* In that introduction he described, in terms of quiet understatement, what he thought of his literary productions. "They have," he said, "the merit of being earnest expressions of the writer's mind, and of giving the results of quiet, long-continued thought." And what he said was true, for the works were the man; and their lack of literary dress was characteristic of their author's mind.

While it is not so, as Renan disparagingly remarked, that none of them exhibited "the least pretension to art or style," they were typical of the unstudied simplicity of his habitual expression. Repetitiousness and an occasional rhetorical flourish sometimes disturb the easy flow of thought, but these faults are attributable to his primary function of preaching.

Like so many of his contemporaries—his cousin, Richard Henry Dana and his brother-in-law, Allston, to mention but two of the more obvious examples—he suffered from the lack of an intellectual milieu larger than himself. As Emerson so cogently put it, "Dr. Channing, had he found Wordsworth, Southey, Coleridge, and Lamb around him, would as easily have been severe with himself and risen a degree higher as he has stood where he is. I mean, of course, a genuine intellectual tribunal, not a literary junto of Edinburgh Wits, or dull conventions of Quarterly or Gentleman's Reviews."

He was with these men in spirit; but the activating principle of personal contact was lacking, so that he could not rise above the level which he himself had created. "The finest writer of his age," he was emphatically not; but neither was he an example of the proverb: "In the country of the blind, the one-eyed man is king."

CHAPTER FIFTEEN

THE DISCIPLES

WHEN AMOS BRONSON ALCOTT came to the tangle of streets, roads, lanes and alleys that was Boston in the spring of 1828, he was searching for "Minds." A country boy from Wolcott, Connecticut, Alcott was quite unlike any other product ever turned out by the little community of Spindle Hill where he had been born.

Nearly thirty when he first saw the Massachusetts Capital standing on her three hills, Alcott had enjoyed a variety of experiences but none that had ever completely satisfied his longing for something that seemed almost to lie beyond his reach of experience. When he had arrived at manhood, instead of staying on the land like his father before him, or going into one of the factories that were beginning to invade the New England countryside, he had become a peddler—and an unsuccessful one, too, as his father, who always had to make up his deficits, could sadly testify.

Fairly early, too, he had acquired the habit of seeing all things double—the fact and its significance; the event and its universal meaning; the concrete temporal instance and the everlasting law. Perhaps it had been fostered by his favorite book, the great allegory of John Bunyan, or maybe it was a trait of mind that had been born into him. Whatever its source, it needed only nourishment to become a fully developed philosophy of idealism.

Peddling had given Alcott a wonderful opportunity to see human nature in all its aspects. His experience among the traders of Virginia had been particularly enlightening; but it had not begun to satisfy his wants, either bodily or spiritual, and so he had turned to school teaching. And what a teacher he had been! Children had learned quickly and painlessly under his benevolent and progressive methods, but that was the trouble—parents didn't expect learning to be either painless or easy. Besides, they were shocked at some of the tales their sons and daughters brought home about the newfangled ideas of the young man who was instructing them. He seemed to believe that even the youngest child had a mind of its own, and he encouraged all his pupils to think for themselves. He had even been known to talk to them about their souls and to discuss questions of morality—which everyone knew was the exclusive prerogative of parents.

Alcott was a revolutionary, and his doctrines were not acceptable on their face value to the conservative folk of Connecticut, who had been brought up on the stern doctrines of Calvin. He decided to try out his ideas elsewhere, and what better place was there than Boston, the Capital of "the Monarch Thought's dominion"?

Upon his arrival, Alcott hastened to call on William Russell and Ezra Stiles Gannett. He bore letters of introduction to both from Samuel May, his friend in Brooklyn and Channing's former assistant in the Berry Street School. They received him cordially and gave him advice on how to get settled in Boston. Russell listened attentively to his ideas for starting an infant school, and Gannett answered his queries about the clergy of the city. Although Alcott had made up his mind sometime before that the teacher performed a more important function than the preacher, because he was on the ground earlier (while the soul was still "trailing clouds of glory," so to speak) and because he was more practical (actually molded conduct), he had no illusions about where the "mind" of Boston was concentrated. It was in the clergy!

To Alcott, the ministers of Boston were a brilliant group of individuals. Although he seldom mentioned such Trinitarians as Lyman Beecher, the "father of more brains than any man in America," he was full of praise for the twenty or more Unitarian ministers who were serving the city when he arrived.

Nathaniel Frothingham was at First Church, Ralph W. Emerson at Second, Francis Greenwood at King's Chapel, John Palfrey at Brattle Square, Francis Parkman at the New North, Alexander Young at New South, John Pierpont at Hollis Street, Charles Lowell at West Church, Joseph Tuckerman at Bulfinch Street, Samuel Barrett at the Twelfth Congregational, George Ripley at the Thirteenth Congregational, Lemuel Capens at Hawes Place, and finally, leading them all, Gannett and Channing at Federal Street.

On his first Sunday in "Channing's" city, he heard him preach on the "Dignity of the Intellect," and he realized then why Sam Jo May and Gannett had been so fulsome in their praise. Listening to Channing was like taking an introductory course to immortality, and good discipline for the soul besides. In the months that followed they became firm friends. Alcott confided to his journal that he thought Channing the most original thinker in the city and added: "His mind is a remarkable one. It soars high. It leaves the region of material vision and seeks affinity with the objects and essences of spiritual forms."

He met many other people who were interested in educational matters; but wherever he turned, the trail always seemed to lead back to Channing. There was Elizabeth Peabody for example, whom he had met out in Roxbury, where she and William Russell were teaching school. The two of them were always discussing Channing, though it was usually Elizabeth who brought him up in their conversations. She had not impressed him at first because she seemed "offensively assertive"; but later he changed his opinion and decided that she had more mind than any other woman he had met.

There was Dorothea Dix also. When he was trying to get his school underway and was looking about for advice, she had been recommended as one of Boston's most experienced teachers. He had found it difficult to associate the word *experienced* with the young lady of twenty-six whom he met shortly afterwards, but he soon learned it was no misnomer. Miss Dix had taught school in her grandmother's house when she was only fourteen and, at nineteen, had conducted one of the most successful Dame schools in the city. She, too, had come under Channing's spell.

Like many other young ladies in Boston—Elizabeth Peabody was of course the prime example—Miss Dix had found his liberal gospel a refreshing change from both the "excitements" of her father's religion (he was a Methodist minister) and the coldness of her uncle's Congregationalism. Only last year, when her strength had become overtaxed by a constant round of teaching and writing, she had spent the spring and summer at Channing's summer home, tutoring his children and listening to him unfold his ideas on self-culture. She had learned from him also, she told Alcott, that no mind in the community must be overlooked and that all avenues of learning should be explored. She was now looking around for more useful ways in which she could play a part in such work. Dorothea was a very determined woman, Bronson decided, but very nice; and if she was not an enthusiast like Miss Peabody, she was nevertheless just as earnest, and just as sincere a disciple of Channing as Elizabeth was.

Meanwhile, Channing found Alcott himself an interesting companion, although he sometimes felt Bronson carried his enthusiasms a little too far. How different he was from Ezra Gannett! Ezra was over-scrupulous, inclined to value himself too meanly, and in need of constant encouragement. Alcott, on the other hand, was too much inclined to rely on his own intuitions when there was no justification. Channing was far from wishing to discourage such self-reliance, but Alcott should be taught that there were limits even to individualism. He needed a broader perspective—a little theory to counter-balance his practical knowledge. His knowledge of history, for example, was sadly wanting. He seemed to think one could conceive of man's future without knowing about his past. He tended also to put too much faith in the powers of education, and his conception of the powers of comprehension of the childish mind was grossly exaggerated.

The two men often gathered in Channing's study to discuss these and other matters. When their conversation turned to such topics as retribution, government, art, education, they were usually able to agree on basic principles, although there was always some difference of opinion regarding details. Alcott told his host that he needed more practical experience of human nature, which Dr. Channing did not deny; but he always came away from these meetings with renewed faith. And Alcott needed encouragement. Although the glow had not entirely disappeared from the bright hopes that he had held out for Boston upon his first coming to the city, he now felt even "the splendid genius of Channing . . . inadequate to break through the remaining clouds of prejudice and intolerance which linger on its horizon." Only two years before he had written a little prose-poem celebrating "the city that is set on high" as the source of "every pure stream of thought and purpose and performance." Now he was beginning to come down to earth and to see it in more realistic perspective—a perspective born of the memorable evenings in the study on Mount Vernon Street, where he and Dr. Channing had struck sparks from each other.

If there were lowering clouds of prejudice and ignorance on the Boston intellectual horizon in 1832, new winds of doctrine were also beginning to fill up its mental sky, eddy about its avenues and streets, and circulate through its temples of worship and learning. There was more than one indication that precedent and tradition were becoming stifling to the more spiritually minded members of the community and that the "corpse-cold" Unitarianism of Brattle Street and Harvard College might once again have breathed into it the spirit of life which Channing had originally inspired. There were hungry seekers after the bread of new truth to whom the old loaf of institutionalism was no longer satisfying—most of them had been nourished on Channing's doctrine of self-trust and free inquiry.

Waldo Emerson was the first of the Boston Unitarians to seek a wider freedom than institutionalism provided. Although he had served the Second Church less than three years, he knew without further trial that he could no longer conscientiously administer its simple rites, and so he had resigned. An article in *The New England Magazine* hinted broadly that his defection was owing largely to Channing's liberal preaching, and his Aunt Mary Moody, who all along had warned against "humanitarianism," was inclined to agree. Channing himself was unperturbed, although Ezra Gannett hastened to defend both him and Emerson against the imputations contained in the *New England* article.

But Emerson was not the only "seeker." George Ripley, who liked to call himself "a child of Channing," was beginning to grow restive down in the little meeting-house on Purchase Street, although he had not progressed as far along the road to rebellion as his friend Emerson. Ever since his Harvard days he had been an ardent admirer of the Federal Street pastor. In his senior year, he had written some pieces for the *Christian Register* under the initial "C," and nothing had given him greater pleasure than to hear their merits attributed to Dr. Channing.

Ordained in 1826, he had begun his career under the conservative auspices of John Kirkland, Henry Ware, Jr., and Ezra Gannett; but his naturally inquisitive mind had not long remained content with their beliefs or with the Lockean doctrines that Professor Andrews Norton had tried to impress upon him. He had never forgotten Norton's *ex cathedra* pronouncement, "We have the teaching of experience in regard to the facts of the material universe; and concerning the realm of spiritualities, we are dependent on the authority of divine revelation"; but neither had he ever believed that it was so. Channing had taught him instead that man's ultimate reliance must be on his own mind and that the Scriptures could not contradict human reason. That was sounder doctrine; besides, there was room in Channing's system for intuition, and intuition, contrary to what Dr. Norton might believe and say, was a very important channel of truth.

When Ripley preached his sermon, "Jesus Christ the same Yesterday, To-Day, and Forever," it caused no alarm among his Unitarian friends and parishioners; nor were there any raised eyebrows when James Walker's tract, "The Philosophy of Man's Spiritual Nature in regard to the Foundations of Faith" appeared at approximately the same time. Yet Ripley's discourse contained the basic substance of the South Boston sermon that Theodore Parker was to deliver seven years later on the "Transient and Permanent in Christianity"; and Walker's pamphlet (published, incidentally, by the Unitarian Association) was an exposition of transcendentalism. Perhaps the vigilance of the custodians of "revealed" truth was momentarily dulled; whatever the cause, Channing was all for encouraging men like Alcott, Ripley, and Walker, and—yes, even the unpredictable Orestes Brownson.

Orestes was that mercurial spirit whose religious journeyings (to some they seemed like a trip on a merry-go-round) were always a good topic for conversation. Beginning almost as soon as he had been able to pry into the somber tomes of the tiny Congregational library that was his introduction to the world of literature, he had gone from the extremes of Presbyterianism to Universalism, detoured with Fanny Wright, whose doctrine of "Wright Reason" was nearly as attractive as Fanny herself, into the sloughs of infidelity, and come to rest finally in the bosom of Unitarianism.

For Brownson it was the "everlasting yea" of Channing's gospel that brought him out of the depths and restored him to spiritual health. He was already convalescing from the effects of his excursion into the materialistic ethics of Miss Wright and Robert Dale Owen, son of the famous philanthropist, when a friend read him Channing's sermon on "Likeness to God." This eloquent affirmation of the potential divinity of man, which Brownson later called "the most remarkable [sermon] since the Sermon on the Mount," raised him from the darkness of doubt and made him feel that he had found a spiritual father. That was in 1830. Returning to his post as an independent minister in Ithaca, New York, early the following year, he told his congregation, "I belong to no party, I disclaim all sectarian names. . . . Should I assume the name of any party, it should be Unitarian, as that denomination approximates nearer, in my estimation to the spirit of Christianity than any other." The next year when his magazine, the *Philanthropist,* failed, he accepted a Unitarian pulpit in Walpole, New Hampshire, only a hundred miles from Boston and Unitarian headquarters.

Almost immediately he had begun to contribute articles on French philosophy and on the alliance between Christianity and social progress to the *Christian Register* and the *Examiner* and later, when it was founded in 1834, to the *Unitarian.* His contacts with these magazines brought him frequently to Boston, and there he met Channing and George Ripley.

Channing remembered their first meeting very clearly. He had been pleased when Brownson confessed his indebtedness to the Farley Sermon, because Orestes's words were tangible proof of the efficacy of the truths contained in that address; but he had not warmed to his tall visitor immediately. He had written him a letter shortly afterwards, however, telling him that although he could not regard a stranger "not brought up among us, and who has made important changes of religion" as an old friend, he nevertheless approved of his treatment of Christianity as a principle of reform.

Brownson demonstrated his pleasure at receiving even this much of a welcome by naming his third son, William Ellery Channing Brownson. Soon he was exchanging pulpits with Channing as well as with Ripley, who became his closest friend. Ripley suggested that he come to Boston and establish a church for people "who are disgusted with Orthodoxy and insensible to Liberal Christianity in any of the modes, in which it is now presented, but who would gladly hear the gospel preached in the spirit of Jesus, in a way to meet their intellectual and moral needs." The voice was Ripley's but the words belonged to Channing.

For a number of years Channing had been thinking of a "Church of the Future," and one of the means that he had considered to bring about a more progressive Christianity was the preaching of the gospel to large numbers of workingmen who were "unchurched" because of the artificial distinctions that existed between them and the so-called "respectable" members of Boston society. These people needed someone who could talk to them in their own idiom—someone who had knowledge of their wants, who could grapple with the problems peculiar to their state in life. The poor had the gospel preached to them— Joseph Tuckerman and his assistants were seeing to that; and the rich sat sedately every Sunday in the pews of the several dozen churches in the city to listen to the word of God; but the man of labor was left alone to struggle with intemperance, immorality, and infidelity. Clearly there was a need; only the man was lacking. Brownson's background with the Workingman's Party made him an ideal candidate.

Early in 1836 Brownson moved to Chelsea and began to hold independent meetings in Boston. His "Church of the Future" bore the rather fancy title of the "Society for Christian Union and Progress," but its program was contained in three simple articles: intellectual liberty, social progress, and a more spiritual morality than animated the ministers who took care not to offend State Street. Channing's conservative friends regarded this new manifestation of radicalism with suspicion, but Channing himself was hopeful for its future. He wrote Elizabeth Peabody that he preferred Brownson's "morbidly sensitive vision to prevalent evils, to the stone-blindness of the multitudes who condemn him" and gave freely of his money and counsel to the new missionary.

The Society did not continue to justify his complete confidence, however. He found Brownson inclined to default now and again on his program of inner reform, looking instead among social conditions for possible solutions to the problems of the laboring classes. He couldn't agree either with all of Brownson's philosophic ideas, believing many of them beyond the comprehension of the men whom Orestes was trying to reach. Brownson agreed with him, however, that manual-labor schools were the best and most direct way of helping the workers. They discussed the Boston Farm School, which Joseph Tuckerman had worked so hard to establish and which was proving so successful in rehabilitating indigent boys, and decided something similar might prove effective for young tradesmen. Such schools not only would make labor more respectable by placing it on a level near that of the white-collar professions but would also help to refine the workingmen by making them aspire to something higher than their usual sensory pleasures. On Channing's advice, Brownson even took steps toward preparing a specific plan for enlisting the readers of his *Boston Reformer* in a search for relevant information.

The plan was dropped, however, when the Bank Panic of 1837 opened Brownson's eyes to the havoc that could be wrought when a complicated financial system burst the bonds of a personal morality. He told Channing there was more hatred of the rich than he had ever expected and, in the face of this bitterness, he would have to recast his plans for reform. He decided that he could not ask *hungry* people to put their trust in religion and manual-labor schools. Prayer would not call down manna from heaven; and, while State Street might feed those in the food lines, it did not choose to. The only way to achieve social amelioration appeared to be political action, and the only party that seemed likely to be helpful was the Democratic party. He would support it.

When Elizabeth Peabody informed Channing of Brownson's treason, he was grieved. He told her he had hoped that the study of great truths and universal principles would give Brownson a calmness and stability of mind. He added, "So they would, were it not for an unhappy organization." Channing was sadly disappointed, but he did not desert the man who had once believed wholeheartedly in "likeness to God." He did, however, look for someone else to carry out the work of internal reform. For a time it looked as if his own nephew, William Henry, might do something about it; and he wrote Charles Follen, "I earnestly hope that he will enjoy sympathy and encouragement in this philanthropic work."

There had always been a soft spot in Channing's heart for his nephew. He had tried to be a father to him and, if the truth were told, had found him a more responsive spirit than his own son, Francis. They had much in common, he knew—he and this nephew who tried to be as much like him as possible—and they suffered from the same scrupulosity and sense of personal unworthiness.

When Henry graduated from Harvard and told him of his intentions to prepare for the ministry, Channing had been pleased but had urged him to consider the step very carefully. Henry had completed his theological studies satisfactorily but was unable afterwards to settle upon a field for his future endeavors. For a time he had considered joining his boyhood friend, James Freeman Clarke, in the latter's plan to found another Boston in the West; but a feeling of personal insecurity had deterred him from going through with the idea. Channing had been just as satisfied, because he thought Henry much more suited to preach in a "cultivated" society than in the rough-and-ready frontier communities of the middle West. He gave Henry money for a European trip instead and rejoiced when he returned with a new sense of determination and purpose.

In Paris Henry had given much attention to the Baron de Gerando's plans for alleviating the misery of the poor. Gerando's *Le Visiteur du Pauvre* had recently been crowned by the French Academy, and Henry had learned it by heart. He had also studied the widespread charitable organizations of the Catholic Church while he was in Rome. On his return to Boston he had talked to Joseph Tuckerman and his uncle about a ministry for the poor in New York, and they had urged him to undertake the task. Channing was still interested in fighting infidelity among the workers of the large cities, and he thought Henry might combine a ministry among the under-privileged with a program of instruction for the workingmen. Where Brownson had failed, Henry might be able to succeed. He knew at least that his nephew's attitude toward reform was the correct one.

The new undertaking proved to be short-lived. Henry found orthodoxy firmly intrenched in New York and could neither compete with the existing agencies for reform nor cope with the financial problems resulting from the Bank Panic. Faced with a situation analogous to that which had confronted Brownson in Boston, he withdrew from the competition rather than take Brownson's way out. Returning to Boston, he set out shortly afterwards for Ohio, where James Freeman Clarke was waiting for him. During the next few years, he preached "Channing Unitarianism" to the good burghers of Cincinnati.

Although Channing regretted his nephew's failure, he was not despondent. He was enough of a philosopher to realize that a defeat here and there was to be expected, and he never looked for smooth sailing in the work of reforming character. Recently, for example, he had been somewhat disturbed by the actions of Bronson Alcott. When he got Alcott and his Temple School off to a good start three years before, he had expected great results from it; but he soon discovered that Alcott had his particular hobby horse and sometimes lost sight of his goal in his preoccupation with method. He had discussed with Alcott and Elizabeth Peabody his objections to the mental self-analysis which Alcott employed in his classes; but Alcott had not been able to see his point. No amount of talk was sufficient to convince him that the soul of a child was jealous of being watched or that analysis could impede the development of the spiritual nature. He confused man's nature with God's. His *Record of Conversations on the Gospels* proved that, although Channing could not agree with Andrews Norton that the "*Record* was one-third absurd, one-third blasphemous, and one-third obscene."

Channing's concern for Alcott was more than compensated by his elation over the recent decision of his young lawyer friend and parishioner, Horace Mann. For some five years he had watched with interest Mann's career in the Massachusetts legislature and had predicted a great political future for him. But when Mann threw aside his excellent opportunities for political preferment to accept the secretaryship of the newly organized Massachusetts Board of Education, Channing was overjoyed. He wrote him a letter of enthusiastic approbation, exclaiming, "You could not find a nobler station. You must allow me to labor under you according to my opportunities. If at any time I can aid you, you must let me know." Shortly afterwards, he accepted Mann's invitation to attend an educational convention in the town of Taunton. When he saw the enthusiasm with which Mann's address was received, he got up himself and delivered a lengthy extemporaneous speech on the value of common school education. Mann was eager to have him repeat his performance on other occasions, but Channing's health prevented him from indulging his friend. He gave him moral support, however, and Mann frequently called on him for advice.

Although common school education was of great importance to Channing, he regarded his province to be more the encouragement of progressive thought among the "minds" of the community—those young men who were thinking for humanity in general rather than for any specific group or purpose. The power of acting upon minds was the greatest power in the world, and he had tried many times to impress that idea upon his friends and acquaintances—upon his parishioners in Federal Street and upon the lawyers and politicians of the State House; upon the farmers and fishermen who had come to hear him preach summers in the little white church at Portsmouth; and upon the apprentices and mechanics at the Franklin lectures.

A short time before Ralph Emerson's *Nature* appeared, Channing had suggested to George Ripley that he and a few others ought to found a society for "mutual inquiry." Ripley thought the suggestion excellent and proposed a meeting for the near future. The following September, a group composed of Alcott, Emerson, Frederick Hedge, Convers Francis, Brownson, and James Freeman Clarke met at Ripley's home; and the Symposium or Transcendental Club, as it was later named, was born. Channing himself did not attend the first meeting of the Club, but his spirit of independence and free inquiry was well represented; and in succeeding meetings, many of the topics to which he had long directed attention were discussed.

As a matter of fact, Channing appeared at the gatherings of the Transcendental Club only once or twice, because he was beginning to feel that he had too often taken the leading role in such organizations and thereby prevented other from speaking their minds. There was another group, however, in which he continued to participate as actively as ever. This was the informal association which met at irregular intervals in the rooms of Jonathan Phillips in the Tremont House. The Friends, as the members of this club called themselves, included—besides Channing, Phillips, and Charles Follen—three members of the Transcendental Club—Alcott, Hedge, and Ripley. Wendell Phillips, Jonathan's cousin, joined them occasionally; and early in 1838, Theodore Parker, the youthful pastor of the Spring Street Church in West Roxbury, became a regular participant in their discussions.

Parker had come to Boston seven years before, a raw country boy of twenty-one, without even the dignity of a Harvard degree to offset his rustic ungainliness and lack of social grace. After fighting the battle against ignorance alone for several years, he had entered the Harvard Divinity School, where men like Professor Henry Ware, Jr. opened up new vistas of thought to him. After graduation, he had welcomed the call of the little church in Roxbury and had entered upon his ministry with a resolution "to preach nothing as religion that I have not experienced inwardly and made my own."

Before Parker had been long at his new work, he had become acquainted with Channing, and the two of them had spent many afternoons together discussing such big words as "conscience," "miracles," "materialism," and "inspiration." As they grew to know each other better, their conversations became warmer, and Parker even dared to take issue with his illustrious friend.

In some things Channing had been more conservative than Parker; in others, less. He shocked Parker by his doctrine that conscience must be educated—an idea which Parker ridiculed, believing instead that conscience was infallible and maintaining that it would always decide rightly, if the case was fairly put before it and old habits had not darkened its vision. Channing even went so far as to question whether men needed an infallible guide, whether such a guide would not be more a disadvantage than a help. In regard to the morality of the gospels, Channing was inclined to think that Parker did less than justice to Christianity. He maintained that the character of Jesus was different *in kind* from his own and asserted that Biblical miracles were distinct in genus from those of other nations or books. In all these opinions, Parker, of course, dissented vigorously.

When Channing introduced Parker to The Friends, he was pleased to see how well the newcomer fitted into the group. He always enjoyed the evenings at the Tremont himself, because the level of conversation was unusually high, the company congenial, and the points of view interesting. When Follen and Wendell Phillips were both present, the conversation usually came round to the subject of slavery, and then things really became warm and exciting. Channing liked particularly to encourage discussions about the progress of civilization and, in his favorite role as the Socrates of the group, to draw out different views. He could always get George Ripley or Bronson Alcott to voice his ideas on progress, and interesting ideas they were too. The Friends were pretty well agreed that society had made progress; but they were also of the opinion that there were certain disadvantages accompanying it; men's actions, for example, were often assessed at unreal values; and vanity and love of show—in short, all forms of selfishness—were more common than in other days.

Sometimes, instead of talking about such broad topics as progress, the group came down to more specific subjects. They discussed Emerson's Address at the Divinity School, for instance, and whether Emerson was a Christian or a Pantheist. Parker defended Emerson, declaring that the charge of pantheism was too vague to have any validity. Pantheism meant that God was only an idea of man's mind, and he could not accept such a definition of Emerson's views. Channing thought Emerson's ideas were essentially the same as his own, although he objected to the ambiguity of some of Emerson's language. He agreed completely with Emerson that the age of inspiration was not past and that the Bible was not closed. He referred to the recent sermon that Henry Ware, Jr., his old friend and Emerson's former colleague, had preached in an effort to exonerate the teachers and students of the Divinity School from any blame for Emerson's "transcendental" heresy, and he said he thought Ware, in attempting to answer Emerson, was only fighting with a shadow. Ware, he added, had charged Emerson with denying the personality of God, but he had not understood Mr. Emerson so. The significant thing to remember, he concluded, was that "Mr. Emerson expressly says, and makes a great point of it, that God is *alive* not *dead,* and would have the gospel narrative left to make its own impression of an indwelling life, like the growing grass."

Channing believed that Emerson was a great moral and Christian teacher, and he admired him for the purity and benevolence of his personal life. He told Elizabeth Peabody, who thought nearly as much of Emerson as she did of Channing, that he did not have the slightest respect for those persons who had abused Emerson because of his Divinity Address and remarked that they did not have "a tittle of the moral earnestness which makes him a most powerful person." Somehow he felt that Emerson was gifted to speak to an audience which he himself could never reach.

In general, Channing knew that men were governed by their affections and that any preacher who expected to reach all men—from the highest to the lowest—must touch the affections of the multitude. "But pure love," he said, "is an idea; and to purify men's love of Jesus it may be in some instances desirable not to think of his individuality." He could never do it; but if Emerson found it a better way to reach men's hearts, then he gave him his blessing.

Similarly, when Channing heard of attempts to "put down" Parker for his sermon on the *Transient and Permanent in Christianity,* he wrote that he wished him "to preach what he thoroughly believes and feels." The great idea of the discourse—the immutableness of Christian truth—he responded to entirely. He was grieved, however, that Parker had not given some "clear, direct expression of his belief in the Christian miracles"; for, as he said, "I see not how the rejection of these can be separated from the rejection of Jesus Christ." But he was one of the few among Parker's Unitarian friends who did not desert him after the South Boston Sermon. While such Unitarian pillars as Francis Parkman, Ezra Gannett, and Nathaniel Frothingham—even Convers Francis, Parker's oldest friend in Boston—stood aloof, Channing cried out, "Let the full heart pour itself forth." He had never been able to stomach attempts to silence sincere and earnest speech, and he was not going to change the habits and convictions of a lifetime at the ninth hour.

It saddened Channing, however, to see the young men leaving Unitarianism. First Emerson had departed; then Parker had alienated the majority of the old guard, which was just about the same as bidding it goodbye; and now there was George Ripley, whose farewell discourse to his congregation had only recently set new rumors buzzing in Boston religious circles. Ripley's resignation came as no surprise to him, because he had known for some time that George had no heart for the prevailing philosophy of the majority of the Unitarian Churches. After the clash between Ripley and Norton over the latter's address on "The Latest Form of Infidelity" two years before, he had foreseen that George would soon seek a freer atmosphere.

Channing could not blame Emerson and Parker and Ripley for blazing new trails. Unitarianism had begun as a protest against mental slavery and had pledged itself to progress. But gradually it had grown stationary, and now it was just another orthodoxy. There was really not much in it to attract youthful and vigorous minds. Perhaps that was the way of things; perhaps all reforming bodies were doomed to stop, once they had made a perceivable gain, in order to hold on to it. One thing he was sure of: "they become conservative, and out of them must spring new reformers, to be persecuted generally by the old." Knowing this, he watched all new movements with interest. His own life was nearly at an end, but he could lend encouragement to those whose careers were still before them.

Although he had grown increasingly dubious about associations and preferred the monarchy of individual freedom to the democracy of a public opinion that forced man to extremes, Channing was attracted by several cooperative experiments then getting underway. Ripley spoke to him about his plans for the "Brook Farm Institute of Agriculture and Education," and Channing told him there were fine possibilities in the enterprise. The "Fraternal Community" at Mendon also appealed to him. He wrote to Adin Ballou, the founder of "Hopedale," as the community was called, that he had "for a long time dreamed of an association, in which the members, instead of preying on one another . . . should live together as brothers, seeking one another's elevation and spiritual growth." At the same time he foresaw the danger "of losing in such establishments individuality, animation, force, and enlargement of mind."

Channing told Elizabeth Peabody that he hoped to see "a union of *labor* and *culture*," and he found "Mr. Alcott hiring himself out for day labor, and at the same time living in a region of high thought . . . the most interesting object in our Commonwealth." He did not care for "Orpheus in the 'Dial,'" but "Orpheus at the plough" was after his own heart.

He sympathized with Brownson's feelings for the *masses* ("an odious word!" he exclaimed, "as if spiritual beings could be lumped together like heaps of matter"), but he had little patience with his essay on "The Laboring Classes." He thought Brownson greatly exaggerated the hardships of the workingmen, and he questioned whether they were not better off than a good many professional men or merchants.

"We all have a hard battle to fight," he said somewhat piously. "To me the matter of complaint is, not that the laboring class wants physical comforts,—though I wish these to be earned by fewer hours of labor,—but that they live only for their physical natures; that so little justice is done to their souls. . . ."

Brownson's remedies for the inequalities of the social classes he thought "shocking, or absurd." It was pure foolishness to talk of abolishing the law of inheritance, and dividing the estates of the dead among the people. "An equal distribution of the world's property would solve no problems! "No good can come but from the spread of intellectual and moral power among all classes, and the union of all by a spirit of brotherhood."

Later, however, when Brownson sent him his letter on "The Mediatorial Life of Jesus" and told him that he had at last found peace in his new doctrine of "communion with man, and through the life derived from Jesus with God," he congratulated him but warned, "Some passages of your letter would lead an incautious reader to think you a thorough-going Universalist and as asserting the actual appropriation of the life of Christ to the whole human race, past and present, will they or nill they." Then, fearing perhaps that Brownson might feel this criticism too strongly, he added, "Let us see you at the head of a really earnest and vital society of your own. God made you for something more than to scatter random shot, although these shot may sometimes be grand ideas and may hit old errors between wind and water."

When James Freeman Clarke returned in 1841 from Kentucky, where he had made his *Western Messenger* the organ of Channing's anti-slavery opinions, he set about establishing a Free Church. Its support was to be voluntary, its worship congregational, its method social.

To most Bostonians, it seemed a daring innovation, but Channing was delighted with the prospect. He welcomed Clarke to frequent consultations about ways and means and encouraged his parishioners and family to become members of the new society. Clarke's formula for his new church was "Our faith is in Jesus, as the Christ, the Son of God"; Channing preferred "in Jesus as the divinely appointed teacher of truth." "He said," wrote Clarke, "that the danger would be a tendency to conform to the old established way, as the mass exerted a great power of attraction. He said again, emphatically, that we must be more afraid of formality than of eccentricity."

"Too many of our young men," Channing once wrote, "grow up in a school of despair. Instead of hearing a generous kindling voice, summoning them to the service of their country and mankind, they hear the palsying tones of cold derision or desponding prophecy. . . ." He could look back, however, at his own life, when his long years of service were nearly over, and feel fairly confident that he had never been one of the prophets of gloom. He could remember, for example, the time when George Hillard, fresh out of Harvard as first scholar in his class, had come to visit him. Only a short time before, reports of the Revolution of 1830 in France had reached him, and he had been comparing the moderation of the present generation's celebrations with the uproarious ones of his own college days. He had spoken to Hillard of the difference, and George had replied, "Sir, you seem to be the only young man I know." His answer then had been "Always young for liberty, I trust," and that was the principle upon which he had always based his actions.

Channing could not agree, of course, with all the ideas that filled the intellectual atmosphere in the late '30's, but he tried to keep an open mind. He had never seen a stranger assortment of humanity than the group that assembled for the reformers' convention in Chardon Street, but still he expected more from the soil that yielded such vagaries than from Beacon Street respectability. "Nothing," he declared, "terrifies me in these wildest movements. What has for years terrified and discouraged me is *apathy*."

As far as the Transcendentalists were concerned, he thought they sometimes mistook their individualities for the Transcendent. Not realizing that "what is common to men and revealed by Jesus transcends every single individual," they were in danger of falling into a kind of "ego-theism," of which a true understanding of Jesus Christ was the only cure. But he believed in the purity of mind and conscience of those who were active in the new movement, and he felt that men like Emerson would be able to avoid the pitfalls that lay in its path.

He had good reason to place such confidence in Emerson. Since the days of Emerson's graduation from college, when he had helped the gaunt boy to become aware of himself and of his future, Channing had watched his development carefully. And he had been pleased to see how Emerson had taken advantage of the freedom that he himself had fought for in the years when Emerson was still a growing boy. His idea of man's future greatness, his stress on the benevolence in the universe, and his emphasis upon self-reliance and self-culture had all been taken over by Emerson now, and fortunately so, because the problems facing the new day required the strength of a young man and a more powerful voice than Channing himself possessed.

On the other hand, Emerson recognized his indebtedness. There were occasions when he had criticized Channing for being "tame," and Channing's proportions had tended to diminish somewhat as he himself had broadened out. It had not always been easy, either, to show Channing his point of view; but that was not an uncommon experience with great men, even one as liberal and open-minded as Dr. Channing. When all was said and done, there was no one like him, and the age bore his stamp as it did that of no other man. As he told Elizabeth Peabody; "In our wantonness we often flout Dr. Channing, and say he is getting old; but as soon as he is ill we remember he is our Bishop, and we have not done with him yet."

CHAPTER SIXTEEN

THE SLAVERY QUESTION

DURING THE LAST ten years of his life Channing found himself between two fires, never pleasing the conservative part of the Boston community and of his own society; seldom satisfying the Abolitionists, that group of religious and moral zealots whose sympathies went out so strongly to the enslaved and suffering Negroes of the South. Denounced by many of his own parishioners as an Abolitionist and regarded at times by the Abolitionists themselves as an open enemy, he became a storm center around which took place a number of the major skirmishes leading up to the Civil War.

Channing was born in a slaveholding state and in a town noted for its "triangle" trade. When he died, the gradual manumission of slaves in his beloved Rhode Island was not quite complete. In his early youth he had mingled freely with his grandfather's slaves; and while he was at Harvard, he showed his awareness of injustice toward "the poor African" by writing themes about his plight. Slavery, however, had not really made any great impression upon him at that time. After graduation, his experience with the Randolphs in Richmond gave him a closer view of the Negro field-hand; but even then he was seeing "paternalism" at its best, for the Randolphs abhorred the system which they had inherited along with their birthright as Southerners.

During the early years of his ministry, when he was busily engaged in fighting "mental" slavery, he evidently paid no attention to the physical variety, for neither his journals nor his sermons contain any reference to it. Even the Missouri Compromise of 1820 had little effect on him, except as it related to the neighboring state of Maine and the consequences for religion there. By 1825 he was beginning to take a deeper interest in the evil, however; one of his parishioners even wrote Edward Everett that he was "half mad on the subject of slavery." Three years later he was corresponding with Jane Roscoe about the intellectual and moral harm it inflicted.

When Benjamin Lundy, the publisher of *The Genius of Universal Emancipation,* visited Boston to organize abolition societies in 1828, Channing sent Daniel Webster, who was then in the Senate at Washington, some suggestions for allaying the fears of Southern plantation owners, who "interpret every word from this region on the subject of slavery as an expression of hostility." "It seems to me," he told Webster, "that, before moving in this matter, we ought to say to them distinctly, "We consider slavery as your calamity, not your crime, and we will share with you the burden of putting an end to it." If the South, he added, could be made to believe that the North was really its friend, something could be worked out between them. Otherwise, he was fearful that the Union might be endangered, and he asked from the national government "hardly any other boon than that it will hold us together, and preserve pacific relations and intercourse among the States."

Soon afterwards he took advantage of another opportunity to see slavery close at hand. Since his wife's health as well as his own was none too good, he took her to Santa Cruz in the fall of 1830 for a rest cure. "Here," he said, "was a volume on slavery opened always before my eyes, and how could I help learning some of its lessons?" He wrote Joseph Tuckerman of the wretchedness that he saw on every side and declared that the greatest misery of the slaves was still "that their condition dooms them, generation after generation, to a merely animal and unimproving existence, and does as much as can be done to extinguish their intellectual and moral nature." No spot exists on earth, he concluded, where man has done more to countenance the doctrine of total depravity.

Returning to Boston after six months spent in learning the sad lesson of man's inhumanity to man, he used his experiences as the text of a sermon. He began by admitting that he had found slavery in its mildest form in Santa Cruz. "Still," he declared, "I think no power of conception can do justice to the evils of slavery. They are chiefly moral, they act on the mind, and through the mind bring intense suffering on the body. As far as the human soul can be destroyed, slavery is that destroyer." He ended by urging his listeners to cultivate the same public feeling that was leading England along the road to emancipation in the West Indies. Here he seems to have overlooked a basic difference between the situation of the two countries. Britain, who had complete control over Crown and Free colonies, could abolish slavery in the West Indies by a simple act of passing a law. In the United States, on the other hand, abolition was a matter for the individual states. Passing a single law that would suit every one of them was no simple matter.

From this time on, the affection of many members of his congregation began to cool. Even before this, his attacks upon the love of gain in the community had not set well with the more affluent members of his Church. Wealth, he had begun to say with monotonous regularity, was at the root of slavery, and was as much a Northern as a Southern fault. Certainly his impressive generalizations about the benevolence of God and the greatness of man were more congenial to them than his specific references to their faults.

The proximate cause of his congregation's hypersensitivity was not Channing himself but a much more outspoken advocate of freedom for the Negroes. In January, 1831, William Lloyd Garrison had started his *Liberator* in Boston. "I will be heard" had been his battle cry, and Bostonians were beginning to learn that he had not been idly boasting. Many of them, however, were like Elizabeth Peabody, who thought Garrison's editorials "the most unchristian and unreasonable violence and indiscriminate rage against the whole South, and most of the North as well."

Channing became a subscriber to Garrison's paper at once and read it diligently. He agreed completely with Garrison's main principle, that it was wrong to make a chattel of a human being, but he had serious doubts about the methods Garrison was using to present his ideas. He was sympathetic towards Garrison's demolition of the colonization fallacy, and he could accept his demand for immediate emancipation by interpreting "immediate" to mean "at the earliest practicable moment"; but he was unable to look upon slaveholders in the aggregate as Garrison did. To him they were individuals, and they bore an individual responsibility for their share in slavery. Their guilt, therefore, could not be measured collectively.

Unhappily, the first effects of Abolitionism upon Channing led him to defer his own participation in the growing opposition to slavery. While still at Santa Cruz, he had planned and already begun to write an essay on slavery, which he thought of addressing to the South in the form of an open letter. But when he returned to find Garrison and his allies agitating for immediate action, he decided to bide his time. Ill health and self-distrust could have been his reasons for delaying, but it was more than likely that he was unwilling either to be leagued with the Abolitionists or to criticize them publicly.

The most unfavorable construction of his motives came from one of his own parishioners, Maria Weston Chapman. Miss Chapman had joined the Abolitionist movement against Channing's wishes, and she felt no sympathy for anyone who did not support the abolition program wholeheartedly. A passage from the appendix to the autobiography of Harriet Martineau, which she edited many years after Channing's death, reveals the extent of her bias and bitterness.

"He had neither insight, courage nor firmness," she wrote. "In his own church had sprung up a vigorous opposition to slavery, which he innocently, in so far as ignorantly, used the little power he had to stay . . . he was terror-stricken at the idea of calling on the whole American people to take counsel on so difficult and delicate a matter in antislavery associations; and above all he deprecated the admission of the colored race to our ranks. He had been selected by a set of money-making men as their representative for piety, as Edward Everett was their representative gentleman and scholar, Judge Story their representative jurist and companion in social life, and Daniel Webster their representative statesman and advocate looking after their interests in Congress."

Nothing could have been farther from the truth, but Garrison had no more loyal supporter than Mrs. Chapman. By depreciating Channing, she felt that she was establishing the true stature of the man whom Channing had slighted. While Garrison's own resentment of Channing's coldness towards him and his methods in the early thirties softened with the lapse of time, Mrs. Chapman's only grew more bitter.

Harriet Martineau's conception of Channing's role differed widely from her friend's. In the fall of 1835 she met Channing at Oakland and spent some time at his home there and in Boston. When his antislavery work was only well begun, she wrote, "He dislikes associations for moral objects: he dislikes bustle and ostentation; he dislikes personal notoriety; and, of course, he likes no better than other people to be the object of popular censure, of popular dislike. He broke through all these temptations to silence, the moment his convictions were settled;—I mean not his convictions of the guilt and evil of slavery, but of its being his duty to utter his voice against it." And she concluded, "He has shown what his moral courage is by proofs which will long outlast his indications of slowness in admitting the full merits of the Abolitionists."

But Channing did not have to depend on visitors from abroad like Miss Martineau for a favorable estimate of his attitude toward the antislavery cause. There were American Abolitionists of the highest authority who respected and admired Garrison, but who, at the same time, differed totally from Maria Chapman in their opinions of Channing. Lydia Maria Child, one of the most popular women writers in the country, was one; Samuel Joseph May, another.

In 1833 when Miss Child published her *Appeal in Favor of That*

Class of Americans Called Africans, she brought down upon her head the interdiction of the proprietors of the Boston Athenaeum, who had been proud to have her use their facilities when she had devoted her talents to more "romantic" subjects. She sent Channing a copy, and in a few days he came to see her. He had walked all the way from Mt. Vernon Street to her home on Cottage Place, and he was tired; but he was still good for nearly three hours' talk. He expressed his satisfaction at the publication of the *Appeal* and urged her never to desert the cause, "through evil or through good report." In some respects, he thought she went too far. "He then entertained," said Mrs. Child, "the idea, which he afterwards discarded, that slavery existed in a milder form in the United States than elsewhere." She became somewhat vehement in her opposition to this idea, and he sought to moderate her "with those calm, wise words which none spoke so well as he."

Whenever Mrs. Child was in Boston, Channing sent for her to get a complete report of the latest developments in the antislavery struggle. At first she thought him timid and even slightly time-serving, but it was not long until she revised her judgment completely. She discovered that his caution was due to his desire to secure justice for all instead of popularity for himself. He constantly grew in her respect, until she came to regard him "as the wisest, as well as the gentlest, apostle of humanity." Eventually they were both pretty much of the same mind on the antislavery question. It was important but not the *only* question of interest to humanity.

Soon after Channing's return from the West Indies, Samuel May discovered his interest in the Abolitionists. Whenever they met, Channing would inquire about the purposes, measures, and progress of the group, and he repeatedly invited May to his home for the express purpose of talking over their affairs.

The most memorable of these meetings took place in the autumn of 1834. So thoroughly convinced was May of the truth of the leading doctrines of the Abolitionists by this time that he forgot his usual deference for Channing and began to debate with him on the subject of Abolitionism. "His principal, if not his only objections," May declared, "were alleged against the severity of our denunciations, the harshness of our language, the vehemence, the heat, and excitement caused by our meetings."

Channing dwelt upon those objections, until May became impatient, then indignant, and finally broke out warmly: "Dr. Channing, I am tired of these complaints . . . it is not our fault, that those who might have managed this reform more prudently have left us to manage it

as we may be able. It is not our fault that those who might have
pleaded for the enslaved so much more eloquently, both with the pen
and with the living voice, than we can, have been silent. We are not
to blame, sir, that you, who, perhaps more than any other man, might
have so raised the voice of remonstrance that it should have been
heard throughout the length and breadth of the land,—we are not to
blame, sir, that you have not spoken. And now because inferior men
have begun to speak and act against what you yourself acknowledge
to be an awful injustice, it is not becoming in you to complain to us,
because we do it in an inferior style. Why, sir, have you not moved,
why have you not spoken before?"

When May had finished this rather impassioned statement, there
was, or so it seemed afterwards to him, a long silence. He waited, somewhat painfully, for it to be broken. When Channing's reply came, it
was uttered in a low but steady voice, "Brother May, I acknowledge
the justice of your reproof; I have been silent too long."

From this time on, Channing was consistently active in "raising the
voice of remonstrance." When May became the General Agent and
Corresponding Secretary of the Massachusetts Antislavery Society a
few months later and moved to Boston to begin his new labors, Channing was the only one of the Boston ministers who invited him to
preach during his stay in the Massachusetts capital, although in all
fairness to Channing's friends, it should be pointed out that Charles
Follen, Henry Ware, Jr., James Clarke, and Theodore Parker—to
mention the most prominent—were not in Boston at the time.

Channing, however, had not been entirely passive before May ad-
monished him. In a letter of July, 1834, he wrote Charles Follen, who
was an active participant of the Cambridge Anti-Slavery Society, that
there was no need of unanimity in the Abolition movement, but that
there should be a body of men, not Abolitionists themselves, "who
uncompromisingly maintained that abolition of slavery ought *immediately* to be decided on, and means used for *immediately commencing*
this work."

Three weeks later he was "much shocked by the late riots in New
York" which had greeted Garrison's return from his first trip to England. "The duty of the Abolitionists seems to me clear," he wrote.
"Whilst they ought to review their principles with great deliberation,
they ought not, at this moment, to *recant* anything, because recanta-
tion will certainly be set down to the account of fear." Upon his return
to Federal Street in October, he was still thinking of the riots, because
he warned his congregation, "Every great city has materials for them."

But, he concluded, "when a good cause suffers from the excesses of its friends, the true course is, not to abandon it in despair,...but to espouse it with calm wisdom, enlightened zeal, and unfettered, fearless resolution."

Dr. Follen hailed his discourse as an "Abolition sermon"; others denounced it for the same reason. Channing himself refused to publish it, because along with his condemnation of the mob spirit and his defense of the Abolitionists' right of free speech, he had mingled adverse criticism of their violence of denunciation. "Were I to publish," he wrote, "I should feel myself bound, not only to vindicate more fully the invaded right of Antislavery societies, but to enlarge on what I deem their errors." It was with this sermon fresh in his mind that Samuel May had rebuked Channing.

Despite Channing's hope that Boston might be spared the disgrace of public riots, mob violence came to Boston in the autumn of 1835, and William Lloyd Garrison was its victim. On October 21, Garrison was stripped of much of his clothing and dragged in the noose of a rope over the ground of Boston Commons, barely escaping with his life, when Mayor Lyman finally shut him up in jail as "the instigator of the mob." The mob was not the result of unpremeditated action but originated in an anti-Abolition meeting which had been held the preceding August. Two days before the meeting, Channing wrote to the *Daily Advertiser,* protesting against such "unwise proceedings":

> Any resolve passed at the proposed meeting, implying, however indirectly, that a human being can rightfully be held and treated as property,—any resolve intended to discourage the free expression of opinion on slavery, or to sanction the lawless violence which has been directed against the Anti-slavery societies, any resolve implying that the Christian and philanthropist may not strive to abolish slavery by moral influences, by appeals to the reason, conscience, and heart of the slaveholder,—any resolve expressing stronger sympathy with the slaveholder or with the slave, or tending at all to encourage the continuance of slavery,—will afflict me beyond measure. . . . That Boston should in any way lend itself to the cause of oppression would be a dark omen indeed.

Four days after the meeting, he wrote as if his fears had been confirmed by the event. The Abolitionists, he said, "have a deep consciousness of the truth and excellence of their cause. They have, too, the immense advantage of acting from great principles; and these alone give permanent strength. Such men cannot be put down."

In November, when the "highly respectable gentlemen" of Boston who had taken part in the Garrison mobbing were feeling some traces of mortification, Channing's lengthy article on *Slavery* appeared. His

purpose, as stated in the introduction, was "to aid the reader in forming a just moral judgment of slavery"; and he proposed to show that
slavery was a great wrong without passing sentence on the character
of the slaveholder, for "these two subjects are distinct. Men are not
always to be interpreted by their acts or institutions." Underlying the
whole work was his confidence in the dignity of human nature and the
fatherhood of God.

His first task was to show that man cannot be justly held or used
as property. "He cannot be property in the sight of God and justice,
because he is a Rational, Moral, Immortal Being; because created to
unfold godlike faculties, and to govern himself by a Divine Law written on his heart, and republished in God's word. . . . Such a being was
plainly made for an End in Himself. He is a person, not a Thing. He
is an End, not a mere Instrument or Means." Next, he proceeded to
show that man's rights come directly from God rather than from the
social unit in which he lives and cannot therefore be abrogated by
man-made law. The rights which are sacred above all others are those
which enable a man to unfold his moral and intellectual nature. Slaves
are given no such chance.

Under the title of "The Evils of Slavery," he listed a formidable
array of instances in which the institution had violated human rights.
Finding it evil "from its own nature," he charted its ruinous effect on
both slave and master, declaring, after the total was complete, "an
institution so founded in wrong, so imbued with injustice, cannot be
made a good."

When he came to the question of the "Means of Removing Slavery,"
he characterized it as one which the slaveholder alone could fully answer; but he was certain that any workable proposal would have to
begin with "the great principle, that man cannot rightfully be held as
property." To rely on colonization to cure or even mitigate the evil
"would be the equivalent to a resolution to perpetuate the evil without end." A system of gradualism was preferable to immediate emancipation, because it would make possible the adjustments involved in a
change affecting such large numbers of people. To the common objection that inter-marriage would result from emancipation, he said,
"Can this objection be urged in good faith? Can this mixture go on
faster or more criminally than at the present moment? Can the slaveholder use the word 'amalgamation' without a blush?"

Such statements as these gave little pleasure to the slaveholders and
their apologists, but they were most satisfactory to the Abolitionists.
The chapter on "Abolitionism," however, tended to reverse the pro-

cedure. "Of the Abolitionists I know very few," Channing said; "but . . . I honor them for their strength of principle, their sympathy with their fellow-creatures, and their active goodness." He characterized the party as "singularly free from political and religious sectarianism, and . . . distinguished by the absence of management, calculation, and worldly wisdom." He denied that it had ever proposed or desired insurrection among the slaves, and he denounced the hounding that its members were subject to. He criticized its motto of "Immediate Emancipation," believing that it required "labored explication" to rescue it from misunderstanding.

But Channing's most serious charges were leveled against the inflammatory and bitter denunciations of some of the Abolitionists. He never would become reconciled to their "showy, noisy mode of action," although later on he would decide the substance rather than the form of the Abolitionist attack on slavery infuriated the Southern slaveholders and their apologists in the North. In the meantime, he exonerated the majority of Abolitionists from blame upon this score: "I know that many of their publications have been calm, well considered, abounding in strong reasoning, and imbued with an enlightened love of freedom."

The appearance of "Slavery" excited varying kinds of censure and blame. Garrison summed up his objections under twenty-five heads, denouncing the book as "utterly destitute of any redeeming, reforming power"; as "calumnius, contradictory, and unsound"; and, as such, it "ought not to be approbated by any genuine abolitionist. 'He that is not with us is against us.' " Other Abolitionists, however, were inclined to believe rather that "He that is not against us is for us."

Ellis Gray Loring, a friend of both Channing and Garrison, wrote, "It is the most elaborate work on the *philosophy* of Anti-Slavery I have ever seen, and appears most seasonably when iniquity is claiming to pass for an angel of light. I am grieved at some few censures of the abolitionists in it . . . but nineteen-twentieths of the book are sound in principle, and I will not grudgingly bestow my gratitude and praise for this splendid testimony to the truth." Halfway between the extreme of Garrison's criticism and Loring's stood John Quincy Adams, objecting that slaveholders could quote parts of the "Slavery" as a palliation of their system, "but it is in fact an inflammatory if not incendiary publication."

The most virulent attack upon Channing's pamphlet, however, came from James Trecothick Austin, Attorney-General of Massachusetts, devout Unitarian, writer for the *Christian Examiner,* and a distinguished member of Channing's own congregation. "I charge him—in spite of his disclaimer—with *the doctrine of* INSURRECTION," exclaimed Austin. According to Austin, public sentiment in the Free States in regard to slavery was perfectly sound, and ought not to be altered; in the slaveholding states, whether right or wrong, it could not be altered; consequently all such attempts as Channing's were bound to cause additional evil—moral, social, and political.

Since Channing had no solution to the slavery problem, why did he preach? "If there is no known remedy," said Austin, "why taunt a man with his condition?" The Bible, history, and the United States government all recognize slavery. Where, then, did Dr. Channing receive the authority to shout that "no property can be made to exist in a human being?" It would seem that he had derived it "from a refined and elaborate metaphysical subtilty wholly incomprehensible to a great part of mankind—from new light in the recesses of his study, from some double distillation which by a novel process of alchemy he has been able to effect on the dry bones of ancient morality."

According to Samuel May, Channing's pamphlet found its way into many parlors from which a copy of *The Liberator* would have been spurned. His exposé of the "sinfulness of holding slaves and the vices which infested the communities where human beings were held in such an unnatural condition" aroused the Southern slaveholders and their Northern partisans to such a pitch of anger that they came to regard him as even a more dangerous opponent than Garrison. Austin's *Remarks* precipitated a controversy over Channing's pamphlet; and, as a result, the subject of Negro servitude was fully broached among a class of people who had paid no heed to *The Liberator* and the numerous antislavery tracts being broadcast at the time.

That Channing was drawing closer to the Abolitionists was demonstrated on several occasions early the following year. On a wintry day in March, when he might easily have been expected to remain in his study, he appeared at the State House, muffled in cloak and shawl-handkerchief, to give his moral support to a group from the Massachusetts Antislavery Society, who were protesting before a committee of the legislature against a recent proposal to abolish by law all abolition societies.

Samuel May, who was one of the protestants, declared afterwards, "Nothing . . . gratified us so much as seeing Dr. Channing approach Mr. Garrison, who until then he had appeared to avoid, shake him cordially by the hand, and utter some words of sympathy."

The next spring Channing made his first appearance at a meeting of the Antislavery Society. His principal object in attending it was "to judge for himself of the spirit of this society. I wished to ascertain whether there was no diminution of the bitterness and intolerance of feeling which had characterized too many of its proceedings." Although he detected "a tendency to unsparing invective," he heard "nothing so exceptionable as the vituperations, and coarse unfeeling personalities which too often dishonor Congress." The most gratifying circumstance at the meeting was a short address from a man "of pure African blood."

"I felt," Channing wrote, "that he was a partaker with me of that humanity for which I unceasingly thank my Creator." He was struck by the life of the members present: "Nothing was said or done mechanically. . . . You know by instinct whether you are surrounded by life or death. This body was alive. I am sure, that, if the stirrers up of mobs could have looked into the souls of these Abolitionists, they would have seen the infinite folly of attempting to put them down by such persecutions as they can bring to bear on them."

After attending this meeting, Channing decided that Abolitionism had most to fear from the indifference of people who worshipped prosperity. Its basic strength resided in the religious conviction on which it was founded. Thus its adherents would not be discouraged easily, and unexpected events might bring many new supporters into the fold. Boston's proslavery spirit and its opposition to all antislavery speech and action, he attributed to its scepticism concerning human progress. The average social temper of its people was well represented, he thought, by the reception accorded to Harriet Martineau after she had attended a ladies' abolition meeting in Boston. Because she had expressed a favorable reaction to the antislavery movement, she had been excluded from the hospitality of many of Boston's best families and had become the target of insults from Boston newspapers.

In the autumn of 1836 Channing found himself compelled once again to come before the public. The previous July a mob in Cincinnati had destroyed the press on which James G. Birney, a former slaveholder but now an ardent Abolitionist, had been printing his antislavery paper, *The Philanthropist,* and had driven editor Birney from the city. It was plain to Channing that liberty of speech was in danger when such actions were allowed to go uncensured. He wrote a public letter of some twenty-six pages to Birney, in which he eloquently defended the right of the Abolitionists to speak freely against slavery while lecturing them on the violence of their denunciations. Always on firm ground where freedom of expression was concerned, he used to telling advantage the experience he had gained in the years of the Unitarian Controversy to expose the most dangerous of all pretenses for restoring to lawless force, "the *tendency* of measures or opinions."

Garrison copied the letter to Birney in its entirety and reprinted it in *The Liberator* with the comment, "A million letters like this would never emancipate a single slave, but rather rivet his fetters more strongly." Yet this letter was more vigorous and concrete than Channing's earlier and more philosophic treatment, and it offered consolation to the majority of the Abolitionists. Birney realized that it could be used to excellent purpose in *The Philanthropist,* and Garrison would hardly have reprinted it had he believed it such a futile piece of writing.

The letter to Birney was the beginning of Channing's friendship with the Ohio antislavery leader and of a fairly steady correspondence between them. Both were agreed on the question of free expression of opinion, but Channing could see no good in the rapidly growing political activity of that wing of the Abolitionist party which Birney represented. Instead, he felt, as did Garrison, that "Antislavery is to triumph, not by force or appeals to interest, but by becoming a living part of the public conscience and religion. Just in proportion as it is complicated with political questions and feelings it is shorn of its strength." "There is a class of politicians," he added, "who will use Abolition to rise by, but will disgrace it by want of principle."

As far as threats to secede were concerned, Channing was convinced that "On this point the South does not merely bluster, but is in earnest." He wrote Follen on Christmas Day, 1837, that "The great obstruction to Antislavery sentiments at the North is the fear of dissolving the Union"; but he was then already upon record as saying that dissolution of the Union was a lesser evil than spreading the dominion of slavery. On August 1 he had completed his open letter to Henry Clay on the "Annexation of Texas." Of all his contributions to the antislavery movement, this was the most cogent and best adapted to its end. Harriet Martineau thought it "perhaps the most honoured in England of all his writings"; and even Maria Chapman gave it credit for delaying the annexation of Texas for a number of years. William Hickling Prescott wrote to Channing "as one of the people," expressing his thanks for the latter's "patriotic and well timed effort" and declaring that he, too, thought "separation better than union with a preponderance of slave states."

Channing's ostensible motive in addressing his "Letter" to Clay was to secure a wider reception of the ideas in it by linking them with the name of a well known statesman, whose "great influence, if exerted in promoting just views on the subject . . . would accomplish a good, to which, perhaps, no other man in the country is equal."

Although Channing wrote that he had been "driven to a task lying beyond my province, by the unwillingnes of others to undertake it," he had made careful preparation; and his "Letter" carried an authoritative and legal tone. It reviewed the insurrection against Mexico and overwhelmed it with righteous indignation. It denounced annexation as an act by which the United States "will enter on a career of encroachment, war, and crime. . . . The seizure of Texas will not stand alone. It will darken our future history. It will be linked by an iron necessity to long-continued deeds of rapine and blood."

The South wants Texas to become part of the Union because it must have new territory in which to breed and sell slaves and thereby perpetuate its "peculiar institutions." Rather than be a party to any such immoral action as this, he would prefer national disunion. "Earnestly as I deprecate the separation of these States," he said, "and though this event would disappoint my most cherished hopes for my country, still I can submit to it more readily than to the reception of Texas into the confederacy. I shrink from that contamination. I shrink from an act, which is to pledge us as a people to robbery and war, to the work of upholding and extending slavery without limitation or end. I do not desire to share the responsibility, or to live under the laws of a government, adopting such a policy."

He concluded, "To me it seems not only the right, but the duty of the Free States, in case of the annexation of Texas, to say to the Slaveholding States, 'We regard this act as the dissolution of the Union. . . . We will not become partners in your wars with Mexico and Europe, in your schemes of spreading and perpetuating slavery, in your hopes of conquest, in your unrighteous spoils.' "

This last remark was still reverberating when news reached Boston that Elijah P. Lovejoy had been shot and killed while defending his antislavery press in Alton, Illinois. Channing suggested to Samuel Sewall a protest meeting in Faneuil Hall and headed up a petition of a hundred names for the use of the Hall. It was followed immediately by a counter-petition, and the request of Channing and his supporters was denied. He wrote a stirring appeal "To the citizens of Boston," which was published in the *Daily Advertiser* with opposing editorial comments. The result was a gathering of citizens on December 3 to consider the reasons for the city officials' refusal of the petition for a peaceful assembly. Channing was thanked for his eloquent defense of the citizens' liberties and requested to prepare resolutions for a meeting in Faneuil Hall, if the request to use it was not again denied.

The city authorities agreed to the second petition, and December 8 was selected as a suitable date. At ten o'clock in the morning, Faneuil Hall was packed with nearly five thousand spectators. Jonathan Phillips presided, and after the opening prayer was offered, Channing addressed the assemblage.

His first remarks were a disavowal of any partisan purpose in calling the meeting. If that were so, he would not be present, he assured his listeners. But "when a great question of humanity and justice is discussed here, when a number of my fellow-citizens meet here to lift up their voices against violence and murder and in support of the laws and the press, I feel that my place *is here.*" The resolutions which he had prepared were then read and were supported by George Hillard.

Everything was quiet and the meeting promised to end uneventfully, until Attorney-General Austin jumped up to speak. He pronounced Channing's resolutions "abstract propositions"; demanded to know why Lovejoy, who had incited slaves to rise upon their masters, should be thus commemorated; declared that Lovejoy had "died as the fool dieth"; and likened the mob of Alton to the fathers of the Revolution.

After Austin finished speaking, a tremendous roar filled Faneuil Hall, and it appeared that Austin might prevail against the resolutions for freedom. Jonathan Phillips then turned to Channing, "Can you stand thunder?" "Such thunder as this," was Channing's answer, "in any measure." Then occurred a sight that he never forgot. Young Wendell Phillips, who had already risked his career as a lawyer to speak at several antislavery meetings, strode to the speaker's platform and began to talk the crowd down.

Expressing surprise at the sentiments of the last speaker and even more surprise at the applause that they had received, he made an impassioned defense of the principles of freedom which were at stake.

Reaching a point of climax, he paused and then said with all the disdain he could master; "Sir, when I heard principles laid down that place the murderers of Alton side by side with Otis and Hancock, with Quincy and Adams, I thought those pictured lips would have broken into voice to rebuke that recreant American, the slanderer of the dead. The gentleman said, that he should sink into insignificance, if he dared to gainsay the principles of these resolutions. Sir, for the sentiments he has uttered, on soil consecrated by the prayers of Puritans and the blood of patriots, the earth should have yawned and swallowed him up."

When Phillips's last word was uttered, bedlam broke loose. His bravery and eloquence had turned the tide of sentiment, and Channing's resolutions were passed. Freedom of discussion in Boston had once more been vindicated.

Channing's participation in the Faneuil Hall meeting was further cause for more of his parishioners and friends to fall away from him. But while his actions on behalf of the right of Abolitionists like Lovejoy to free speech had identified him, in the minds of many people, with the Abolitionists, a letter from him to *The Liberator,* within a week of his appearance at Faneuil Hall, did much to offset whatever gains he had made among the Abolitionists themselves. In that letter, he called upon them to disavow the appeal to force which Lovejoy had employed in defending his property.

Garrison, even more of a non-resistance advocate than Channing, had already expressed his regret over Lovejoy's armed defense; but he thought very justly that it was too much for Channing to demand that *all* Abolitionists should repudiate Lovejoy's actions. After Channing's "Letter" to Clay and after his Faneuil Hall appeal, Garrison had begun to hope that Channing's "vision was becoming more clear, his spirit more intrepid, and his acquaintance with the real state of the hearts of slaveholders more accurate." But he was greatly disappointed by Channing's latest production: "This Letter shows no improvement: nay, it bears marks of new infirmities."

The same motive that led Channing to defend Lovejoy's right to operate his antislavery press, while deprecating his use of force to defend that right, led him in 1838 to place his name at the head of a petition to remit the prison sentence of Abner Kneeland, editor of the "infidel" newspaper, *The Investigator.*

Kneeland, a one-time orthodox and Universalist preacher, had been indicted for blasphemy four years previously. The charges against him were three: he had quoted a scurrilous passage from Voltaire touching the virgin-birth of Jesus; he had published an article affirming the absurdity of prayer; he had said in a public letter in his paper: "Universalists believe in a God, which I do not, but believe that their God, with all his moral attributes (aside from nature itself) is nothing more than a chimera of their own imagination."

The case had dragged along for four years, with James Austin, the prosecuting attorney, working hard to secure a conviction. When Kneeland was finally given a two months' sentence for having, in the language of the judge, "wilfully denied the existence of God," Ellis Loring prepared a petition which Channing afterwards edited. The storm raised by this petition and its inevitable counterpart was considerable. Kneeland's sentence was carried out, and Channing lost more of his friends. As usual, however, he could not have acted otherwise. Atheism was detestable to him, but even an atheist was entitled to express his views. So thought Emerson, Ripley, Parker, and Follen also, for their names followed Channing's on the petition.

The last four years of Channing's life were illustrated by as many antislavery documents: Three of them were published in printed form, and the last was given as an address and printed posthumously. In 1839 he wrote an open letter to Jonathan Phillips, in which he took issue with Henry Clay's recent expression of slavery sentiment. In his "presidential" speech on February 7, 1839, Clay had made a bid for Southern votes by voicing opinions that had long been cherished by the South. "That *is* property which the law declares *to be* property," he had said. He had also defended slavery in the District of Columbia, opposed antislavery petitions touching that matter, affirmed the inviolable permanence of slavery in the slave States, and demanded immunity for it from Northern criticism. Channing, on the other hand, refused to believe that slavery was a permanent institution; he opposed its existence in the District of Columbia and defended the right of petition against that existence; also the right of the North to criticize and condemn slavery in the South.

Although he claimed to have "no thought of defending" the Abolitionists, because "they must fight their own battle," he had much praise for them. "Abolition in its more general form, or regarded as an individual principle of settled, earnest opposition to slavery," he said, ". . . is in harmony with our institutions, and with all the tendencies of modern civilization." He denounced the burning of the Hall of Freedom in Philadelphia and similar acts of violence against Abolitionists and asked, "Are they the only intolerant people in the country?"

As far as colonization was concerned, he thought it would succeed in draining off slavery about as soon as one could drain off the Atlantic. "Colonization may do good in Africa," he said. "It does only harm among ourselves. It has confirmed the prejudice, to which slavery owes much of its strength, that the colored man cannot live and prosper as a freeman on these shores."

Northern complicity in the evil of slavery was not overlooked. "As our merchants and manufacturers cast their eyes southward, what do they see? Cotton, Cotton, nothing but Cotton. This fills the whole horizon of the South. What care they for the poor human tools by whom it is reared? . . . What change do they desire in a system so gainful? Men call it in vague language an evil, just as they call religion a good; in both cases giving assent to a lifeless form of words, which they forget whilst they utter them, and which have no power over their lives."

Strong as Channing's statements were, they did not satisfy Garrison completely. Channing was still convinced that he could separate the slaveholder from his deed, and he made the unfortunate slip of saying, "To me, the slave-holder is very much of an abstraction." Garrison, of course, could not let such an opportunity pass to point out Channing's basic weakness. Referring to the "Remarks," he said, "It separates the subject from personalities—i.e., it shoots at nothing, and hits it."

In the latter part of 1840, Channing started Elizabeth Peabody on her career as a publisher by entrusting her with his manuscript on "Emancipation." He had received the inspiration for this work from Joseph John Gurney, a Quaker, who had spent some time in the West Indies surveying post-emancipation conditions there. Gurney had just returned from the Indies when he visited Channing, and he gave him glowing reports of the healthy situation he had found among the free Negroes in the Tropics. His book, entitled *Familiar Letters to Henry Clay,* led Channing to think that he might publicize Gurney's views and, at the same time, drive home some lessons to be derived from the success of the British plan. He had begun his antislavery publications with "Slavery"; what more fitting way to end them than with "Emancipation"?

While he found much in Gurney's letters to praise, Channing was critical of their emphasis on the economic success of emancipation. "This concern for property," he said, "this uncommon concern for human nature, is a sign of the little progress made even here by free principles, and of man's ignorance of the great end of social union. . . . . A better age will look back with wonder and scorn on the misdirected industry of the present times. The only sure sign of public prosperity is, that the mass of the people are steadily multiplying the comforts of life and the means of improvement. . . . My maxim is, 'anything but slavery! Poverty sooner than Slavery!' "

From the cheering spectacle of Christianity unriveting the chains of the slave in the West Indies, Channing turned "with deep sorrow" to the record of the Christian ministry in America. "The very men," he said, "whose office it is to plead against all wrong, to enforce the obligation of impartial, inflexible justice, to breathe the spirit of universal brotherly love . . . have enlisted under the banner of slavery." And what kind of a race were they helping to keep down? The history of West-Indian emancipation teaches that it is "one of the best races of the human family."

Once again he deprecated the disposition of part of the Abolitionists to organize themselves into a political party. "Their strength has always lain," he asserted, "in the simplicity of their religious trust, in their confidence in Christian truth. Formerly the hope sometimes crossed my mind, that, by enlarging their views and purifying their spirit, they would gradually become a religious community, founded on the recognition of God as the common, equal Father of all mankind, on the recognition of Jesus Christ as having lived and died to unite to himself and to baptize with his spirit every human soul, and on the recognition of the brotherhood of all God's human family. . . . I thought that I saw, in the principle with which the Abolitionists started, a struggling of the human mind toward this Christian union." This was his finest compliment to Garrison, for it was Garrison who had steadfastly stuck to this principle and who had refused all along to turn Abolitionism into a political weapon.

The last few years of Channing's tenure at Federal Street were marked by growing strain between him and his congregation. Before he had begun his antislavery publications, there had not been noticeable friction. As late as 1835 Maria Chapman wrote that the Boston Female Antislavery Society was notified of an address by the English Abolitionist, George Thompson, "in the Rev. Dr. Channing's church, where a notice of our meeting has never been refused a reading." A little later this could not be said. Antislavery notices were intercepted by the standing committee before they reached Channing. Such treatment was, of course, humiliating; but worse was still to come. In 1837 the Antislavery Society was refused permission to use the church for a meeting, although Channing had indorsed its request as "very agreeable" to him personally. Not long afterwards, in direct opposition to his wishes, the church was granted to the Colonization Society for the same purpose.

The crowning humiliation occurred when the committee refused to permit the Massachusetts Antislavery Society to hold memorial services in the church for Charles Follen. Follen had died under tragic circumstances on January 13, 1840, while en route by boat from New York to Boston. Channing's people knew very well how shocking this tragedy had been to their pastor, and they knew he would appreciate having tribute paid to Follen in his church; but "public" considerations outweighed "private" appeals; and they preferred to hurt him rather than allow Abolitionists to "defile" their church.

According to Channing's nephew, "this manifestation of a want of high sentiment in the congregation to which, for so many years, he had officiated as pastor, made him question the usefulness of his whole ministry. To what end had he poured out his soul, if such conduct was a practical embodiment of the principles and precepts which he had so earnestly inculcated." Channing could not, however, be prevented from delivering a discourse of his own on Follen's character; and his remarks on that occasion must have put to shame those who had a share in his humiliation.

The last year of Channing's life produced two anti-slavery publications. These were the double pamphlet, "The Duty of the Free States" and the Lenox Address. The former was inspired by the case of the *Creole,* a brig sailing from Hampton Roads to New Orleans with a cargo of tobacco and 135 slaves in late October of 1841. On November 7 the slaves revolted, killing the slave dealer and severely wounding the officers of the boat. The crew was forced by the mutineers to steer for Nassau, where the British attorney-general took charge of the ship, holding nineteen of the Negroes for mutiny and murder and releasing the rest. Southern senators and their representatives were indignant; and Daniel Webster, who was then Secretary of State, sent a letter of instructions to Edward Everett, the United States minister to England, demanding the restitution of the slaves—not, of course, as slaves—but as mutineers and murderers. Hence Channing's pamphlet, one of the most outspoken utterances he ever wrote.

Even before Webster had written to Everett, Channing saw important issues in the case. He wrote to his congressman for documents relating to such matters as jurisdiction on the high seas and consulted with Charles Sumner, who had just returned from Europe, about procedures in developing his arguments. In the first part of his pamphlet, he censured Webster's position. It signified, he said, that the United States was bound to protect slavery abroad as well as at home. In the second part, he re-emphasized his belief in the duty of the Free States to relieve themselves of all complicity in the South's crime, withdrawing even from the Union if Texas were annexed. Above all he declared the Free States have "the duty of Faith in the intellectual and moral energies of the country, in its high destiny, and in the good providence which has guided it through so many trials and perils to its present greatness."

On August 1, 1842, Channing gave his last public address. It was the eighth anniversary of Emancipation in the West Indies, and he chose the occasion to hold up the example of England, as an object lesson to his countrymen. He was vacationing at Lenox in the Berkshire mountains; and the beautiful valley of the Housatonic, which had been the scene of Jonathan Edwards's Indian labors, was the inspiration for one of his most moving tributes to human freedom. There was nothing startling or new in the Lenox address, but his arguments gained added force from the persuasiveness of his personality and the eloquence of his voice. He was an old man near death's door; but no one would have realized it from the ardor of his speech and the youthfulness of his ideas. Progress and peace were the goals that he set before the people of Lenox, and while he talked of them, they seemed readily attainable.

Even before slavery had become a live issue, Channing had shown his distaste for controversy. Yet he had never shrunk from it when great principles were involved. Men like Jedidiah Morse and William Lloyd Garrison were always at their best in a good fight, but not Channing. His was a nature that tended naturally to desire peace and tranquility. But no man ever possessed more moral courage. Once he had evaluated all the aspects of a problem and knew where the path of justice lay, he never failed to follow it. John Greenleaf Whittier, a man of great principles himself, realized this and wrote to Channing's son: "As to the matter of courage and self-sacrifice very few of us have evinced so much of both as thy father. He threw upon the altar the proudest reputation, in letters and theology, of his day. With the single exception of Lydia Maria Child, I know of no one who made a greater sacrifice than thy father."

CHAPTER SEVENTEEN

A SWEETER CUP

ON HIS SIXTY-SECOND birthday Channing stood in the Federal Street pulpit and read to his congregation from Paul's Second Epistle to the Corinthians. Using as his text, "the things which *are* seen are temporal; but the things which are not seen *are* eternal," he preached upon his favorite subject—the greatness of man's soul. The sermon was the last he ever gave to his people.

Before the month was out, he had completed his plans for a trip into Pennsylvania. He had long hoped to visit the banks of the Juniata and the Wyoming Valley, and something told him to do it that spring. Fearing the summer heat, he started too early. The roads were either seas of mud or washed out, and he was forced to continue his journey by canal boat. The inevitable happened. His lungs were unable to withstand the damp night air and he fell sick.

For nearly a month he was held prisoner in a hotel room in Wilkes-Barre. As soon as he was able to leave his bed, he found some compensation for his confinement in sitting at his window, which overlooked the Susquehanna River, and viewing the beautiful valley spread out before his eyes. Nature was as good for him as the medicine his physician prescribed. He wrote Harriet Martineau, "the burden of life—never overpowering—has been unspeakably lightened by my intercourse with Nature. . . . I feel as a stranger in new cities, and often in well-known circles; but I am at home amidst streams, mountains, valleys which I have never known before. Nature does not alienate me from society, but reconciles me to it."

The combination of rest and Nature's soothing influence brought a quick recovery. By July 1 he was in Lenox, Massachusetts, with his friends the Sedgwicks. Using the Lenox Inn as headquarters, he made several excursions into the neighboring countryside, visiting the Bashpish Falls on one occasion and, on another, spending an entire week at Stockbridge. Most of his time, however, was spent with Catherine Sedgwick's family. They found him a delightful companion. As Catherine's sister-in-law put it, "The man was never lost in the saint, nor the friend in the prophet and seer."

242

Whatever the cause, Channing seemed to have discovered a new sense of freedom that summer. His hopes for mankind were never more sanguine. He wrote a letter of reassurance to Ellen Cabot, who had written anxiously about his health, saying he had never felt better. Then he added, "What mysteries are we to ourselves! Here am I finding life a sweeter cup as I approach what are called its dregs, looking round on this fair, glorious creation with serener love, and finding more to hope for in society at the very time that its evils weigh more on my mind." When he was asked what period of life was the happiest, he smiled and said, "About sixty."

On the first of August he delivered his address on "Emancipation." The day was exceedingly fine—the air pure and clear—and he spoke with great eloquence and power, as though his strength were inexhaustible. But when his speech was ended, he was completely spent. He remained in his room for several weeks, fighting to regain his health, but recovery was slow. Early in September, when he seemed well enough to travel, he set out for Boston, taking the long way home through the Green Mountains. At Bennington, Vermont, an attack of typhoid fever laid him low again, and his family was called to his side.

For twenty-six days he lingered between life and death. His mind did not wander, although it was extraordinarily active. He begged his family to talk of "common things," so that he might be relieved of "these crowds of images, these visions of immensity, and rushing thoughts." As his hold on life became weaker, his faith in man's "common spiritual nature" grew stronger. "We need to feel the *reality*," he said, "the *reality* of a spiritual life." He liked to hear the most minute details about friends, and nothing pleased him more than to hear of sacrifices in behalf of the Antislavery cause.

As September came to a close, he knew that he was going to die. He told his doctor, "I should wish, if it is the will of Providence to be able to return home—to die there." Then he added quickly, "But it will all be well; it *is* all well." The following Sunday, October 2, as he heard the bells of the church ring, he urged his family to attend services. Knowing that he might die at any moment, they persuaded him that it would be best for them to remain at his side. He asked one of them to read from the Sermon on the Mount. At the end of the Lord's Prayer, he said, "That will do now . . . I take comfort, Oh, the greatest comfort, from these words. They are full of the divinest spirit of our religion." His last words were, "I have received many messages from the spirit." Turning toward the window, he looked out at the setting sun and closed his eyes. The end had come.

His body was taken immediately to Boston. On Friday afternoon, October 7, funeral services were held at the Federal Street meeting-house in compliance with the wish of the Society. Ezra Gannett preached the funeral discourse. At the close of the services, those who were present passed slowly up the middle aisle of the church to take a last look at their departed leader. As the procession moved from the church on its way to Mount Auburn cemetery, the bell of the Catholic Cathedral tolled a final tribute.

There were countless testimonies to Channing's greatness both in America and abroad, but none more sincere or moving than the "humble tribute" Theodore Parker preached to his congregation in West Roxbury. "I hesitate not to say," declared Parker, "that since Washington, no man has died amongst us whose real influence was so wide, and so beneficent, both abroad and at home. . . . He did not see all the truth that will be seen in the next century. He did what was better, he helped men to see some what of truth in this, and blessed all that aided others to see."

LITERATURE AND SOURCES

THE WRITINGS OF Channing and his contemporaries constitute the main sources of this biography. Unfortunately, little manuscript material is available to the modern scholar, because most of Channing's sermons, letters, and journals were destroyed some fifty years ago.

The American Unitarian Association in Boston has a few items—the most valuable being the notes of the Baltimore sermon. The Meadville Seminary in Chicago holds the scripts of numerous published and unpublished sermons together with the original of the fragmentary treatise on Man. Some letters are to be found in the A. U. A. Library in Boston, the Houghton Library at Harvard, the Massachusetts, Rhode Island, and Newport Historical Society libraries. The Arlington Street Church in Boston owns a number of interesting mementos of Channing's ministerial career as well as a few records of his preaching at the Federal Street Church.

Channing's writings have been collected in two editions. Five volumes of *The Works of William E. Channing* were published at Boston in 1841, and a sixth volume was added in 1843. *The Works* went through seventeen editions by 1867. A revised edition was issued in 1875. In 1886 the American Unitarian Society brought out a "complete" one-volume edition of Channing's works which included *The Perfect Life,* a series of twelve discourses edited by William Henry Channing from his uncle's unpublished sermons. This is the most usable of all editions of the *Works,* because it contains a fairly complete index.

William H. Channing's *Memoir* (Boston, 1848, 3 vols.) is an invaluable source of correspondence and manuscript material, although the editor's role of "moral censor" leaves much to be desired in the way of completeness and unbiased reporting. It was re-issued in 1880 (Boston) in one volume under the title: *The Life of William Ellery Channing.* The *Correspondence of William Ellery Channing and Lucy Aikin, from 1826 to 1842* (London and Boston, 1874), edited by Anna LeBreton, gives an illuminating picture of Channing's interest in European affairs and reveals sides of his character not exemplified in the *Memoir.* Dr. *Channing's Note-Book* (Boston and New York, 1887), edited by his grand-daughter, Grace Ellery Channing, contains some manuscript notes left out of the *Memoir.*

245

No bibliography of Channing has been published. He is listed incompletely in the *Literary History of the United States* (III, 438-439), and some of his nephew's writings are confused with his. Marie Hockmuth's unpublished dissertation (Wisconsin, 1945), *William Ellery Channing, D. D.: A Study in Public Address,* contains excellent bibliography. The selective bibliography in Arthur W. Brown's *Always Young for Liberty: A Critical Biography of Dr. William Ellery Channing* (unpublished dissertation, Syracuse, 1950) brings the record up to date.

Although twentieth-century scholars have neglected Channing, he does not lack for biographers. His nephew's *Memoir* provides a rich background of autobiographical information marred only by chaotic organization and the editor's process of moral distillation.

René La Vollee's *Channing: Sa Vie et Sa Doctrine* (Paris, 1876) received high honors from the Academy of Moral and Political Science. The first complete attempt to present Channing to Europeans, it is soundly based on the *Memoir* and Channing's published writings. Its main weakness is its author's lack of knowledge about Channing's intellectual milieu. Charles T. Brooks's brief, popular life, *William Ellery Channing* (Boston, 1880), adds several personal reminiscences to the *Memoir* but lacks documentation and interpretation.

Valuable primary source material relating to Channing's personal experiences from 1825 to 1842 is contained in Elizabeth R. Peabody's *Reminiscences of William Ellery Channing, D. D.* (Boston, 1880). Its author reflects the "great man's" shadow and tries to be his mouthpiece. Rich in Channing's letters, it is often inaccurate in details of time and place.

An excellent biography is that of John White Chadwick: *William Ellery Channing: Minister of Religion* (Boston and New York, 1903). Written by a liberal Unitarian minister, it relies heavily on the *Memoir* and is pardonably biased in favor of subject and his religion. Sources are used with considerable dexterity, although Channing's European experience is slighted. It contains no bibliography and a minimum of "apparatus."

Anne Holt's *William Ellery Channing: His Religious and Social Thought* (London, 1942) emphasizes Channing's blindness toward evil and argues that the antislavery struggle showed Channing's optimism at its weakest.

In no sense a biography, Robert L. Patterson's *The Philosophy of William Ellery Channing* (New York, 1952) is still the fullest and most discerning analysis of the growth of Channing's mind. The author, a professor of philosophy at Duke University, has established a unique position for Channing between orthodox Protestant and Roman Catholic theologians. Channing's doctrine of "essential sameness": his explanation of the relationship between human and divine nature, makes him, according to Patterson, the greatest of all perfectibilitarians.

Of great importance for an understanding of Channing and his times are the many volumes written by and about his contemporaries. The most important are listed below under chapter bibliographies, but special mention should also be given to the following: *The Diary of William Bentley, D. D.* (Essex Institute, Salem, 1905-1914, 4 vols.) ; *The Journals of Ralph Waldo Emerson* (Boston, 1909-1914, 10 vols.) ; *Ezra Stiles Gannett, A Memoir,* by William C. Gannett (Boston, 1875) ; John Ware's *Memoir of the Life of Henry Ware, Jr.* (Boston, 1854, 2 vols.) ; *The Works of Charles Follen with A Memoir of His Life* (Boston, 1841, 5 vols.) ; *The Journals of Bronson Alcott,* edited by Odell Shepard (Boston, 1938); *Autobiography and Letters of Orville Dewey, D. D.* (Boston, 1883) ; and *Memoir of Samuel Joseph May,* edited by Thomas J. Mumford (Boston, 1873) .

For general information concerning the New England of Channing's youth, Walter Channing's *My Own Times, or 'Tis Fifty Years Since* (Boston, 1845) is humorously interesting. Edward Everett Hale's *A New England Boyhood* (New York, 1893) provides gossipy social notes, while William W. Story's *Life and Letters of Joseph Story* (Boston, 1851, 2 vols.) contains important material about the world of politics. Sidney Willard's reminiscences in *Memories of Youth and Manhood* (Cambridge, 1855, 2 vols.) reflect a wide-eyed interest in nearly every aspect of New England life in the first half of the century. Among the many worthwhile books of Octavius B. Frothingham, *Boston Unitarianism, 1820-1850: A Study of the Life and Work of Nathaniel Langdon Frothingham* (New York, 1890) is a sound and penetrating analysis of religious history during Channing's lifetime.

There is also important background material in the following autobiographies, biographies, and memoirs: *Memoirs of John Quincy Adams,* edited by Charles F. Adams (Philadelphia, 1876) ; Dwight L. Dumond, *Letters of James Gillespie Birney, 1831-1857* (New York, 1938, 2 vols.); Eliza B. Lee, *Memoirs of Rev. Joseph Buckminster, D. D., and of His Son, Rev. Joseph Stevens Buckminster,* (Boston, 1851, 2 vols.) ; *Letters of Lydia Maria Child* (Boston, 1883) ; *James Freeman Clarke: Autobiography, Diary and Correspondence,* edited by Edward E. Hale (Boston, 1891) ; William Allen, *Memoir of John*

Codman, D. D. with Reminiscences of Joshua Bates (Boston, 1853) ;
Francis Tiffany, *Life of Dorothea Lynde Dix* (Boston and New York,
1891) ; Josiah Quincy, *Figures of the Past* (Boston, 1926) ; Wendell P.
Garrison and Francis Jackson, *William Lloyd Garrison: The Story of
His Life* (New York, 1885, 4 vols.) ; *Harriet Martineau's Autobiography,* edited by Maria Chapman (Boston, 1877, 2 vols.) ; John Weiss,
Life and Correspondence of Theodore Parker (New York, 1864, 2
vols.); Carlos Martyn, *Wendell Phillips: The Agitator* (New York,
1890) ; Octavius B. Frothingham, *George Ripley* (Boston, 1882) ; Nina
M. Tiffany, *Samuel E. Sewall: A Memoir* (Boston and New York,
1898) ; Joseph B. Felt, *Memorials of William Smith Shaw* (Boston,
1852) ; Herbert B. Adams, *The Life and Writings of Jared Sparks*
(Boston and New York, 1893, 2 vols.) ; George Ticknor, *Life, Letters
and Journals* (Boston, 1880, 2 vols.) ; James Walker, *Memoir of Hon.
Daniel Appleton White* (Boston, 1863) ; Henry Ware, Jr., *Memoirs of
the Rev. Noah Worcester, D. D.* (Boston, 1844) ; Samuel M. Worcester, *The Life and Labors of Rev. Samuel Worcester, D. D.* (Boston,
1852, 2 vols.).

CHAPTER ONE

Information about Channing's ancestry and childhood must be
gleaned largely from William H. Channing's *Memoir.* Channing himself made occasional references to his early years, particularly in the
discourse, "Christian Worship," delivered in Newport in 1836. Edward
Tyrell Channing's *Notes on the Channing Family,* the one serious
attempt during Dr. Channing's lifetime to prepare a genealogy, is an
amateurish job. The genealogy in the Newport Historical Society
Library is not much better. The entry in the *Abridged Compendium
of American Genealogy* (1925) is as good as any. Additional information about Newport connections of the family can be found in *The
Gibbs Family of Rhode Island and Some Related Families* (New York,
private printing, 1933) .

George Channing's *Early Recollections of Newport, R. I.* (Newport,
1868) and Elizabeth P. Channing's *Kindling Thoughts* (Boston, 1892)
give first-hand information about Newport in the late years of the
eighteenth century. William Updike's *Memoirs of the Rhode-Island
Bar* (Boston, 1842) contains some references to Channing's father,
and Edward T. Channing's *Life of William Ellery,* vol. VI of Sparks's
The Library of American Biography, gives a good account of his
maternal grandfather. *The Literary Diary of Ezra Stiles* (New York,
1901, 3 vols.) is a treasure house of material on Stiles and his times.

Samuel Hopkins is memorialized in *Sketches of the Life of the Late Rev. Samuel Hopkins, D. D.* (Hartford, 1805) as well as in Williston Walker's *Ten New England Leaders* (New York, 1901) and *Early Religious Leaders of Newport* (Newport, 1918). F. B. Dexter's *Biographical Sketches of the Graduates of Yale College,* IV (New York, 1907) contains a write-up of the Reverend Henry Channing, and James McCosh's *The Scottish Philosophy* (New York, 1875) furnishes a workmanlike account of Witherspoon and his influence on American education.

CHAPTER TWO

For Justice Dana, see H. W. L. Dana's *The Dana Saga* (Cambridge, 1941). Channing's experiences at Harvard are detailed in the *Memoir,* but this information must be supplemented by the accounts of contemporaries. The "College Records" in the Harvard Archives give statistical data about Channing's class and the "Library Charging List" for the years 1795-1798 offers an accurate index to Channing's college reading habits. Perhaps the most complete picture of Harvard and Cambridge during Channing's tenure can be secured from Sidney Willard's *Memories of Youth and Manhood* (Cambridge, 1855). Andrew P. Peabody's *Harvard Reminiscences* (Boston, 1888) is also useful.

For a brief account of the philosophical instruction at Harvard, see Benjamin Rand's article in the *Harvard Graduates' Magazine,* XXXVII (September, 1928). The ideas of Richard Price are accurately discussed in Roland Thomas's *Richard Price, Philosopher and Apostle of Liberty* (London, 1924). Professor Tappan's discourse to the Freshmen in 1794 was published in *Sermons on Important Subjects* (Cambridge, 1807). The best introduction to Francis Hutcheson is *An Inquiry into the Originals of our Ideas of Beauty and Virtue* (London, 1726).

One of the finest treatments of Joseph Tuckerman is that by Channing himself in the *Works,* VI. Daniel T. McColgan's *Joseph Tuckerman, Pioneer in American Social Work* (Washington, 1940) documents Tuckerman's philanthropy thoroughly. For Channing's classmates in general, see James Walker, *Memoir of Hon. Daniel Appleton White* (Boston, 1863); Felt, *Memorials of William Smith Shaw* (Boston, 1852); W. W. Story, *Life and Letters of Joseph Story* (Boston, 1851). Yale contemporaries are described in the *Autobiography and Correspondence of Lyman Beecher,* edited by Charles Beecher (New York, 1864).

Deism and free thinking are thoroughly treated in Herbert Morais's *Deism in Eighteenth Century America* (New York, 1934) and G. Adolph Koch's *Republican Religion: The American Revolution and the Cult of Reason* (New York, 1933). The definitive study of "Illuminati" influence is Vernon Stauffer's *New England and the Bavarian Illuminati* (New York, 1918).

CHAPTER THREE

The account of Channing's Southern experience must be gathered largely from his personal correspondence as edited in the *Memoir*. Fragments of letters are also printed in Felt's *Memorials of William Smith Shaw*. For his reaction to slavery, one is dependent on the scattered comments in his own publications. Leslie Stephen's *History of English Thought in the Eighteenth Century* (1876-1881) offers a sympathetic treatment of the English historians who delighted Channing. To follow the transition from Edwardian piety to eighteenth-century morality, one can hardly improve on Joseph Haroutunian's *Piety Versus Moralism* (New York, 1932).

CHAPTER FOUR

Jared B. Flagg's *The Life and Letters of Washington Allston* (New York, 1892) reveals Allston's early aspirations. Channing's discourse on "Christian Worship" is the best source of the nature influence.

There is little available information about the divinity program at Harvard during Channing's day, but the atmosphere was not radically different from that depicted in John Ware's *Memoir of the Life of Henry Ware, Jr.* (Boston, 1849, 2 vols.). Buckminster's brief career is sketched in Lee's *Memoir of Rev. Joseph Buckminster, D. D., and of His Son, Rev. Joseph Stevens Buckminster* (2nd ed.; Boston, 1851). Channing's reading on divinity follows the pattern outlined in "Remarks on the Character and Writings of Fenelon," in volume I of the *Works*. For an extremely critical view of Channing's theological background, see Ernest Renan's "Channing and the Unitarian Movement in the United States, A. D. 1780-1842" in *Leaders of Christian and Anti-Christian Thought,* translated by William M. Thomson (London, 1891). Information regarding ministers already settled when Channing entered the ministry can be found in W. B. Sprague's *Annals of the American Pulpit* (New York, 1865). Extracts from Channing's first sermon are quoted in Charles Brooks's *William Ellery Channing* (Boston, 1880). The Federal Street Meeting-House is described in *Sketches of Some Historic Churches of Greater Boston*

(Beacon Press, 1918). George Ticknor's associations with Channing are related in *Life, Letters, and Journals* (Boston, 1880, 2 vols.).

CHAPTER FIVE

The *Memoir* must be relied upon for most of the information regarding Channing's early ministry. There are scattered comments regarding his effectiveness in the articles on his contemporaries in Sprague's *Annals of the American Pulpit*. Little has been written about Channing's brothers, but the article on Edward Tyrell in the *Dictionary of American Biography* is useful; and Octavius B. Frothingham's *Memoir of William H. Channing* (Boston, 1886) touches briefly upon Francis Dana.

M. A. DeWolfe Howe has written an introduction to the *Journal of the Proceedings of the Society which conducts the Monthly Anthology and Boston Review, Oct. 3, 1805 to July 2, 1811* (Boston Athenaeum, 1910). For Palfrey, see volume VIII of *Annals of the American Pulpit*. Emerson's "Historic Notes of Life and Letters in New England," *Lectures and Biographical Sketches*, X (Boston, 1883) provides valuable commentary on the period during which Channing carried on his labors.

CHAPTER SIX

The best account of Morse's activities is James Morse's *Jedidiah Morse: A Champion of New England Orthodoxy* (New York, 1939). The *Diary of William Bentley* (Salem, 1904-1914, 4 vols.) contains an amazing amount of information about the "liberals" in Boston and the surrounding communities, and the survey of the Harvard Controversy in E. H. Gillett's "History and Literature of the Unitarian Controversy," *The Historical Magazine*, IX (April, 1871) is exhaustive.

The Harvard of Edward and Walter Channing's day is described in Andrew Peabody's *Harvard Reminiscences* (Boston, 1888) and the *Autobiography, Diary and Correspondence of James Freeman Clarke* (Boston, 1891).

For Codman, see William Allen's *Memoir* (Boston, 1853). Channing's sermon at his ordination is not in the collected *Works*, but it was published in Boston (1808). Horace Bushnell's famous sermon on "Christian Nurture" (1847) is reprinted in *American Philosophic Addresses*, edited by Joseph L. Blau (New York, 1946). The review of Channing's New York sermon was first published in the Rhode Island *Religious Messenger* (Providence, May 1, 1827). See *A Memorial of*

the Federal-Street Meeting-House (Boston, 1860) for an account of
Ezra Gannett's sermon at the dedication ceremonies.

CHAPTER SEVEN

Washington Irving recalls his association with Allston in *Spanish
Papers, Biographies and Miscellanies,* II (Boston, 1866). For portraits
of the Channing family, see plates in Edgar P. Richardson's *Washington Allston: A Study in Romantic Painting* (Chicago, 1948). For
Thacher, see article in *Annals of the American Pulpit,* VIII. There
are frequent references to Andrews Norton in the letters of his contemporaries; see also Sprague's *Annals* and Allen R. Clark's *Andrews
Norton: A Conservative Unitarian* (Honors thesis, Harvard, 1940).

Channing's fast-day sermons are not in the collected *Works.* They
were published in Boston shortly after each was delivered. Extracts of
the August, 1812 sermon are given in volume V of the *Works.* Channing's *Discourses on War* were published in Boston in 1903. John
Lowell's *Mr. Madison's War* (Boston, 1812) describes the Federalist
attitude toward conflict with Britain. Henry Adams gives an account
of the Baltimore riot, which contemporary historians have generally
disregarded, in his *History of the United States,* VI.

Channing's article on "The Union" is reprinted in volume I of the
Works. For an interesting criticism of our "national vanity" by a visiting Englishman, see John Bristed's *The Resources of the United States
of America* (New York, 1818).

CHAPTER EIGHT

For details of the Half-Way Covenant and its results, see William
W. Sweet's *Religion in Colonial America* (New York, 1947) and Perry
Miller's "Solomon Stoddard," *Harvard Theological Review,* XXXIV
(1941). Kenneth Murdock's *Increase Mather, the Foremost American
Puritan* (Cambridge, 1925) is a scholarly account of the great Puritan
conservative. The Synod of Dort is ably reviewed in James Elson's
John Hales of Eton (New York, 1948). The best treatment of Edwards
is Perry Miller's *Jonathan Edwards* (New York, 1949). The only
thorough study of Arminianism in New England is Conrad Wright's
Arminianism in Massachusetts, 1735-1780 (Unpublished dissertation,
Harvard, 1943). Chauncy's emphasis on good behavior as the result of
conversion shows up in *The New Creature* (Boston, 1741). The different psychological positions of Chauncy and Edwards are illustrated
by Chauncy's *Seasonable Thoughts on the State of Religion* (Boston,

1743) and Edwards's *A Treatise Concerning Religious Affections* (Boston, 1746).

James Freeman's "liberal" trinitarianism is outlined in *Sermons on Particular Occasions* (Boston, 1821). Jonathan Mayhew's *Seven Sermons Delivered at the Boston Lecture* (Boston, 1749) demonstrates antipathy to creeds. The insistence on morality as the test of Christianity is revealed in *Letters from the First Church in Glocester to the Second in Bradford with Their Answers* (Boston, 1744). For Dana's confutation of Edwards, see *An Examination of the Late President Edwards's "Enquiry on Freedom of Will"* (Boston, 1770). Gad Hitchcock's *Natural Religion Aided by Revelation* (Boston, 1779) argues for the harmony of natural and revealed religion. The discussion of Universalism in Richard Eddy's *American Church History*, X (New York, 1903) is excellent.

CHAPTER NINE

For details of Codman's struggle with his parishioners, see Allan's *Memoir of John Codman* and Morse's *Jedidiah Morse*. E. A. Park's *Memoir of Nathanael Emmons* (Boston, 1861) describes one of the Hopkinsian leaders, and William Bentley's *Diary* reflects the liberals' point of view toward Andover Seminary. Channing's sermons on infidelity were published in Boston (1813). Andrews Norton reviewed the controversy over infidelity in *The General Repository and Review*, IV (October, 1813). Channing's catechism, which is invaluable for showing his early views of Christ, was published under the title of *Elements of Religion and Morality in the form of a Catechism* (Boston, 1813).

For the Worcester brothers, see Henry Ware, Jr., *Memoirs of the Rev. Noah Worcester, D. D.* (Boston, 1844). Joseph Allen's *Historical Sketch of the Unitarian Movement Since the Reformation in American Church History*, X (New York, 1894) contains a full treatment of English Unitarians.

The literature on the so-called Unitarian controversy is voluminous. The *Memoir* contains considerable information on Channing's role in it, and his discourse on "The System of Exclusion and Denunciation in Religion Considered" (1815) is printed in the *Works*. Extracts from his letter to Thacher appear in the *Memoir*, I; the complete letter was published June 20, 1815. Gillett's "History and Literature of the Unitarian Controversy," *The Historical Magazine*, IX (April, 1871) gives a masterly account of both sides in the contest. For the purely orthodox side, see Sam W. Worcester's *The Life and Labors of Rev. Samuel Worcester, D. D.* (Boston, 1852, 2 vols.) .

CHAPTER TEN

Though not always completely reliable, Elizabeth Peabody is the best witness to her association with Channing. See her *Reminiscences of William E. Channing* (Boston, 1880) . Channing's memorial to the Congress is printed in the *Memoir,* II. His letters to Eloise Payne are in the A. U. A. Library in Boston. For the Ticknor correspondence, see *Life, Letters and Journals of George Ticknor* (Boston, 1880, 2 vols.) . Orie W. Long's *Literary Pioneers* (Cambridge, 1935) gives excellent accounts of American students abroad.

Channing's estimate of Thacher is printed in the *Works,* V. The attitude of American Unitarians toward English necessitarianism is described in Frederick R. Griffin's "Joseph Priestley, 1733-1804," *Proceedings of the Unitarian Historical Society,* III (1934) . For Sparks, see Herbert B. Adams, *The Life and Writings of Jared Sparks* (Boston and New York, 1893, 2 vols.) . The most complete account of the Baltimore ordination is Charles H. Lyttle's *The Pentecost of American Unitarianism* (Boston, 1920) . Letters relating to Channing and the Baltimore sermon are contained in the Jared Sparks collection in the Houghton Library. The Stuart-Norton controversy resulted in a number of published pamphlets that can be found in any library with a fairly complete Channing bibliography. The aftermath of the split between the Unitarians and the orthodox is traced in Jacob C. Meyer's *Church and State in Massachusetts from 1740 to 1833* (Cleveland, 1930) .

CHAPTER ELEVEN

For Channing's son, William Francis, see article in *Dictionary of American Biography.* The interest of New York Unitarians in Channing is described in the *Life and Letters of Catherine M. Sedgwick,* edited by Mary E. Dewey (New York, 1871) . For the Berry Street organization, see Charles Lyttle's "An Outline of the History of the Berry Street Ministerial Conference," *Meadville Theological School Quarterly,* XXIV (July, 1930) . The Sparks Collection in the Houghton Library contains Channing's correspondence relating to *The Unitarian Miscellany.* His blind spot toward Priestley shows up in the *Correspondence of William Ellery Channing, D. D. and Lucy Aiken,* edited by Anna L. LeBreton (London and Boston, 1874) .

The constitutional convention of 1820 is covered in *Journal of De-*

bates and Proceedings in the Convention of Delegates Chosen to Revise the Constitution of Massachusetts (Boston, 1853). Channing's sermon, "Religion a Social Principle," is not in the *Works*. It was published as a pamphlet in Boston (1820). For Emerson's ideas at this time, see his *Journals,* edited by E. W. Emerson and Waldo Emerson Forbes (Boston and New York, 1909-1914). Orville Dewey's career is traced in Mary E. Dewey's *Autobiography and Letters of Orville Dewey, D. D.* (Boston, 1883).

The only account of Channing's European itinerary is contained in a memorandum book in the possession of the A. U. A. Library in Boston. The *Memoir* is more useful for his European experiences in general, although it mixes up chronology and omits significant dates and persons. Elizabeth Peabody's *Reminiscences* paraphrases Channing's reports on his trip. For his attitude toward Catholicism, see the article "On Catholicism" in *Works,* II. Coleridge's religious views are analyzed in Hoxie Fairchild, *Religious Trends in English Poetry,* III (New York, 1939); Herbert L. Stewart, "The Place of Coleridge in English Theology," *Harvard Theological Review,* XI (January, 1918); and C. R. Sanders, *Coleridge and the Broad Church Movement* (Durham, 1942). Margaret Fuller's article on Coleridge appeared in the *American Monthly Magazine* (September-October, 1836). For a good account of Miss Aikin, see Philip LeBreton's *Memoirs, Miscellanies, and Letters of Lucy Aikin* (London, 1864). Some personal reminiscences of Channing and Miss Aikin are given in Catherine Dall's "Dr. Channing and Miss Aikin," *The Unitarian Review,* II (November, 1874).

CHAPTER TWELVE

The Cheverus letters are in the Rhode Island Historical Library in Providence. Louis Warner's "Channing and Cheverus: A Study in Early New England Tolerance," *Christian Register* (May 4, 1939) lacks personal details but is useful for an estimate of Cheverus. For comments on the Wood n' Ware controversy, see volume IV of *The Works of Leonard Woods, D. D.* (Boston, 1851, 5 vols.). Channing and Gannett are discussed in William C. Gannett's *Ezra Stiles Gannett, A Memoir* (Boston, 1875).

For various aspects of Boston in the '20's and '30's, see the following: Charles P. Huse, *The Financial History of Boston* (Cambridge, 1916); Edward Everett Hale, *A New England Boyhood* (New York, 1893); and Josiah Quincy, *A Municipal History of the Town and City of Boston* (Boston, 1852).

The eulogy of Channing the writer appeared in *Blackwood's,* XVI (September 4, 1824). For nineteenth-century estimates of Felicia Hemans and Joanna Baillie, see articles in *Encyclopedia Britannica,* ninth edition. The *Memoir* gives fullest treatment of Channing's interest in social reform. The *History of Labour in the United States,* edited by John Commons, *et al* (New York, 1918, 2 vols.) deals with labor trouble in New England at the time.

Channing's "Remarks on Associations" is printed in *Works,* I. For Channing's conduct at meeting to discuss the establishment of a Unitarian association, see James Walker's article on Andrews Norton in *Annals of the American Pulpit,* VIII. There is also a complete account of Channing's role in this matter in George W. Cooke's *Unitarianism in America* (Boston, 1902).

Channing's attitude toward the predicament of the American artist should be compared with James F. Cooper's in *Notions of the Americans* (1828). The letter criticizing Channing's authorship was written by Mrs. S. P. Hale to Edward Everett on March 28, 1826. The manuscript is in the Massachusetts Historical Library. Emerson's references to his studies with Channing are in volume I of *The Letters of Ralph Waldo Emerson,* edited by Ralph Rusk (New York, 1939, 6 vols.). For a list of readings Channing considered necessary for an informed minister, see T. P. Doggett's manuscript in the Harvard Divinity School Library. Charles Follen's life and writings are admirably dealt with in Eliza Lee Follen's *The Works of Charles Follen with a Memoir of His Life* (Boston, 1841, 5 vols.).

CHAPTER THIRTEEN

A good example of orthodox spleen against the New York sermon is Joseph McCarrell's *Answer to A Discourse preached by Dr. William Ellery Channing, at the Dedication of the Second Congregational Church, New-York, Dec. 7th, 1826* (New York, 1827). For a contemporary definition, see "What Constitutes Infidelity?" *Spirit of the Pilgrims,* III (1830). The Finney revivals in Oneida, Auburn, and Troy, New York, are described in Gilbert H. Barnes's *The Antislavery Impulse, 1830-1844* (New York, 1933).

Channing's *The Great Purpose of Christianity* (1828) should be compared with Emerson's *The American Scholar* (1837) to see the similarity of their views on self-reliance. Channing's failure to recognize evil in man and the universe is criticized by William Shedd in *Letters to the Rev. William E. Channing, D. D. on the Existence and Agency of Fallen Spirits* (Boston, 1828).

George Combe's most popular book was the phrenological work, *The Constitution of Man* (London, 1828) ; his views on American life are expressed in the *Notes of the United States of America during a Phrenological Visit in 1838-9-40* (Philadelphia, 1841, 2 vols.) . Emerson's journal entries on Taylor (volume IV) are illuminating. De Tocqueville's visit with Channing is briefly commented upon in George W. Pierson's *Tocqueville and Beaumont in America* (1938) . Reino Virtanen's "Tocqueville and William Ellery Channing," *American Literature*, XXII (March, 1950) lacks convincing evidence of Channing's influence.

Channing's first book, the *Discourses, Reviews, and Miscellanies* (Boston, 1830) contained his "Examiner" and "Disciple" articles, nine of his most important discourses and extracts from his miscellaneous writings. The Glasgow edition in 1829 was not edited by Channing.

Stuart's pamphlet, *A Letter to William E. Channing, D. D. on the Subject of Religious Liberty,* was published at Andover in 1830. Orthodox Episcopal views of Channing are set forth in Frederick Beasley's *A Vindication of the Fundamental Principles of Truth and Order in the Church of Christ from the Allegations of the Rev. William E. Channing, D. D.* (Trenton, 1830) . For an excellent treatment of the entire argument of "tendency," see Clarence H. Faust's "The Background of the Unitarian Opposition to Transcendentalism," *Modern Philology*, XXXV (February, 1938) .

CHAPTER FOURTEEN

Dewey's tribute to Channing is in the *Discourse on the Character and Writings of Rev. William E. Channing, D. D.* (New York, 1843). The manuscript of the work on man is in the Meadville Theological Seminary in Chicago. A transcription was made by Norton de Corcey Nachlas for a B. D. thesis at Meadville in 1942. Brief but sound discussions of Kames and Blair and the philosophers Stewart, Alison, and Reid are given in William Charvat's *The Origins of American Critical Thought* (Philadelphia, 1936) .

The complete documentation of English periodical criticism of Channing in Robert E. Spiller's "A Case for W. E. Channing," *The New England Quarterly*, XXX (January, 1930) makes mention of specific periodicals unnecessary here. The letter to Mrs. Prescott (May 8, 1839) is signed by Joseph Cogswell and is in the possession of the Massachusetts Historical Society. Channing's "Remarks on a National Literature" appeared first in the *Christian Examiner*, VII (January, 1830) . It is reprinted in *Works*, I. For a good survey of the kind of articles in the *Examiner* at this time, see Pedigo's *Literary Criticism in the Christian Examiner 1824-1839* (Unpublished M. A. thesis, University of N. Carolina, 1946).

CHAPTER FIFTEEN

The best introduction to Alcott is *The Journals of Bronson Alcott,* edited by Odell Shepard (Boston, 1938). Shepard's biography *Pedlar's Progress: The Life of Bronson Alcott* (Boston, 1937) is an excellent companion volume. Helen E. Marshall's *Dorothea Dix, Forgotten Samaritan* (Chapel Hill, 1937) is a definitive study. A good nineteenth-century account of Ripley is O. B. Frothingham's *George Ripley* (Boston, 1882). Ripley's article on "Philosophic Thought in Boston" in volume IV of *The Memorial History of Boston,* edited by Justin Winsor (Boston, 1881, 4 vols.) gives insight into the way his mind worked. For the best modern biographies of Brownson, see Arthur Schlesinger, Jr. *Orestes A. Brownson: A Pilgrim's Progress* (Boston, 1939) and Theodore Maynard, *Orestes Brownson: Yankee, Radical, Catholic* (New York, 1943). Both contain excellent bibliographies. O. B. Frothingham's *Memoir* (Boston, 1886) is fullest treatment of William Henry Channing.

Gerando's *Le Visiteur du Pauvre* was translated by Elizabeth Peabody and published in Boston (1832). For a discussion of the role of the *Western Messenger,* see Clarence Gohdes's *The Periodicals of American Transcendentalism* (Durham, 1931). Mann's struggles to organize the educational system of Massachusetts are narrated in Raymond B. Culver's *Horace Mann and Religion in the Massachusetts Public Schools* (New Haven, 1929). For details of the first meeting of the Symposium, see Emerson's *Journals,* IV. Information on the "Friends" is scanty, but there are some details in O. B. Frothingham's *Theodore Parker: A Biography* (Boston, 1874). Henry Steele Commager's *Theodore Parker* (Boston, 1947) is an excellent modern biography. The exchange of letters between Henry Ware, Jr. and Emerson over the "Divinity School Address" is published in James E. Cabot's *A Memoir of Ralph Waldo Emerson* (Boston, 1887, 2 vols.). The publications called forth by the quarrel between Andrews Norton and George Ripley are listed in C. W. Wendte's bibliography in the Centenary edition of Parker's *Works* (Boston, 1907-1913).

Much has been written on the various communal societies of the '40's. Bestor's *Backwoods Utopias* (University of Pennsylvania) is a good general account. Gilbert Seldes's *The Stammering Century* (New York, 1928) is popular but erratic. J. T. Adams's chapter in *New Eng-*

land in the Republic (Boston, 1926) is better. Channing's visits to Brook Farm are mentioned in John Weiss's *Life and Correspondence of Theodore Parker* (New York, 1864, 2 vols.). Ballou's Hopedale is reviewed in Seldes's work.

Brownson's essay on "The Laboring Classes" was published in his own *Boston Quarterly Review* (July, 1840). *The Mediatorial Life* was published as a pamphlet in Boston (1842). It is also in *Brownson's Works* (Detroit, 1882–1887, 20 vols.), IV. For details of the "Church of the Disciples," see *James Freeman Clarke: Autobiography, Diary and Correspondence,* edited by E. E. Hale (Boston, 1891). There are excellent accounts of the Chardon Street Convention in Emerson's article in *The Dial,* III (1840), and in his *Historic Notes of Life and Letters in New England.* The discussion of Emerson's relationship to Channing in Lenthiel Downs's "Emerson and Dr. Channing: Two Men from Boston," *New England Quarterly,* XX (December, 1947) touches only on tangential contacts; and Arthur Ladu's "Channing and Transcendentalism," *American Literature,* XI (May, 1939) fails to show why Channing did not follow the lead of Parker and Emerson.

CHAPTER SIXTEEN

The account of Channing's role in the antislavery struggle given in the *Memoir* must be supplemented by Channing's articles in the *Works* and by the many references scattered throughout the writings and correspondence of his contemporaries.

Channing's letter to Webster is printed in volume V of *The Works of Daniel Webster* (Boston, 1864). The sermon he preached after his return from Santa Cruz (June, 1831) is in manuscript in the Meadville Theological Seminary. W. P. Garrison and F. J. Garrison's *William Lloyd Garrison: The Story of His Life* (New York, 1885, 4 vols.) contains material on Maria Chapman. Her edition of Harriet Martineau's *Autobiography,* 2 vols., was published in Boston (1877). Her uncompromising attitude shows up in her account of *Right and Wrong in Massachusetts* (Boston, 1839). For Harriet Martineau's opinion of Channing, see volume II of her *Retrospect of Western Travel* (London, 1838, 3 vols.). Lydia Child's *Letters* were edited by Whittier and published with his introduction in Boston (1883). Samuel May's early experiences with Garrison are narrated in *Some Recollections of Our Antislavery Conflict* (Boston, 1869).

The most unfavorable view of Channing's antislavery efforts is that of the Englishman Edward Abdy in volume III of his *Journal of a*

Residence and Tour in the United States of America from April, 1833, to October, 1834 (London, 1835, 3 vols.). The New York riots against Garrison and his adherents are discussed in Gilbert H. Barnes, *The Antislavery Impulse 1830-1844* (New York, 1933), the best account of the religious motivation of abolitionism. For an excellent survey of Catholic attitude in this country toward slavery, see Madeleine H. Rice's *American Catholic Opinion in the Slavery Controversy* (New York, 1944). John Quincy Adams's remarks on Channing's *Slavery* are given in volume IX of *Memoirs of John Quincy Adams,* edited by Charles F. Adams (Philadelphia, 1876, 12 vols.).

For both sides of controversy resulting from Channing's *Slavery,* see the following: George F. Simons, *Review of the Remarks of Dr. Channing's Slavery by a Citizen of Massachusetts; Reply to the Reviewer of the Remarks; A Friend of the South in Answer to Remarks on Dr. Channing's Slavery* (all published in Boston in 1836). For graphic picture of State-House meeting, see Harriet Martineau's "The Martyr Age of the United States," *Westminster Review,* XXXII (December, 1838). Birney's conversion from slaveholding to abolition is described in Dwight L. Dumond's *Letters of James Gillespie Birney, 1831-1857* (New York, 1938, 2 vols.).

Channing's "Letter" to Clay is printed in *Works,* II. See Robert C. Winthrop's *Memoir of Henry Clay* (Cambridge, 1880) for Clay's connection with Channing. Channing's research for "Letter" is described in manuscript letters in Rhode Island Historical Society. The violence of the Southern reaction is illustrated in Sidney's *Letters to William E. Channing, D. D. occasioned by his Letter to Hon. Henry Clay on the Annexation of Texas to the United States"* (Charleston, 1837). Austin's remarks appeared in *The Daily Advocate* (Boston, December 9, 1837). For Wendell Phillips, see Carlos Martyn's *The Agitator* (New York, 1890) and Theodore D. Weld's "Lesson from the Life of Wendell Phillips" in *Memorial Services upon the Seventy-fourth Birthday of Wendell Phillips* (Boston, 1886).

The Kneeland affair is discussed fully in Henry S. Commager's "The Blasphemy of Abner Kneeland," *New England Quarterly,* VIII (March, 1935). There are copious extracts of the "Letter to Abolitionists" in W. H. Channing's *Memoir,* but the full text appears in Garrison's *The Liberator,* VII (Boston, December 14, 1837). The Follen address is in volume V of Channing's *Works.* Whittier's tribute is printed in S. T. Pickard's *The Life and Letters of John Greenleaf Whittier* (Boston, 1894, 2 vols.).

CHAPTER SEVENTEEN

Channing's last days are discussed at length in the *Memoir*. For an intimate glimpse of him during the summer of '42, see Cora M. Ritchie's *Autobiography of an Actress or Eight Years on the Stage* (Boston, 1854). Parker's *An Humble Tribute to the Memory of William Ellery Channing, D. D.* was published in Boston (1842). Russell Bellows has edited a round-up of commemorative discourses in *The Channing Centenary* (Boston, 1881), and similar tributes are to be found in *The Centenary Commemoration of the Birth of Dr. William E. Channing* (London, 1880).

INDEX